The Compositor in London

To my grandchildren with my love.

Isidore Cyril Cannon

The Compositor in London

The Rise and Fall of a Labour Aristocracy

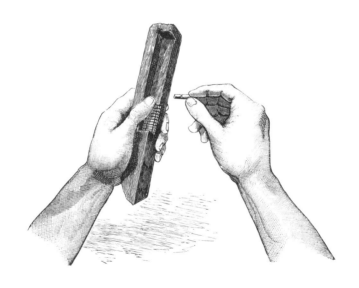

St Bride Library

St Bride Foundation, Bride Lane, Fleet Street, London EC4Y 8EQ
Registered Charity Number 207607

First edition 2011

British Library Cataloguing in Publication Data
A catalogue record for this book is available from the British Library

ISBN 978-0-9504161-7-5

Designed by Chris Kouppis and Matthew Lickiss, students in the
Department of Typography and Graphic Communication,
University of Reading

Typeset in 11/13pt Celeste

Printed in Great Britain by MWL Print Group, Pontypool

Contents

Illustrations

Unless otherwise ascribed, the illustrations are to be found within St Bride Library. The two trade posters and the map were in the original thesis but the remainder have all been selected for this edition.

Foreword

The invention of printing created not only an entirely new craft, but also an entirely new kind of artisan. Printing itself was not new; impressions of inked blocks, some including letters, predate the first use of separately cast mobile types, the distinctive feature of the invention. It was the need to manipulate the latter that brought the new craft into existence; those who practised it were called 'compositors' because they put the types together. To do this they had to have or acquire a skill that no other craft demanded, literacy. Literacy is capable of many definitions: at its lowest, it means knowing the names and pronunciation of the letters of the alphabet or the ability to 'sign' a document by writing the letters of the signer's name; at the other end of the scale, it means not only reading and writing words, but understanding what is written at a high level of intellectual competence. Bookbinders, whose craft long predated the compositors', had need only to know the letters of the alphabet and those that made up roman numerals in order to gather quires thus signed correctly; some could certainly read and write in more than one language, but it was not obligatory to the performance of their work. The compositor had not only to read letters and find their metal equivalents in the case in which they were held, but also to arrange them in the correct order and to perform the subsidiary tasks of justification of lines, breaking words where necessary at logical places. The compositors' task was thus predicated upon literacy, and that above the simple level at which bookbinders and other artisans could be literate.

It was literacy that distinguished compositors from all other kinds of manual workers. This distinction constituted their craft as a bridge between those of humbler manual workers and those, not artisans, with whom they worked, clergy, lawyers, authors of other kinds, who were as literate as they but expressed their literacy with a pen, not the manual dexterity, this new skill of manipulating letters in three-dimensional form, that isolated the compositor from those on either side of the bridge. This isolation gave them from the outset, or at least from 1466 when Johannes Borne, the first to write on the subject, identified them as 'logothetae', a unique position and status. Two centuries later, when Moxon described their work in his *Mechanick Exercises*, they have built up not only a distinctive way of doing their work, but a special social position, and even a special language. They were, by their individuality, in the forefront of society's attempts to define and regularise those in the new trade. Printers were early subject to legislative control, and compositors closed ranks to defend their position, within the trade of printing, both vis-à-vis other workers, printers and labourers, and management, overseers and foremen, and outside it, as a class within the growing number of classes defined by trade or occupation, with a place on a graduated social scale.

This development, this sense of being different, is the subject of the author's admirable book, and both as a practitioner, a comp himself, and as an academic social scientist, as he later became, he has done a wonderful job of both subjective and objective analysis. It was a world that he entered in 1942 and I five years later in 1947. We shared the common experience of seeing a trade that had survived the war in central London by the skin of its teeth; all around were ruined buildings or holes in the ground where once large printing and publishing firms had been. Amid this desolation, small firms selling printers' sundries had escaped the blitz; you could still buy a compositor's stick, the immemorial basic tool of the trade, as if nothing had happened. But both he and I grew to become part of the trade, working in and then watching it, not, perhaps, with an imminent sense of foreboding, but certainly aware of the fragility of what had taken five hundred years to build up.

Dr Cannon has divided his subject into two parts: the social history of the compositor in Britain and the practice of what he has called 'the present-day compositor'. Early evidence up to the middle of the eighteenth century is hard to come by, but such as can be found or deduced is all here. From then on, as evidence is commoner, the picture is clearer. Business records like the Strahan ledgers, scales of costs of composition and of wages, and the earliest descriptive texts, from Charles Manby Smith's *The Working Man's Way in the World* to *London Labour and the London Poor*, add colour to the narrative. This period he aptly characterises as the passage 'From Group Awareness to Artisan Consciousness'. Robert Owen's social experiments with an increasingly industrial society sharpened the compositors' already alert sense of their position to a new 'class-consciousness' (Marx, obsessed by the phenomenon of class itself, was oddly disinclined to explore the social individuality of different working trades). Change has to be seen against an economic situation that changed remarkably little from 1810, when the relative payments for piece-work and 'stab hands' (those with an established weekly wage) were fixed, to 1891, when the scales were rewritten *ab initio* on the eve of the successful introduction of machine-composition. Although wages at first remained remarkably static, the fall in the cost of living and relatively full employment enabled compositors to keep up their position. Guild status migrated into trade unionism without affecting this. The compositors' 'London Typographical Society', later the 'National Graphical

Association', played a part in this, but they were less inclined to associate this with political activity than other unions.

A sense of being paid a better wage in comparison with other 'workers' survived both world wars and the intervening depression. Both managers and men (women compositors were still rare) were protected by a shared conservatism. Changes in education, even the 1944 Act, hardly altered this (they did alter the position of the printer's reader, another specialist trade closely allied to the compositors', but without their inbuilt sense of cohesion). Most compositors, characteristically, read the *News Chronicle*, designed for the thoughtful but politically uncommitted working class. The 'chapel' was more important than the 'union'. Rather surprisingly and despite their tenacious grip on their 'literate' status, the compositors saw themselves as 'working class'; they were, above all else, an 'occupational community'.

Having survived the transition from hand- to machine-composition with little strain, the industry was unconcerned by experiments with photo-composition, such as George Westover's experimental 'Rotophoto', going back to 1936. The revolution finally came from the least expected quarter, when in the late 1960s, for reasons unconnected with the printing trade, the price of lead increased sevenfold overnight. This revolution was still in progress, its ultimate consequences still unforeseen (save by Ellic Howe), when Cannon, by now graduated into an academic world, presented the thesis that forms the basis of this work. He was asked at the time whether his experience in the trade would not damage the objectivity proper to his subject. He brushed the suggestion away confidently. Now, looking back over a lifetime that has become the subject of industrial archaeology, he is not so sure. His 'Epilogue', written in 2011, when the compositor has ceased to exist and anyone writing words for print on a computer has taken his place, leads him to wonder whether a romantic sense of *temps perdu* has not coloured what he has previously written.

To me, viewing the same story both as historian and participant, that is of no consequence. Whether written from the inside or viewed with scientific detachment, this is an absorbing history, well worth writing in the first place and all the more so now that it comes to publication fifty years later. Cannon's last picture shows two young women who run the Corridor, a small press in north London. Both trained as graphic students, they turn out good quality work using hot metal and electronic type-setting with letterpress and litho. 'These are hardly green shoots for hot metal', writes Cannon, 'rather ignited embers kept alive by enthusiasts, but they help keep a light on a technology now largely in the past.' Long may they continue to do so.

Nicolas Barker

Acknowledgements

This book could be eligible to join the ranks of publications taking a lifetime to complete, in this case over fifty years in two bisected periods. Many have been involved and deserve credit.

The first period was when the thesis was prepared in the late fifties. Tom Bottomore, then at the London School of Economics, later Professor of Sociology at Sussex, was my supervisor; now sadly deceased he introduced me to a number of distinguished historians, especially H.L. (Lance) Beales and Eric Hobsbawm, resulting in memorable discussions. Interested and helpful others included Ellic Howe, George Rowles, and Harold Waite. Professor Asa Briggs, my external examiner, made my viva in 1961 a pleasurable experience (even without being aware that it was my birthday!). Professor Donald MacRae of the LSE, now also deceased, invited me to contribute the thesis to the sociology series he was editing, but other life changes led me to withdraw from the contract; had I not done so my advancing years may have provided a little more gentle leisure, but be much less interesting.

A number of book and other documentary collections have been especially important. The British Museum's library then housed in that splendid circular reading room; St Bride Printing Library, with its librarians, initially Turner Berry, later James Mosley; the library was brought into satisfying use again for this publication. The library of the London School of Economics and Political Science was valuable, as were the records at the Stationers Company (an extraordinary search in their roof space revealed important items I was seeking which had been discarded in piles of papers!), and especially those of the London Society of Compositors, later the London Typographical Society. The thesis would not have been possible without the one hundred anonymous compositors who agreed to take part in the survey, facilitated by the senior management and Fathers of Chapels in the 28 firms sampled. The LSC/LTS gave access to their records and permission for the interviews, as did the former British Federation of Master Printers (now the British Printing Industries Federation) and the London Master Printers Association who enabled me to sample their members. Also making their contributions were students in my apprentice classes at the London School of Printing (now absorbed into the London College of Communication), and students attending my adult education sociology evening class.

For this second stage my very warm thanks are due to Nigel Roche, Librarian at St Bride Foundation, for suggesting that St Bride publishes my thesis, a copy having been deposited in the library half-a-century ago. He felt that a record of a now departed occupation should be more widely available. Always a delight to work with, he has been most supportive and helpful throughout and undertook the onerous task of preparing and updating the bibliography and modifying the footnotes. Others associated with the Foundation have given their support: the Director, Glyn Farrow, Ben Weiner, the library assistants and Rob Banham, former chair of the Friends of St Bride Library, together with Chris Kouppis and Matthew Lickiss, his able typography students at Reading University who have designed the book. I trust they found it a useful learning experience. I am also aware that many others have contributed to this publication in a variety of ways, all their efforts are appreciated.

I am delighted to place on record my very special thanks to Ursula Jeffries, granddaughter of a compositor. Initially she was asked if she would be willing to retype the thesis, product of an old manual type-writer, onto a computer. She soon became the project manager, keeping an eye on all stages of the production, chivying unobtrusively and usually effectively anyone in danger of falling behind in their role, and locating many of the illustrations and writing the captions. Without her enthusiasm and suggestions it is difficult to think how the production would have been completed, certainly not in the time-span envisaged.

I also wish to express my deep gratitude to the eminent print historian, Nicolas Barker, for most generously agreeing to write the Foreword. Appreciation is due to all those who gave time to assist my understanding of the technological changes which had to be faced by the compositor. In addition to staff in numerous institutions, such as the BPIF and Proskills, I especially wish to thank John Finn, Barry Felstead, Dave Fairbairn, Ron Harris, Peter Laxton, Peter Shea, Peter Smith and John Voller, all former compositors, for sharing with me their experience of change. Alf Parrish, a former senior official of the National Graphical Association, and now involved in the Retired Printers section of Unite, invited me to meet some of the former comps. Deepening my understanding of the impact of change on other printing occupations were conversations with a former stereotyper, Denis Gomm, and Monotype-caster, John Ford.

I found all discussions illuminating and enjoyable. I, of course, remain responsible for any errors, and apologize if I've missed out on any who have provided help.

One of the joys of the research has been not only the insight it has given me into social change and the satisfaction of renewal with my past, formative working life, but has also brought me into contact with a wide range of new, interesting people, though regrettably not always as much as I would have liked.

My wife Charmian and son Jon made helpful comments on the new chapters. All my children and their families were as ever a great source of interest, hope, concern, enjoyment and relaxation. They were probably relieved by my having another project to keep me out of mischief, and one that this time didn't take me off alone to gather information in distant parts.

The book is dedicated to my numerous grandchildren. They are likely to experience occupational change in their lives, hopefully less dramatically than that faced by the compositor.

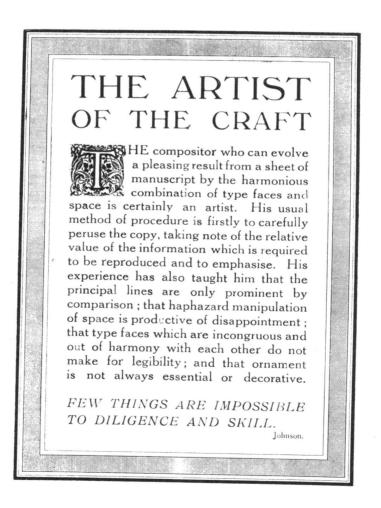

THE ARTIST
OF THE CRAFT

THE compositor who can evolve a pleasing result from a sheet of manuscript by the harmonious combination of type faces and space is certainly an artist. His usual method of procedure is firstly to carefully peruse the copy, taking note of the relative value of the information which is required to be reproduced and to emphasise. His experience has also taught him that the principal lines are only prominent by comparison ; that haphazard manipulation of space is productive of disappointment ; that type faces which are incongruous and out of harmony with each other do not make for legibility; and that ornament is not always essential or decorative.

FEW THINGS ARE IMPOSSIBLE TO DILIGENCE AND SKILL.

Johnson.

General Information

Currency and Cost of Living

For readers unfamiliar with British currency before decimalization, an explanation may be useful. The pound Sterling was divided into *shillings* (s) of which there were 20 to the £, and *pence* (d) which were 12 to the shilling. Other terminology was also used, such as a *florin* for two shillings, or *half-a-crown* for two shillings and sixpence (in the text this would be shown as 2s 6d; the 'd' derived from *denier*, the name of a small coin).

Comparing the cost of living and its impact on living standards over time is extremely difficult, often impossible. A wider variety of goods has come onto the market, and the relative price of the same goods can vary considerably over time; some, such as books, becoming relatively cheaper with changes in the cost of production, others, such as housing, became much more expensive especially in recent years with wide regional variations. One readable account of what has happened in Britain, which also discusses some of the problems of comparison, can be found in John Burnett's *A History of the Cost of Living* (Penguin, 1969), but this only goes up to the 1960s. Also see his *A Social History of Housing, 1815–1970* (Methuen, 1978). Readers are referred to search engines such as Google to ascertain more recent movements.

The Text Notes

The original thesis contained nearly 700 notes and it was deemed desirable to reduce these, partly by indicating the source in the text. Readers wishing to pursue sources in detail can do so by referring to a copy of the original which has been deposited in the following libraries: St Bride Library, University of London and the London School of Economics.

Major sources for the historical material, such as Howe's *London Compositor* documents, are usually obvious from the context, the nature of the item or the date; where this is not the case the source has been retained either in the text or the note. A word of explanation is due for the seeming disparity between the date of the thesis and the dates of certain publications. Since the thesis was written many of the quoted items have been updated by new editions. It was felt that these would be more readily locatable and a page reference to the latest edition is given where appropriate.

Union Records

Many of the union records used, such as delegate meetings, annual reports, and journals have over the years been collected by or donated to various collections. For example, those of former print unions which have all undergone amalgamations, such as the LSC, the LTS, and the NGA may now be found, inter alia, in the Modern Records Centre at Warwick University, the TUC Archives Collection at London Metropolitan University, and the Marx Memorial Library; St Bride Library also has some union records. After ascertaining specific sources from the thesis, the reader will need to check which collection holds the item.

Abbreviations

ACAS	Advisory, Conciliation and Arbitration Service
BFMP	British Federation of Master Printers
BPIF	British Printing Industries Federation
C&G	City and Guilds
EETPU	Electrical, Electronic, Telecommunications and Plumbing Union
FoC	Father of the Chapel
GFTU	General Federation of Trade Unions
JIC	Joint Industrial Council
LCP	London College of Printing
LGTS of C	London General Trade Society of Compositors
LMPA	London Master Printers' Association
LRC	Labour Representation Committee
LSC	London Society of Compositors
LSP	London School of Printing
LTC	London Trades Council
LTJ	London Typographical Journal
LTS	London Typographical Society
LTS of C	London Trade Society of Compositors
LUC	London Union of Compositors
MRC	Modern Records Centre, University of Warwick Library, Coventry
NATSOPA	National Society of Operative Printers and Assistants
NGA	National Graphical Association
NTA	National Typographical Association
NVQ	National Vocational Qualification
PKTF	Printing and Kindred Trades Federation
PMMTS	Printing Machine Managers' Trade Society
PTA	Printing Trades Alliance
SLADE	Amalgamated Society of Lithographic Artists, Designers, Engravers and Process Workers
STA	Scottish Typographical Association
TA	Typographical Association
TUC	Trades Union Congress
WPS	Women's Printing Society

Prologue

This Prologue is a personal statement; its aim is to acquaint the reader with a brief account of my background in printing to explain my connection with the occupation of compositor, to convey something of my thoughts and feelings when visiting the firm I had left well over half-a-century before, and how the book came about.

Entering 'the print'

My mother determined that I needed to have a trade; having seen her two nephews 'do well' in 'the print' (they had become Linotype operators but were then in the forces), she decided I was to be a printer. My father, then in the army, was a tailor, an industry fraught with uncertainties as demand for work rose and fell especially during the 1930s; following him was not considered desirable, nor did I wish to do so. Printing proved a good choice: after having experienced a very ragged education with frequent school changes due to house moves, evacuations, and the London Blitz, I was ready to leave school as soon as possible. My main interest apart from reading was maps; this was seen as somewhat quirky and no one considered map-making as an occupation. So at the age of thirteen, in the Spring before leaving school, my Mother and I trudged depressingly around several printing offices in the City of London, searching for an opening in 'the print'. It's a sign of the importance she attached to my securing a position that she accompanied me, for she would normally have expected me to deal with such things on my own; an attractive woman, she relied a good deal on persuasion by a winning smile which she probably felt was needed in this case. The area was filled with bomb-sites from the 1940/41 London Blitz, several with half-destroyed buildings displaying desks in bombed offices, and abandoned cooking stoves, baths, and even beds, still to be seen on now exposed upper-floor residential flats. The experience was discouraging until late in the day one informant who had no job to offer himself said he thought that Williams, Lea in Worship Street might have a vacancy. I was interviewed, given a reading and spelling test on the spot, and offered employment. I guess it was the smile that did it!

I started work in July 1942, at the end of term, just two weeks after reaching fourteen, the then minimum age for leaving school. Following several months in the reading room as a 'reading boy' (also known as 'copy-holder') to the proof-correctors, in March 1943 I was indentured for seven years to the trade of compositor. My wage was laid down in the indenture: eighteen shillings and sixpence a week for the first year of apprenticeship, rising to a handsome twenty shillings (one pound) for the second, and by two to three shillings a week each following year until coming out of my time. We worked a basic 45-hour week over five-and-a-half days starting at 8 a.m., with one-week's holiday a year. Wages and conditions were further modified as negotiated by the London Society of Compositors, the union that apprentices in union firms, which most were in London, joined after completing two years. In signing the contract I agreed, inter alia, not to 'gamble with cards or dice' during the term, nor 'haunt or frequent taverns'; an agreement which in 'the print' was inevitably honoured more in the breach.

Williams, Lea, a commercial and periodical printers, was large enough to provide a varied experience, and the training I received was, I think, good. The firm had an established procedure for apprentices. Starting with a period in the reading room as a reading boy, where one saw a range of printing matter, there followed a stint in the store. This involved finding the made up type to be used again for a repeat or modified job; and learning the layout of the type case 'boxes' by distributing used type characters of a given font and size into their different sized compartments in wooden cases. These were divided into an upper one for capital letters and numbers, and a lower one for non-capitals (the origin of 'lower case'). We also became familiar with spacing material, sorting leads or wooden reglets of different lengths and thicknesses. After about two years in these preparatory activities, apprentices entered the composing room proper, and were placed under the care of a compositor responsible for a periodical, or a variety of 'jobbing' or one-off items of printing. If more than one comp. worked with others they were known as a 'ship, probably derived from 'companionship', under a head or foreman, known as the 'clicker'. The whole composing department staff would work under an overseer who distributed the work to be undertaken. Apprentices would also be sent for half day a week to a printing school, in my case what was then the London School of Printing in Stamford Street and followed, after returning from the forces, by the North-Western Polytechnic in Kentish Town. As City apprentices, we were all given time off to attend the Lord Mayor's

Day colourful procession through the City which then took place during the week.

The firm, which still exists, relocated to Paddington and Norwich, then specialized in foreign languages and produced many of the journals for those members of armed forces who were able to escape from their occupied countries such as the free Belgians, Poles, and Norwegians. The wide range of other languages printed included Greek, Russian and Hebrew. Among the compositors and readers were native speakers of several of the languages offered. They were a colourful mix, with a variety of political and religious affiliations and interests; many of the men were World War One veterans and several had a characteristic croaking cough from having been gassed in the trenches. The young apprentice was exposed to a wide range of personalities, attitudes and levels of literacy, encouraging in me an early interest in social and political affairs.

My apprenticeship was interrupted by a couple of years' National Service, serving with the Royal Electrical and Mechanical Engineers. I thought I would take the opportunity to travel a little at government expense by volunteering to serve overseas which took me to Malta and Libya, not as exotic as some places servicemen were sent to, such as the Far East or the Caribbean, but interesting enough. After completing an apprenticeship there was a widely agreed expectation that the fledgling journeyman widened his (and it was always 'his') experience by working elsewhere. Work was easily available and through the union I found employment in a small jobbing firm in the heart of London's West End, and attended an evening class preparing students for the examination of the Association of Correctors of the Press. I then worked as a proof-reader for Keliher, Hudson and Kearns, a large periodical firm, whilst studying part-time for University entrance; this was a precursor to pursuing my interest in social issues more systematically. I was accepted at the London School of Economics to read for a Sociology degree, and having by then a young family, to supplement my grant throughout the three-year full-time course I worked part-time as a reader at several of the daily and weekly newspapers, as well as having an early morning job cleaning parts of a small block of flats. Following graduation I taught full-time at the London School of Printing, teaching general studies to day-release students, economic and social history to management trainees, and proof-correcting to potential proof-readers; I also did some adult education teaching. Research for a doctorate was undertaken part-time. I then moved into the world of higher education where I remained for the rest of my working life.

A revelatory visit

Visiting Williams, Lea after retirement, over sixty years after starting work there, I was shown around by the overseer who had been a young fellow apprentice at the time I left the firm and was now nearing retirement. Printing had changed considerably in the half-century since my time as a journeyman compositor and proof-reader. Of that I was partially aware from the union journal I continued to receive, but this became less informative as the trade union movement underwent major amalgamations, moving from craft to multi-craft, to industrial and later multi-industrial unions;[1] items in the journal focusing specifically on the compositor were much reduced. Until my visit I hadn't fully grasped the import of the technological changes and their impact on the compositor: I was not prepared for the utter transformation that had taken place.

Gone were the rows of frames of dusty type cases where each compositor had his base, separated by the large, heavy stone tables for imposing the made-up type to be printed; gone the workers' short impractically white carpenter aprons with their deep frontal pockets for bits of equipment, such as tweezers, metal 'em' ruler, short composing stick, and the somewhat superior long, brown or grey 'warehouse' coats. Gone also the clatter of Linotype and Monotype composing machines. In their place there were lines of men and women (the latter unknown in London printing firms in my time, except in very few offices), sitting at their computers in shirt-sleeves or blouse, in well-swept, clean, much quieter areas. No longer would the call of 'rat' or 'mouse' be heard, arousing apprentices to compete to stun or kill the beast with a well-aimed implement, earning three old pence for a mouse or a coveted sixpence (the price of a cinema seat) for a rat. Even the lavatory, with its graffiti-covered cubicles and iron trough along which ran a row of water taps, had been replaced by pristine toilets with rows of white enamel washbasins. Gone also were the remnants of gas lighting, cosy in winter, stifling in summer, lit with a taper by an apprentice when he arrived at work in the early morning.

There was also something else missing. Before we departed I recalled what it was: the pervading smell of the print workshop, a blend dominated by printer's ink, modified by lead or molten metal and the dust collected in cases of type, plus a hint of Rozelux, the sweet-scented pink cream rubbed into the hands to make them easier to wash.

The visit was bound to evoke a variety of memories, and they floated to the surface. One seemed more distressing at a distance than it was at the time. The second round of the enemy's attack on London used their 'secret weapons'; the first of these, the V1, known as 'the doodle-bug', was launched on London in June 1944. This pilotless plane crashed when its engine cut out at an approximate predetermined distance; the plane could be heard and usually seen on its preordained trajectory. When they first appeared the public air-raid warning gave its dismal drone and everyone went to the shelters where they usually remained until the all-clear sounded: a costly activity for the firm. An alternative strategy was soon adopted where spotters would go onto the roof when the public siren went off and they would try to assess in which direction the doodlebug was travelling; only when it was clear that it was heading in our direction would the firm's own alarm be set off, and work stopped. Apprentices undertook a rota for this task operating in pairs, doubtless fulfilling that exhortation in their indentures to 'demean and behave himself as a good and faithful Apprentice should'. This was clearly a much cheaper solution for the firm (especially as no danger money was paid); it wasn't that apprentices' lives were expendable, just that their time was. Fortunately, I recall finding the activity exciting rather than scary. The V2, however, the supersonic rocket launched in September of the same year, travelled too fast to be seen for warning to be given.

A more rewarding task was the weekly rota for getting the men's tea from the local cafe, frequently with morning bread and dripping, and afternoon cake; mugs would be collected on a type case modified as a tray. At the week's end a small but welcome tip would be collected, except from the few who gave a cheery 'your reward will be in Heaven' or the promise of 'an orange at Christmas'.

Memories of some of the personalities flooded back, of journeymen and apprentices, and the group of us who made a weekly visit to Sadlers Wells Opera – I being the one whose home was most conveniently located to queue for cheap seats at seven in the morning. My main reader appeared to me very erudite and guided some of my early literary reading. He had developed a nice little earner from the furniture trade periodical he looked after which paid for each letter published; he frequently wrote a provocative one under his own name, and then a reply under a pseudonym. The head reader, another First World War gas victim, who had recently come out of retirement, was familiar with classical Greek and Latin, and was teaching himself Hebrew. My first 'clicker', was responsible for a periodical for Free Norwegian armed forces; though a strong Conservative and an official in his local church, he never tried to influence me in either area, but he did endeavour to get a rather rude cartoon removed from the journal; in this he was unsuccessful, the editor being more concerned with the morale rather than the morals of his readers. A socialist fed me with left-wing books and pamphlets, and a former

Russian anarchist (who had returned to Russia after the 1917 Revolution, but had come back to Britain disillusioned a few years later) likewise produced interesting publications, at the same time cynically cautioning against youthful over-idealism. A Roman Catholic attempted conversion, even arranging a discussion with an impressive, but to me unconvincing, Jesuit priest in his seminary. Working with such people created a challenging milieu.

There was a rhythm to the week, especially for those engaged on weekly journals: a steady pace rising to a concentrated crescendo as the final preparations culminated in the type-matter being imposed, that is encased in a special page order within a metal frame or 'chase', the whole known as a forme which was then taken to the machine room for printing. A less frenetic period followed until the forme was returned to the composing room for dismantling. Someone would start whistling usually a hymn or a popular opera aria, and others would join in singing the words, with the occasional rude variation given by someone; this tended to happen more in the composing room distant from the overseer seated in his raised observation room.

Swearing levels varied: some wouldn't allow a 'damn' to cross their lips, others had a vivid terminological range. One stone-hand couldn't utter a sentence without a crudity every other word, a trait of which I was convinced he was completely oblivious. Some of the men would form groups for a swear box, the fine imposed varying with the strength of the word used; money collected would be distributed for drinks or at Xmas. A journeyman or two delighted in playing a cruel joke by sending a boy on false errands: a couple of pennyworth of chocolate wrappers, or a long weight (wait); the occasional innocent youth fell for it.

Visiting local pubs was widespread even among the under-aged boys, though a few of the men were teetotal; one reader who couldn't start the day without his beer, made an illegal arrangement with a publican and sent his reading boy to collect a mugful each morning before work – echoes of the Eighteenth Century practice, mentioned later, when a pot-boy would do his round of printing offices. Apprentices 'coming out of their time' were expected to treat colleagues to a wet celebration.

Such were just a few of the memories sparked by the visit. Clearly the world had changed.

Publication

Having retained an affection for the occupation that had nurtured my early experience of the world of work and heightened my social/political awareness and intellectual curiosity, I was intrigued to know more about the changes in the compositor's work and the effect on apprenticeships and training. A meeting was arranged in early 2009 at the St Bride Library where I had deposited a copy of my thesis,[2] partly in gratitude for the many hours I'd spent there with the valuable help of the then librarians. Out of the discussions came the suggestion that the St Bride Foundation might be interested in publishing the thesis, to include a new chapter containing something about the nature of the changes that had taken place and, in particular, how they had been experienced by the traditional compositor. I've also included this Prologue which has turned out to be more personal than initially envisaged – perhaps with elements of self-indulgence which hopefully will be forgiven. The target date for publication was set as June 2011, exactly fifty years after the thesis had been approved. The orientation of the study is sociological with a good deal of social, rather than technological, history.

What follows is the presentation of the thesis, basically unaltered apart from some corrections and slight modifications, with an Epilogue, briefly describing what has happened to the occupation since the thesis was written.

An Introduction sets out the context of the study and issues raised by the wider social climate at the time of undertaking the research in the late fifties. The thesis then divides into two parts. Part One consists of four chapters concerned with the social history of the compositor; it presents the conditions in which this relatively well-educated occupation, part of the labour aristocracy in terms of income and status, was drawn into identification with the working class. In Part Two the first two chapters are concerned with the socio-economic position of the compositor, his way of life and political and class identification at the time the material was gathered, around 1959/1960; the second two chapters describe the occupational community that developed among compositors, and attempts to measure the impact of this as a partial explanation for their atypical ideological orientation which had been established earlier.[3] A concluding chapter considers some broader theoretical implications of the findings, probably of more interest to the social historian and sociologist, and stresses the importance of occupational studies which can deepen our understanding of the broader, and in some ways cruder, concepts of class. Appendices cover the compositor's work situation, the samples used for the study, and supply a glossary of the special vocabulary developed by members of the occupation. The new Epilogue follows: this outlines relevant technological developments since the thesis was presented, and includes a few summaries of interviews with initially traditionally trained, hot metal compositors, examples of men who had to face the challenge of change.

Thus the study is a portrait of a well-regarded occupation, mainly covering its history up to the period immediately prior to its decline and virtual extinction; the study also stands as an illustration of an occupational community, its features and power to influence its members. By presenting the material largely unchanged[4] I'm conscious that the reader has to bear with the limitations of a thesis written by a novice academic. I trust sufficient interest is found to compensate for its shortcomings.

The offices of Williams, Lea in Worship Street, London
where the author worked as an apprentice

Notes

1 My craft union, the London Society of Compositors, amalgamated with the Printing Machine Minders Trade Society to form the London Typographical Society in 1955. Then in 1964, the LTS amalgamated with the provincially based Typographical Association, to form the National Graphical Association, which later absorbed several other printing trade unions (including, in 1965, the Association of Correctors of the Press, of which I was also a member) and underwent several metamorphoses as other amalgamations took place: NGA (1982), the Graphical, Paper and Media Union (GPMU) in 1991, which joined Amicus in 2004. Unionised print workers are now covered mainly by the multi-industrial union Unite, formed in 2007 from Amicus and the Transport & General Workers Union. Despite all the changes, the Chapel, the historical workshop unit of organization for print workers discussed in the thesis, still exists in a modified form.

2 Cannon, 'The Social Situation of the Skilled Worker'. Other related articles include two by the present author: 'Ideology and Occupational Community' based on a paper presented at the World Sociological Congress, Evian, Sept. 1966; and 'The Roots of Organization among Journeymen Printers'.

3 A related wider-ranging study was published several years later: Goldthorpe, Lockwood, Bechhofer, and Platt, *The Affluent Worker*. This was a major investigation concerned with the process of 'embourgeoisement'. My thesis had looked at a closely related area, highlighting a neglected aspect in this complex process, namely the role of the occupational community itself, and demonstrating that material well-being was not inevitably associated with a change in ideology. There is a methodological point worth making. I have been asked whether the fact that I had been a compositor affected my findings. When first asked this my immediate response was to defend my new identity as a sociologist by replying that any 'objective' practitioner of the 'science' should be able to arrive at the same results. Later I became doubtful and considered this over-idealistic; it is unlikely that a non-compositor would have had a similar view of what to look for. The image of the good compositor being a strong trade unionist, identifying with the working class and voting for the Labour Party might have emerged (sociologists in particular will find of relevance to this image Weber's non-evaluative 'ideal type' construct, see e.g. *From Max Weber*, edited by Gerth and Mills, p. 59). It is much less likely that the compositor's occupational community, its features and influence, would have been identified, certainly not in the same way.

4 There are in fact a few changes. First, the title; secondly, the Notes have been reduced in number, moved to the end of each chapter and streamlined, and thirdly, a separate bibliography has been abstracted from the notes. The thesis had been typed on a manual typewriter before word-processing became the norm, so had to be transcribed, presenting an opportunity to make minor corrections.

The Social Situation
of the Skilled Worker

a study of the compositor in London

Abstract

The compositor, because of his economic position and the status which is ascribed to him, stands ambiguously in the class structure. His way of life, in terms of material possessions and certain aspirations, is rather higher than that of other skilled workers; yet his ideology, in terms of class and political affiliations, is more radical than obtains among skilled workers in general. This situation is explored in this thesis in two ways. First, the changing position of the compositor is traced historically, and the conditions under which he was drawn into identifying more readily with the labour movement is presented; here are the structural conditions for the establishment of a radical ethos. Second, consideration is given to the way in which the occupation itself, through the kind of community that it has developed, acts as a means of maintaining the ethos, despite changed social conditions.

In discussing the relationship between social conditions and class consciousness, certain criticisms are made of Marx's postulates; in particular, attention is drawn to his neglect of the importance of the role of occupations in the development of class. By indicating the possibility of wide social differences, even within the skilled section of the working class, the importance of further occupational studies is emphasised.

Introduction

Since the Second World War, manual workers have participated in the increasing prosperity of British society. The effects of this phenomenon have been the subject of much controversy, and the original concern of this thesis was to investigate some of the questions that have been raised about the relationship between the levels of living, aspirations, and class and political affiliations of manual workers. Has the adoption of a non-manual, or 'middle class,' level of living (as defined by certain items of ownership, such as a house or car), also involved the adoption of other values associated with this class, such as educational and occupational aspirations for one's children? Was it possible to have, or be in the process of attaining, such a level of living and yet still retain a working class affiliation? If so, then this would suggest that prosperity was regarded primarily as an upgrading of the class as a whole and not as involving the individual in separation from his class.

The relationship between class and politics has received increasing attention in view of the results of the general elections of the 1950s. Growing prosperity has been regarded as the major factor explaining the increasing unwillingness of manual workers to support the Labour Party. The post-mortem on the Labour Party's failure to attract more votes has emphasized that the Conservatives have been identified with this prosperity.[1] On the assumption that the prosperity will continue during the 1960s, it may be argued that more individuals in the working class will support the Conservative Party and that the cohesion of the working class as such will weaken. Political observers are by no means in agreement about all this. It may be pointed out that the shift in political allegiance among manual workers since the previous election cannot be explained in terms of prosperity alone. Other factors, such as nationalization and the party image have been invoked.[2] Also it is far from clear what relationship actually exists between class affiliation and voting behaviour: if it were true that voting Conservative is an expression of weak identification with the working class, or positive rejection of the working class condition, then the Conservative party might be damaging its own interests in trying to appeal to all classes.

Most discussion of these changes has dealt with the working class as a whole. But this is too broad a category. It is unlikely that any changes taking place towards a middle class way of life are uniform: more probably some sections of the working class are being affected more than others. It is, indeed, frequently acknowledged that the skilled section of the working class is different from the less skilled sections; but it seems probable that differences could be found even within the skilled section. The study of a particular occupation could be important in providing more detailed material for the study of social stratification in general. Not all sections of the working class have been equally affected, for example, by the growing educational and occupational opportunities. The selection of a working class occupation on the frontier of the middle class in the social hierarchy ought to prove very illuminating, for in such skilled occupations, it might be expected that a working class ideology would be weakening.

The compositor seemed to be eminently suitable for such a study. He is fairly well paid, and he is certainly regarded as having high earnings. He enjoys considerable prestige through the image that people have of his earnings, education and literary associations, and his work (for an outline of his work see Appendix A). This is an occupation where changes are likely to be taking place: the combination of high earnings, status, and education should facilitate the adoption of both the material levels and aspirations of a middle class way of life. It seemed that this would be a group from which intergeneration social mobility is likely: compositors having the aspirations and the ability to fulfil aims for their children, and at the same time the occupation might have an attraction for middle class sons who are downwardly mobile. The problem was to find out to what extent these features obtained among compositors, and to try to assess what effect this had on their class identification. In addition, the compositors' economic and social position would lead one to expect political conservatism among them, yet personal observation in the past suggested a fairly strong support for the Labour Party. Were the political affiliations of the compositors very different from other skilled workers and if so what were the causes?

Of particular interest was to see whether the occupation itself, through the occupational community that developed, had any influence on the compositors' ideology. Various historical studies have been made of the printing industry that have directly or indirectly made reference to the compositor. Often the union has been the main focus of such studies and the compositor's social position has been under-emphasized. In gathering material for an historical introduction it became evident that the present occupation is affected by the past in many ways; in particular, an ideology developed over the period which is still influential; the history, therefore, merited more than an introduction. The existence of material not hitherto used and the pattern of change that emerged made it desirable to devote half the thesis to a social history of the compositor.

A number of historical questions have been formulated. First, there is the general question of how the association with the working class developed. Before the rise of literacy in this country the compositor must have stood socially very high indeed compared with other manual trades, and tradition has it that he was known as a 'gentleman compositor'; under what circumstances did the compositors become involved in the working class movement and come to support the Labour Party? In addition there are a number of more specific questions: what were the social origins of this group of artisans, when and to what extent were premiums paid to enter the trade and who could afford to pay them? What was the position of the compositors in relation to other occupations and did this undergo change, especially with mechanization?

Thus this investigation became concerned with two broad problems. One was historical: in what circumstances did an occupation with high status, because of high earnings and literacy, become drawn into the working class movement? The other problem was to find out more about the changes that are occurring in certain areas of social stratification at the present day; in particular, the effect of rising levels of living of a section of the working class on its ideology. Straddling both areas was the emergence of an occupational community and its role in sustaining this ideology.

Such problems derive from Marx's interest in the conditions of class consciousness and invite some consideration of his work. How does the historical development of the occupation fit in with Marx's thesis on increasing class consciousness? Also what is the relationship between the changing social conditions of a group and its ideology? The extent to which these theories are applicable to the findings of this thesis are discussed in the final chapter.

Mention may be made here of the sources for the material in this thesis. The historical material, though widely based, is unavoidably weighted by union records. In the absence of other data these records are used as an expression of the attitudes of members. This procedure has its dangers, for it suggests definite attitudes whilst the reality might be indifference; also, opposing attitudes are likely to be minimised. Yet it is probably true that there was a broad correlation between union policy and members' views – though which was cause and which effect is debatable. A useful balance to this bias may be found in the analysis of results of union ballots. But unfortunately their value is restricted: first, records of ballots do not go back far enough, and if they did they would then be less representative of compositors as a whole because a smaller proportion would have been union members; secondly, even these results may be subject to some occupational pressure (though this in itself would be significant); thirdly, voting may change according to temporary political and social conditions and thus may not reflect any more permanent underlying attitudes. Fourthly, and regrettably, they do not always deal with the issues this thesis tries to consider.

There are difficulties in writing history in a neat pattern: man does not make automatic and uniform reflex actions in response to economic change; values and habits may persist, especially when the periods, in terms of a number of generations of men, are relatively short; thus exceptions to delineated trends may be found without great difficulty. In addition, the quantity of material, the interpretation of statements, and the existence of contrary evidence make generalization tentative; yet it is necessary, whilst indicating opposing evidence, to stress the emphasis indicated by the research. The historical section is therefore divided into periods which broadly indicate the major trends.

The study of the present-day compositor is based mainly on samples of journeymen and apprentice compositors in London. Details of the samples are given in Appendix B. It is necessary to stress that the size of the sample is usually too small for statistical significance; nevertheless, it is suggested that some importance can be attached to the consistency of the evidence.

As the area of the investigation had to be limited, a fuller monograph on the present day compositor was not possible. Such a survey of the relationship of an occupation and the social structure would also have included the pattern of family life, leisure activities, and various effects of the occupation on the 'way of life' of its members; the intention to include a more detailed account of these features had to be abandoned.

This then became the frame of reference for the thesis:
a) The relationship between the changing social condition of members of an occupation and their class and political identification; and
b) The influence of the occupation itself, through its institutions, on these identifications.

Notes

1 Crosland, *Can Labour Win?*, p. 10.
2 Abrams, *Must Labour Lose?*: public ownership, p. 31–7; image, p. 69–70.

Part One

The Social History of
the Compositor

I

The Early History of the Compositor: Fifteenth to mid-Eighteenth Century

A Victorian illustrator imagined a seventeenth century print office and composing techniques based on early drawings. From The Pentateuch of Printing *by William Blades.*

The expansion of printing

For nearly three centuries after printing was introduced into England by Caxton, in 1476, the industry changed but little in terms of size and technique. In the fifteenth century printing was practised only in London, Oxford and St Albans. By the early sixteenth century there were printing offices in nine other provincial places but their existence was rather intermittent.[1] In 1586 a decree of Star Chamber restricted printing to London and the universities of Oxford and Cambridge.[2] It was not until 1695 that printing was permitted in the provinces,[3] and by then London had become well established as the centre of printing.

The number of printing offices in London was small but steadily growing. At the beginning of the sixteenth century there were only two to four printers, in 1525 there were ten, and by 1550 the number had grown to 30. These were situated in a small area of London with which printing was to be long associated: within the city walls particularly around St Paul's Churchyard. The trade had been largely in the hands of foreigners in the fifteenth century but these had been ousted by 1550, and in 1523 an Act of Parliament prohibited foreign apprentices and restricted the number of foreign journeymen. Within a generation the aliens were no longer the employers but the employed.[4]

The steady growth of the trade was restricted by legislation during the sixteenth and seventeenth centuries. This legislation was partly in accordance with the general economic policy of the State, and partly motivated by the need to control an important means of communication in a period of political and religious turbulence. To carry out its policy the State used the Stationers' Company which had been given its first charter in 1557.[5] The monopolistic control of the Company probably helped to reduce the number of offices, for not only did it regulate the number who practised printing, but it also granted privileges, patents or copyrights to individual members of the Company.[6]

In 1641 the Court of Star Chamber was abolished and the number of master printers rose from about 20 to 70 by 1662. The years following were sufficiently controversial to provide abundant material for these printing offices, but with the Restoration came the demand for centralized control and state censorship. Thus in 1662 a Licensing Act revived the old regulations, and the number of offices fell to 35 in 1668.

This Act ceased to have effect in 1695 and from this time printing continuously expanded in response to the development of education, the desire for news and to the needs of business.

The following indicates the expansion of printing by showing the approximate number of offices in London.

1525	1550	1583	1637	1649	1662	1668	1724	1785	1808	1826	1855
10[a]	30[a]	21[b]	20[c]	60[b]	70[d]	35[d]	75[d]	124[d]	216[d]	323[c]	423[c]

a. figure derived from Thomas, *Beginnings of Printing in London*, p. 13.
b. figure derived from Musson, *Typographical Association*, p. 5.
c. figure derived from Howe and Waite, *London Society of Compositors*, p. 14, 17, 147.
d. figure derived from Howe, *London Compositor*, p. 33.

It will be seen that the beginning of the real expansion of printing occurs around the mid eighteenth century, and it is reasonable to end the early period, when printing was still on a small scale, at this date.

The social condition of the journeyman

The word 'printer' for the journeyman during the period embraced both the 'compositor' who set the type and the 'pressman' who printed the sheets. It was expected that a journeyman could work at either occupation and men would commonly change according to where work was available. Both Thomas Gent and Benjamin Franklin refer to working at one occupation then the other, even in the same establishment, but these were versatile men. Some specialization developed very early, though not until the mid eighteenth century is there definite evidence of recruitment to specific occupations, when a trade directory specified each branch as an occupation to be entered separately, and suggests that different qualities were required for them.[7]

The question arises whether it is realistic to talk about the condition of the 'journeyman printer' if there was a strong possibility that the craftsman would eventually become a small master. The picture of the journeyman setting up on his own was not generally accurate even in this small-scale industry, or it could have been true only for a very short period. It was not until the mid-sixteenth century that the majority of masters were native-born Englishmen, and within one generation there were important financial and legislative restrictions on the aspiring journeyman. In the latter half of the sixteenth century the copyrights of the most profitable books, i.e. those in common demand, such as bibles, law and school books, were protected by patents and the price of these were beyond the reach of those without a good deal of capital. In 1586 the Star Chamber decree regulated the number of permitted apprentices, but this was far in excess of the score who could become masters. By 1599 there is evidence of some 60 journeymen in London,[8] and this had reached the figure of at least 140 in 1666. This figure is given in a petition by the journeymen to the Stationers' Court, 'The Case and Proposals of the Free Journeymen Printers in and about London', which states that this number was almost doubled by the encroachment of foreigners and by 'supernumerary apprentices and turn-overs', that is boys who were turned over to other masters or journeymen in order to complete their apprenticeship.

The evidence clearly shows that in printing the journeyman-to-master ladder could only be climbed by a minority. A gulf developed very soon between master and men, if it had not existed from the very beginning of printing in this country. As Musson puts it: 'The restriction of the number of printers, the granting of patents, and the evolution of gild government tended to place power in the hands of a small oligarchy of master printers and to create a body of permanent wage-earners'.[9] With the breakdown of regulation and the expansion of printing there were many attempts to set up as a master in a small way. Such attempts often failed, and it was probably only attempted by a small minority. Thus, early in the history of printing a group of permanent journeymen existed.

Wages

Little is known about the condition of these journeymen for the early period. It is surmised that they 'mostly lived in their employers' houses and their pay included board, lodging and clothing'.[10] Instances are cited of living-in: in 1577 a certain John Moore was to be paid £3 a year plus 'meate drink lodginge and wasshinge of his lynen';[11] but he had to buy his own clothing: 'shall finde him selfe apparell with his wages'. In 1581 there is an instance of a weekly wage working out somewhat higher, when a Christopher Hackford lived in with a wage of 1s 6d weekly.[12]

Living-in may have been true of some young journeymen, but the numbers suggest that this could not have been the general practice. At the end of the sixteenth century the number of masters was only about twenty, whereas it is estimated that the journeymen numbered about sixty, *plus* apprentices. It seems unlikely that many journeymen, especially those with families, could have boarded with their masters. Regulations made in 1587 seem to bear out this conclusion: firstly, as they were formulated in answer to complaints made by journeymen, it seems improbable that these latter were living in; secondly, the compensations given to workmen for reprints suggests that spasmodic unemployment created some concern, which would not seem compatible with the practice of living-in. Thus one of the possible conditions for a paternalistic relationship between master and journeyman was not widespread.

When it was convenient to both master and journeyman living-in certainly occurred and these conditions obtained in many country districts into the nineteenth century.[13] But this appears not to be general. A description of various trades in 1747 makes no mention of the custom of living-in as applicable to printers, whereas it is referred to for other trades. In London especially, it was probably not very extensive by this time.

Payment by piecework appears to have existed at this date, judging by the regulations made in 1635. There is further evidence of this later in the seventeenth century. Moxon, describing the customs of the printers' chapel (the organisation of journeymen in the office, of which more later), refers to payment for church Holy days whether the men work or not. He states that they are 'paid proportionably for what they undertake to earn every working day, be it half a crown, two shillings, three shillings, four shillings, etc.'[14] This suggests that there were different known outputs for which the men were paid differently. The same inference that piecework existed at that date is also made by Howe.

Evidence concerning wages is scanty, but legislation of the period, as set out in Regulations of 1587 and 1635, expressly forbade the raising of wages. By the early eighteenth century there existed a weekly payment; about £1 seems to have been the average wage. Further evidence of wages gives the average for both compositor and pressman as 16s to £1.1s. The range of possible earnings was quite wide, 'from 10s to upwards of 30s a week, according to their Capacity, Swiftness, and the Nature of the Work', this range probably also reflects some variability in the amount of work available.[15]

Thus, both fixed weekly wages and piecework seems to have existed at this time.

Another source of income was possible for the journeyman who was also a freeman of the Stationers' Company. These men were able to have apprentices indentured to them. Not all journeymen took up their freedom: those who did so probably anticipated becoming masters or the possibility of needing the benevolent activities of the Stationers' Company. The apprentice was not generally paid, though Plant shows there were exceptions to this, and the value of the work he did accrued to the person to whom he was indentured; in return he was taught the trade and was lodged and fed. The 1586 Decree of the Star Chamber restricted the number of apprentices a freeman could have at any one time to one each. Later, the liverymen of the Stationers' Company made it difficult for a freeman to take an apprentice. For example, a journeyman was fined in the early seventeenth century for 'keeping an apprentice... being himself but a journeyman'. One source of income, which possibly superseded indenturing to a journeyman, was the payment by the master of a gratuity each year to a journeyman who taught the trade to the master's apprentice.

These were extras. To see how the printers compared with other trades at the time in terms of wages, average earnings must be considered. Only a rough comparison can be made for the seventeenth century. Moxon in 1683 gives the average wages of the compositor as 2s to 4s daily. Gregory King at the same time estimates that the income of the artisan family was about £40 yearly.[16] But this was for the whole family. For proper comparisons one would need to know the extent of income for other than the male head and whether the practice of earning by other members of the family was true of printers. Also one needs to know to what extent these averages allow for unemployment. It would appear, however, that it was possible for compositors to earn wages well above the average for artisans. At the mid eighteenth century the earning of carpenters are given at 15s weekly, that of the tin-plate worker at 12s to 15s weekly and the tailor 1 shilling per day at least. A more scholarly account of wage levels[17] gives 15s weekly as the upper limit for craftsmen until the 1720s and 18s until the 1770s. The maintenance of wages at a time of falling prices (as indicated by the price of wheat) meant a real increase in living levels in the first half of the century. Therefore, the wage of the journeyman printer, at about £1 weekly in the first part of the eighteenth century, would place him among the better paid craftsmen in a period which has been designated as the 'golden age of labour'.

Employment

We have then a body of journeymen earning a good wage; yet there is evidence that the actual situation of these journeymen was not entirely satisfactory because of the instability of employment.

Apart from the suppression of unlicensed printing offices, among the most important functions of the Stationers' Company was the control of entry into the trade, the maintenance of wage rates and of full employment. Tudor legislation was paternalistic as well as monopolistic and used the Company as a vehicle for dealing with these problems.

There is sufficient evidence to show that instability of employment was a problem. A petition in 1578 from the 'poore men of this Company' produced an ineffectual reply from the Stationers. But more positive action was soon taken. In 1582 the journeymen of the Company presented a 'humble petition of the pore prynters' to the Privy Council, complaining of lack of work. Some response came in 1587 when the Stationers' Company issued 'certen orders concerning printinge'. These accorded rights to journeymen regarding reprints which were made from standing type and did not require re-setting. The number of impressions that could be made from standing type was restricted, so that the matter would have to be re-set and so provide employment. Also apprentices were not to be employed while journeymen were out of work.

The petition to the Privy Council showed that the journeymen were not content to make their complaints only within the Company. Also in 1613 a petition was sent by the journeymen to the Lord Chancellor of England stating that the Stationers' Company had not listened to their complaints, and that more apprentices were taken on than was legal; and the consequent unemployment encouraged the private printing of seditious books. Thus, though theoretically the Company existed for masters and men, the men felt it necessary to go outside and appeal directly to the State.

Twenty years later the employment situation had not improved. The journeymen forwarded another petition to the Company complaining that an excessive number was entering the trade, some of whom were not properly bound as apprentices; it also appears that the restrictions on standing type and the number of impressions were not being adequately observed. The Company's Regulations of 1635 which were framed in reply to the petition have been described as an 'Arbitration Case', for in addition to the consideration of the complaints by the journeymen, those made of the journeymen by some master printers were also considered; these concerned the use of the masters' equipment, particularly for work for private benefit.

In 1637 the Star Chamber took up the problem of unemployment directly by issuing decrees. These regulations were partly motivated by the problem that had existed earlier in the century: that 'divers libellous seditious and mutinous books have been unduly printed, and other books and papers without license, to the disturbance of the peace of the Church and State.' The Court of Star Chamber agreed with the journeymen by attributing this problem to unemployment: 'a great part of the secret printing in corners' resulted from the absence of employment for journeymen printers and it was laid down that any journeyman who was a freeman of the Stationers' Company had to be employed by a master printer whether there was work or not. Also men who had been apprenticed at Oxford and Cambridge were forbidden to seek employment in London when out of their time, without special permission.

But the main problem of unemployment continued. In 1666, after a major plague and the Great Fire which must have destroyed a great deal of equipment and disorganized the trade, another petition is presented: 'The Case and Proposals of the Free-Journeymen-Printers in and about London, humbly submitted to Consideration'. Again, appeals made to control the entry of apprentices, whose numbers had reduced the 140 workmen printers 'to great necessity and temptation for want of lawful imployment'.

State regulations had become a dead-letter by the end of the seventeenth century. But by the beginning of the eighteenth century, work was becoming more plentiful as the demand for printing matter expanded. Trade and industry were growing, and reading was on the increase. 'A fair proportion of the lower classes could read even in the seventeenth century and from the end of that century onwards there was a great variety of charity schools'; also by 1725 nearly every town of any size had its own newspaper.[18]

There was a good deal of casual work; that is, working for short periods with different employers. Thomas Gent found it more profitable at one time to be a 'smouter' (casual worker) than a 'cuz' (full time worker).

Yet it was probably preferable to be employed permanently over a long period. The amount of work available in printing tends to fluctuate, working at high pressure and long hours for a few days followed by a lack of employment; high wages followed by low. The accounts of William Strahan in 1739–40[19] indicate the amount of casual work done. The amounts expended weekly in wages range in one year from £1 16s to over £9, with no two consecutive weeks alike. The practice was to take on men as work was available, retaining one or two journeymen permanently on the establishment.

Tramping over the country in search of employment or seeking temporary work on the way to a destination is shown by Gent's autobiography to be established among printers as early as 1714. It is not known whether this was a custom just developing or whether, despite the regulations in force until the 1690's, men tramped between printing offices which had been set up illicitly in the provinces during the seventeenth century. This was likely: in 1742 an advertisement stated that a house in York had been used for printing for over 100 years (though this could have been an exaggeration), whereas the Licensing Act permitted York only from 1662. Work was not always available, and it was already customary for assistance to be given to tramps by the journeymen working in the office where the tramp called. Here is evidence of the existence of a sense of an occupational community ready to recognize and help brother journeymen without regard to geographical origins.

Thus despite good wages, the printer could not enjoy a life of steady employment. However, wages were kept up despite unemployment, partly because of state policy for most of the period and partly because of the readiness of the journeymen to express their discontent.

Social status and image of the journeymen

Despite the fact that unemployment modified the condition of the compositor, he appears to have enjoyed considerable social status during the period. Some estimate can be made of this social standing by considering the way the occupation was regarded in terms of the qualifications necessary for the work, and the social source of recruitment.

The early compositor has been regarded as being necessarily highly educated, at a time when books were usually historical or scholastic and printed in Greek, Latin and French.[20] There is no real evidence of the extent of the compositor's education, but he must have been relatively educated in the early period if only in being able to read.

Moxon observed that as far as the work as such was concerned it was not necessary for the compositor to be a scholar, so long as he was able to read his copy; but the carelessness of authors had made it necessary for the compositor to be 'a good English scholar, at least' so that he is 'able to make his copy read well'. The book of trades, in 1747, put the requirements somewhat higher, reflecting probably the image held of the occupation rather than the needs of the job: 'A lad ought not only to read and spell English well, but to be familiar with various written hands; to know somewhat of Grammar, Pointing and the Characters of the Greek, Hebrew, etc.' Moxon also refers to the requirements for press-work with which comparison may be made. This work 'requires a good deal of Nicety, as well as strength ... therefore a lad for this part should be both stout and nimble, and if he can read only it is sufficient.'

As with most crafts at the time, the length of apprenticeship was long: the minimum period was seven years, indentures being arranged to expire when the apprentice was 24. Terms of up to 14 years are recorded for the early part of the period.[21] This was much longer than was usual in parts of the Continent. The length of apprenticeship in France was four years in 1615 – the average for most crafts there – but the major-ity did not begin their apprenticeship before they were 18 to 20. For the compositor in France was well educated: by 1649 an apprentice before being accepted had to pass a formal examination by the Rector of the University proving an acquaintance with Greek in addition to Latin. Later in the century it was asserted that many of the journeymen were gradu-ates of the University of Paris. No wonder the French poet, Lamartine, regarded printing as the most intellectual of the manual trades.[22]

The relatively high wage and the image of educational requirements made it likely that the craft was accredited with high status and this prob-ably affected the source of recruitment into the trade. Some indication of the way the occupation was regarded, early in the eighteenth century at least, can be seen in the obituary of E. Cave (1691–1754), a compositor who became editor of *The Gentleman's Magazine*. The writer says, 'this was a trade for which men were formerly qualified by a literary education and which was pleasing to Cave, because it furnished some employment for his scholastic attainments'.[23]

The practice of paying premiums for the apprenticeship of a boy is also suggestive of social origin. This raises questions of how much was paid, to what extent they were paid and who could afford these payments. The extent of premium paying and the sums involved have tended to be over estimated. There is evidence of premiums being paid in the industry as early as 1614, when sums of between £10 and £20 were paid.

It is not known, however, for which sections of the trade these premiums were paid.[24] Plant states that premiums had become customary by the eighteenth century and gives a figure of about £50 for printing and book-binding.[25] The *Book of Trades* was nearer actual practice in estimating the premium amount as between £10 to £20 for compositors and pressmen.

Fairly accurate answers to the questions of social origin and pre-mium payments are given in the Apprentice Registers of the Stationers' Company. The record after 9 June, 1718 (the first record of the occupa-tion of the person to whom the apprentice is bound) gives the occupa-tion of the boy's father, the amount of premium paid and who paid it. Thus examination of these registers shows the social origin of the boy entering printing, how much was paid in premiums and the extent to which this custom was actually practised. At this time the regulations of the Company were still generally observed and apprentices were bound through the Company so that the records are fairly representative.

There are a number of difficulties in trying to construct a social hierar-chy from these records. In the first place there is the general problem of determining what was the actual social stratification for the period. Then there are the problems of estimating the significance of any occupation which is given without explanation in the records. The social position of a merchant or shopkeeper can vary considerably according to his affluence. And the position of the small shopkeeper was at best generally no better than that of the artisan. One cannot be sure whether a given occupa-tion means an owner or craftsman or both – 'baker' and 'shoemaker', for example. Should surgeons be included with barber-surgeons and what is their social position? What is meant by 'gentleman'? Does 'clerke' refer to clerical work or to cleric? There is also the major problem of comparing a given occupation over time, and deciding whether any change had taken place in its social standing (e.g. between yeoman and farmer).

In the five years from mid 1718 to mid 1723 there were 119 appren-tices indentured, and the following tables show the source of recruitment and the number paying a premium; and a rough hierarchy of kinds of occupations similar to that given by Gregory King in 1688.[26] From this a broader classification can be made into 'above artisan', 'artisan' and 'below artisan' which gives give a rough guide to the source of recruitment.

A large number of the entrants into printing came from among other artisans, but it will be seen that a very substantial element are drawn from the more comfortable groups. The small proportion associated with the printing trades partly reflects the expanding nature of the industry, having to draw on other groups.

Table 1 **Source of Recruitment, 1718–1723**

Occupation of father	No.	Number paying premiums
Gentlemen	1	7
Clerkes	3	3
Sheriff's Officer	1	1
Surgeon (including barber-surgeons)	8	5
Merchants & shopkeepers[a]	16	11
Yeomen	11	5
Printing trades[b]	18	2
Other artisans	41	16
Mariners & fishermen	4	1
Gardeners	2	1
Other unskilled[c]	5	1
	119	53

a These are combined because it is difficult to distinguish between them.
b Includes 12 Stationers, 2 Stationer-Printers, 1 Bookseller, 3 Printers. The premiums were paid by a Stationer and by the Bookseller.
c Includes a Coachman, Porter, Park-keeper, and 2 Labourers. The premium was paid by the Porter.

Premiums accompany nearly half of the entrants (44 per-cent). They range in amount from £4 to £105, but about two-thirds are between £10 and £30 with over half of these between £10 and £12. The mode in fact is £10. In five cases the premiums were paid by charities; these were mainly £4 in amount.

It will be seen that premiums are paid more frequently proportionately by the higher social groups (over half of these as against about one-third from artisans and below). This may mean that they were concerned with getting their son into the trade and were able to afford to pay to do so. Printers did not have a rigid policy about whether they accepted premiums or not. Certain printers accepted premiums from some boys and not from others. This would partly depend on personal factors. But other considerations were likely to affect the amount paid. The Gentleman who

Table 2 **Payment of Premiums**

	% indentured	No.	% paid a premium	No.
Above artisan	54	64	64	34
Artisan	42	50	34	18
Below artisan	4	5	2	1
of whom % printers	2			

paid £105 probably expected his boy to be trained in such a way as to enable him to set up as a master printer when he completed his apprenticeship. But this aspiration cannot be alleged for all premium payments. It is, however, important to point out that premium payments were not made in order to enter the trade but in order to learn the trade and also, most important, they were part payment for being fed and looked after; if this proved unsatisfactory premium payments could be reclaimed.

Another explanation is suggested for the fact that the higher proportion of premiums are paid by the higher social groups. This is that these were familiar with the notion of premium paying, whereas the artisans were more aware of actual practice from experience in their own trades or from contact with printers. It is significant that only two premiums were paid by those connected with printing.

What is shown by the analysis is that premiums were far from universal in printing, nor were the amounts as high as popularly supposed. This supports the view that the system of living-in by the apprentice was far from general; though it could be argued that the master was content to have the earnings of the apprentice as payment for being looked after. Most important, the records reveal that recruitment was drawn from a wide social range but with an emphasis on the higher groups.

This suggests that the image of the printer was high enough for these groups to be willing to apprentice their sons to the trade. And the existence of this source of recruitment in the trade was likely to reinforce the image.

The occupational community

'The Chapel' is the organization of the journeymen in a printing office. This institution of great social importance developed early though its origin is obscure. The earliest known reference[27] to it is in the seventeenth century and states that every printing house is called a Chapel 'by the custom of Time out of mind'. In this, and other accounts, the chapel is presented as an institution for social regulation among the journeymen, rather than as the local means of combination against the employer which it later became.

Moxon's detailed description shows that the chapel was run democratically: judgement on any controversy was by a 'plurality of votes in the Chappel'; the oldest freeman was the 'Father of the Chapel' (FoC). Rules were laid down regulating relations between the men (regarding swearing, fighting and being drunk within the Chapel) and ensuring that due care was taken about certain aspects of work. The penalty for a breach of these rules was a 'solace' which could be purchased at a price ranging from one penny to one shilling, the amount being decided on each occasion by the Chapel members. If a man refused to pay the sum decided by the Chapel he was solaced: the workmen 'lay him on his Belly athwart the Correcting-stone' and gave him 'Eleven blows on his Buttocks'. Different Chapels formulated other, often trivial offences (such as making puns) in good-natured attempts to increase chapel income, which was shared out generally in the form of beer. Other payments illustrate the extent to which it was customary for the personal life of a journeyman to be brought into his occupation. When a man married he paid 2s 6d to the Chapel; the birth of son and daughter required payments of 1s and 6d, respectively; even a visit from a man's wife meant a payment of 6d, but on such an occasion the journeymen each paid 2d 'to welcome her' – presumably with a drink. Moxon also gives an account of the yearly feast, the 'Way-goose' given for the trade on May Day.

Ritual played a prominent part in Chapel activities. This was especially so in the case of initiation ceremonies. A new entrant into the Chapel was initiated by a complicated ceremony, and one such is described by Thomas Gent.[28] Another example occurred when a printing office was established in a house not used before for that purpose. A mock imitation of a religious consecration ceremony was performed by the FoC: 'the chief Ceremony is drinking Success to the Master, sprinkling the walls with strong Beer, and singing the Cuz's anthem'.[29]

Having become so institutionalized the Chapel was a powerful pressure to conformity. It was difficult to refuse to become a member or to avoid payment in conformity to its decisions or rules. In the case of a workman trying to refuse 'it is left to the Majority of the Chapel, in Convocation assembled, whether He shall be continued any longer a Chapellonian; and if his Sentence is to be discontinued, he is then declared a Brimstone; that is an excommunicated person. ...While he continues in this State, he can have no Redress for any Mischief that is done Him; so that, in a short Time, he is glad to pay the Penalty, which He incurred and a discretionary fine besides, to reconcile Himself to the Chapel'. An example of this is recalled by Benjamin Franklin.[30] Every new journeyman in an office was required to pay entrance money (called Benvenue) to the Chapel. Franklin had paid his when he worked as a pressman, but when he moved into the composing room in the same office another payment was demanded. Franklin thought this an imposition, especially as the money was spent on drink and he was a teetotaller, and he refused. 'I stood out for two or three weeks, was accordingly considered an excommunicate, and had so many little pieces of private malice practised on me, by mixing my sorts, transposing and breaking my matter, etc., if I ever stept out of the room; and all ascribed to the chapel ghost (known as Ralph) which they said ever haunted those not regularly admitted; that not withstanding the master's protection, I found myself obliged to comply and pay the money; convinced of the folly of being on ill-terms with those one is to live with continually'.

A document of 1734[31] consists of the rules of a particular Chapel. This gives a detailed list of fines for omissions and carelessness at work, and must be an early example of a professional code for craftsmen. The social functions of this code are shown by the rules on disputes between men and by the prohibition of gambling.

The major part of the day was taken up by work. Hours were long. Customary hours for an apprentice, for example, were from six in the morning till nine at night. These hours for the apprentice would include extra time for opening and closing the shop with its appropriate preparations; even so, the journeyman's day was still very long, especially in a trade notorious for its periodic requirements for overtime. There was little time for leisure outside work so that work had to provide its own diversions. Drinking played a prominent part in these activities. Chapel funds were apparently largely expended on drinking. 'Births, funerals, initiations, and all other social events were made the occasions for drink.' It was alleged of one establishment that it was more like an ale-house than a printing house. Franklin was disgusted with the extent of beer-drinking in the office in which he worked where an ale-house boy was in constant attendance. The intemperate would take off a day to recover after Sunday, hence 'St Monday'. But beer drinking was important for conviviality. And the wide-spread practice of it in an industry which was heavily concentrated in one area probably made for contact with other printers meeting in public houses.

Thus a direct result of this absence of leisure was the development of a community at the workplace. The existence of such an institution as the Chapel with its system of disciplinary rules regulating behaviour in relation to men and the work itself, its social occasions, language, and ritual, is evidence of the strong occupational community among journeymen printers.

Concentration of Firms

This community was facilitated by contact between the men. This was likely to be established in a trade of high status, small in number, and where the firms were heavily concentrated geographically.

Evidence for this concentration is to be found in a list of the master printers in London compiled by Negus in 1724. The list gives the address of each printer so that it is possible to construct a map showing their distribution. There were 75 firms in London (all the provinces as yet contained only 28); for five of these no addresses were given, and 68 of the remaining firms have been located.[32]

It will be seen from the diagram that the main area for printing is bounded by Fetter Lane in the west, Barbican in the north and Moorgate in the east. About 80 per cent of firms (54 out of 68) were in this area. But closer concentrations existed. Within about a quarter of a mile of St. Bartholomew's Hospital, 44 of the 68 firms are to be found. Some streets contained several printers: Old Bailey and St. John's Lane, Smithfields, had seven each; Little Britain and Aldersgate Street, five each; and Jewin Street added another four to the Aldersgate Street area, which contained 20 firms altogether. One interesting fact emerges: despite the popular notion about Fleet Street as an early centre of printing, in fact it had, at this time, only two printers, and its immediate surroundings added merely another three. It is true that Caxton's successor, Wynkyn de Worde, moved into Fleet Street about 1501 and others in the early sixteenth century were also there. This was because of the existence of a number of religious institutions in the neighbourhood, housing people likely to have a demand for books. But the main book trade became established in the Aldersgate Street area, (which contained many literary personages), and printers, who were themselves often booksellers,[33] were concentrated in this area before they moved westward to Fleet Street and the West End.

Otherwise they were somewhat scattered: a group of six near the main area, in the Strand, Covent Garden, and Lincoln's Inn fields; two near the Tower of London and another pair in Bishopsgate; and the odd office off Gray's Inn Road, and in Southwark where a printing office was established as early as 1514.

Such concentration made for easy contact between journeymen: particularly when given the propensity for beer drinking by the men in an area well provided with public houses. It is continued contact with others engaged in similar activities which made possible the development and maintenance of the occupational community. Contact within the firm alone was not sufficient at that time for the development of such a community. The largest firms had only about a dozen men in the late seventeenth century, and the larger firm of the early eighteenth century was an exception. Generally, the size of the firm was very small, so that contact with printers in other offices was essential for the continuance of the social customs of the trade and for group consciousness.

What relations actually existed between the various Chapels is not known. But the records of the earlier petitions by the journeymen indicate that they were coming together to make their demands, though this contact was still of an informal or temporary character. It might be argued that these were hardly demands made by self-reliant journeymen, but humble petitions to the master, though the evidence even for the earlier periods shows that the men were willing to by pass the masters. Certainly by the early eighteenth century the journeymen were more strongly active. An obituary notice by Samuel Johnson of E. Cave (1691–1754)[34] refers to his attempts as a young journeyman to persuade others to combine: 'having summoned his fellow journeymen to concert measures against the oppression of their masters, he mounted a kind of rostrum, and harangued them so efficaciously, that they determined to resist all future invasions'. This was probably in the second decade of the eighteenth century. The outcome of it we do not know, but it was not likely to have been an isolated occurrence; nearer the mid century, in 1748, one master printer wrote 'our compositors, who have wanted to raise their prices, [have] combined for that purpose'.[35] Such incidents were the forerunners of more formal combination; the need alone for combination was not enough, the idea itself had to be formulated and made familiar before more formal organization was possible. So that these activities helped to make a climate receptive to the idea of combination, of which there is evidence later in the century.

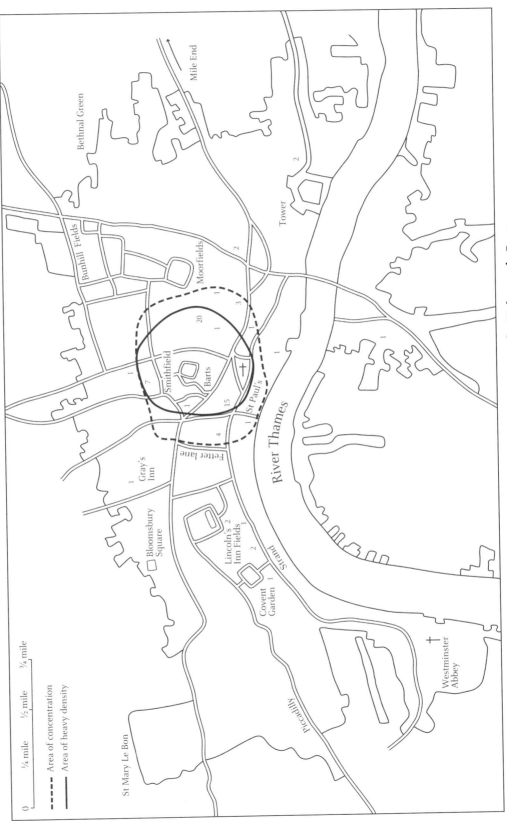

Concentration of Printing Firms in the Early Eighteenth Century

Conclusion

We have then the social conditions out of which it was possible for a section of the working class to emerge, which could be called a 'labour aristocracy'. An 'aristocracy' because these were journeymen of fairly high status, earning relatively good wages (though not far removed, financially, from other artisans); a group able and willing to express itself; being aware of themselves and of the conditions of the trade through contact with others in a similar condition.

A 'labour' aristocracy because these were permanent journeymen, and their condition was one of insecure employment, so that relative comfort throughout life could not be assured.

The economic condition of these early compositors combined with their conditions of work and facilities for easy contact, encouraged the development of a strong consciousness of belonging to an occupational group.

Notes

1 Thomas, *Beginnings of Printing in London*, p. 14.
2 Plant, *English Book Trade*, p. 81.
3 Plant, p. 85.
4 Howe and Waite, *London Society of Compositors*, p. 4.
5 Howe, *London Compositor*, p. 11.
6 Musson, *Typographical Association*, p. 5.
7 *General Description of all Trades*, p. 174–7.
8 Timperley, *Encyclopaedia of Literary and Typographical Anecdote*, p. 435.
9 Musson, *Typographical Association*, p. 10.
10 Howe and Waite, *London Society of Compositors*, p. 3.
11 Greg and Boswell, *Records of the Stationers' Company*, p. 3.
12 Greg and Boswell, p. 12.
13 Smith, *Working Man's Way in the World*, p. 8.
14 Moxon, *Mechanick Exercises*, p. 323–31; quotation from p. 327.
15 *General Description of all Trades*, p. 174–7; quotation from p. 175–6.
16 Hamilton, *History of the Homeland*, p. 264.
17 Gilboy, *Wages in Eighteenth Century England*; London wages are at p. 8–38.
18 Richards, 'Social and Economic Aspects of Combination in the Printing Trade before 1875', p. 6–7; quotation from p. 7.
19 Austen-Leigh, *Story of a Printing House*, between p. 11 and 12.
20 Cornfield, *Effect of the Industrial Revolution on Workers in the Printing Industry*, p. 4.

21 Plant, *English Book Trade*, p. 131–2.

22 Pottinger, *French Book Trade in the Ancien Regime*, p. 269–86.

23 Account of the Life of Mr Edward Cave', *Gentleman's Magazine*, Feb. 1754, p. 55–8; quotation from p. 56. Reprinted, revised, in *The Works of Samuel Johnson* (London, 1796), vol. 12, p. 210–19.

24 Jackson, *Records of the Stationers' Company*, p. 65, 100, 106–7.

25 Plant, *English Book Trade*, p. 151.

26 Displayed graphically as 'The Pyramid of English Society 1688' in Cole and Postgate, *Common People*, p. 70.

27 Moxon, *Mechanick Exercises*, p. 323–31; see also p. 383–5.

28 Gent, *Life*, p. 15–17.

29 A useful discussion of the origin of 'Chapel' and customs is to be found in Musson, *Typographical Association*, p. 12–15.

30 Franklin, *Memoirs*, vol. 1, p. 69–70.

31 Howe, *London Compositor*, p. 29–32.

32 Nichols, *Literary Anecdotes*, vol. 1, p. 288–312.

33 Plant, *English Book Trade*, p. 80–6.

34 'Account of the Life of Mr Edward Cave', *Gentleman's Magazine*, Feb 1754, p. 55–8; quotation from p. 57.

35 Sale, *Samuel Richardson*, p. 27.

Interior of the principal composing room as shown in
Specimens of the Types Commonly used in the Temple Printing
Office, Bouverie Street. *Published 1826*

II

From Group Awareness to Artisan Consciousness: Mid-Eighteenth to Mid-Nineteenth Century

The expansion of printing

The changing social and economic conditions in this period led to a widespread demand for printing. The development of commerce necessitated more printed matter in the shape of catalogues, advertisements, forms, certificates and receipts of various descriptions; political controversy, interest, and activity stimulated the production of newspapers (facilitated by improvements in communications), pamphlets, books, and governmental printing; growing literacy[1] produced a demand for books and magazines varying in their content from the 'blood and thunder' species, to the 'improving'.

The number of different volumes that had been published increased from 1,105 in the year 1828 to 2,934 in 1853.[2] Monthly publications had increased from 177 in 1831 to 362 in 1853, and one popular magazine alone, *The Penny Magazine*, was selling 200,000 copies per issue in 1832.

A good deal of this was the result of the efforts of those who were interested in providing reading matter for the newly literate who could not afford expensive literature. Brougham in 1826 provided the principle and the precedent of cheap literature in forming the Society for the Diffusion of Useful Knowledge. Inexpensive journals and cheap editions of famous books, poets and popular novelists soon followed. By 1854 one million copies each of the following were being sold: *The London Journal, Reynold's Miscellany, Cassell's Paper* and *Family Herald*. Various cheap editions of 'libraries' were issued, though the majority of the reading public would buy only for immediate reading: 'this principle made the essayists, the magazines, the newspapers'.[3]

Demand was stimulated by the growing literature, the creation of circulating libraries, and the development of improvement societies and organizations such as the Literary and Mechanics' Institutes. Reduction in the price of books was an important factor, and later the development of the penny post also helped to stimulate advertising by post.

The growth in the desire for reading and therefore the demand for books and periodicals was accompanied by an interest in political events which was met by the development of the newspapers. By 1854 there were 600 papers in the United Kingdom which could properly be called 'newspapers'. The annual circulation of these in England and Wales had risen from 15 million in 1801 to 29 million in 1836, and then after the reduction of the stamp duty to 1d, to 72 million in 1853. In London alone there were 14 dailies, six two-to-three times weekly, and 71 weekly newspapers.

Thus there was a great expansion in printing. From 1724 to 1785 the number of firms in London rose from 75 to 124; by the early nineteenth century the number was over 200 and by 1855 the number had increased to 423.[4]

Though the number of firms had greatly increased, the size of these firms had not grown substantially. Earlier in the eighteenth century there are one or two instances of relatively large firms. Tonson and Watts employed about 50 workmen.[5] By mid-century Richardson had about 40 employees but these were in three separate houses.[6] William Strahan, the King's printer had seven to nine pressmen constantly employed in 1771, which would probably give him roughly 50 employees. But these were the exceptions. It has been suggested that the size of the average firm in the last quarter of the eighteenth century was probably not much larger than in the past (which would be a total of about four journeymen and apprentices together) and that an employer was doing very well if he had a dozen to 20 men employed.[7] By the turn of the century the largest firms, Strahan's and Hansard's, had about 100 men each. By the end of the period four firms had over 100 compositors each.[8] Several firms had over 50. Altogether, nearly 40 firms had over 20 compositors. Nearly 100 more had between three and 20. Over two-thirds (288 firms) contained three compositors or fewer. Thus over the period a few large firms had developed but the size of the typical firm was still rather small. Probably there were about 4,500 compositors in London by the end of the period.

With this expansion a division of labour developed that was important to the compositor in two respects. Firstly there was an industrial division of labour. The printer, though he had already become separated from the bookselling trade, did all kinds of printing. But it was soon found preferable to specialise; and newspapers, bookwork, parliamentary printing, periodical and general 'jobbing' began to separate. Many had often been separated within the firm – groups of men and possibly different rooms being allotted to the different types of work. Then gradually a firm would increase its specialization until that particular type of work predominated.[9] As will be seen later, the different branches of work were important, because some of them had different wage rates. The second division of labour was occupational. The division between compositors and pressmen had always existed but it was not clear-cut: a 'printer' was one who could and often did work at both, though natural ability, preference and convenience would tend to keep a man at one rather than the other. During the latter part of the period, that is, during the early nineteenth century, it became much more customary to learn only one section of the trade and remain at that throughout life. This was a direct result of the increase in the size of the firm. In the small firm it was easy and desirable for a boy to be adaptable to the demands of the work and he would learn both aspects of printing. As the size of the firm increased it was more convenient to have the labour force permanently in one or the other section and the apprentice would tend to learn only one side of the trade. Theoretically a boy was apprenticed as a 'printer', that is to both occupations, well into the nineteenth century as is shown by the register of apprentices. National censuses retain 'printer' as an occupation till 1911. But in fact the division was taking place well before. It was really with the development of machines for printing in the second decade of the nineteenth century and separate machine departments, that the division became strong.

The existence of compositors as a separate occupational group was not a new development; but as the division became clearer and increasingly isolated from the pressmen the feeling of exclusiveness was likely to be reinforced. This was further emphasized by, and helped to give rise to, the development of separate union organizations.[10]

During this period the authority of the Stationers' Company which had been weakening throughout the eighteenth century was finally broken; this was in common with the general breakdown of the form of protectionism known as Mercantilism. This can be demonstrated in several spheres that affected the compositor. First, the journeymen negotiated disputes directly with the master printers without reference to the Company. Secondly, and at the same time, the journeyman was creating his own benefit clubs and not relying on the benefit of the Company.[11] This illustrates the growing independence of the journeyman and also the need to rely on his own endeavours. Thirdly, the Company's control over the intake of apprentices diminished: employers increasingly ceased to indenture their boys through the Company. For example, by 1818 the proportion bound via the Company was down to 60 per cent and continued to decrease through the period. The custom of doing so became largely ceremonial as it still remains today. This illustrated the increasing failure of employers to recognise the Company as a regulating agency. The Company itself became concerned with trivialities, giving much attention, for example, to the upkeep of the Company's barge.

Though printing was now no longer restricted in size and locality, London remained in this period an extremely important centre. Within the metropolis the location was changing in a westwards direction:[12] a directory of 1785 shows that in a little over half a century the concentration was moving westwards from the Aldersgate area. This process continued during the early nineteenth century[13] and by the mid-century, printing had expanded mainly in these areas with heavy concentrations in the vicinity of Fleet Street and the Strand.[14] This location coincided with the establishment of the area as a fashionable literary centre. It will be seen that despite the expansion, the area for printing was still sufficiently concentrated to facilitate contact between the offices.

The social condition of the compositor

Wages

Any attempt to determine a specific wage rate for this occupation at a particular period would be unreal. Wages varied considerably. A detailed treatment of these rates and the causes of them would require a separate study. Some compositors' wages were paid by a fixed weekly rate, others were based on a scale of prices, that is a piece scale.

The piece scale was extremely complex – for it tried to cover all the different kinds of work which the compositor might have to set: the intricate work being paid differently from straightforward matter. Thus the bookwork compositor and the jobbing compositor (the compositor working in a general printing firm) would have different earnings because of the different matter to be composed. Individual offices would also vary considerably depending on the relationship between the employer and the journeymen and the ability to arrive at mutual arrangements for certain kinds of work. The strength of the chapel in the firm would be an important factor in this, or the profitability of a given job; also customs in charging which had developed in one period would carry over to another. For example, during the period when the Stationers' Company was strong, reprinted work was restricted because it affected the employment prospect of the compositor; either the extent of reprint was limited, in order that the job be reset, or a special rate was paid to the compositor for reprinted jobs which entailed little of his time, so that he would not lose unduly from not having work which was profitable to his employer. When the restrictions could no longer be applied to reprints, a firm which did a large amount of reprinting would pay to the compositor the recognised special rate, and this would be regarded as 'fat' or easily earned work. Or charging would become obsolescent because of technical changes, but the compositor still claimed the old rates which no longer corresponded to the amount of work involved; this claim might be disputed but often it was agreed to because the job was profitable.

Specialist sections of compositors developed, also with their own rates. For example, newspaper rates, though not based on piecework, varied according to whether the paper was a morning, evening or a Sunday one. And later, with the development of printing in connection with government and the legislature a special piece scale 'the parliamentary scale' was introduced in 1836.

One journeyman, Charles Manby Smith, has left behind a useful picture of practices with reference to a period around 1833. He writes: 'My bills were rarely less than forty shillings and often above fifty weekly' (it was often hinted by the management that he was earning too much) whereas one old compositor in the same office earned about 12s weekly. Because Smith was not fully acquainted with the scale he lost 'fat' and did not claim extra for work at night; thus he received less than he was entitled to by custom. Even so, he felt that he earned more than he would have been able to do in a larger office because he worked as many hours as he chose. At one time he earned 12s daily on a Greek volume with Latin notes; though the more profitable work was done by the apprentices. Some of the larger and stronger chapels tried to make the earnings of the men in the firm more uniform. When Smith later moved to a larger firm he found the hours were more rigid, 'he could not work before 8 a.m. or after 6 p.m.' and that no man could be paid for more than 60 hours' work in a week, no matter how quickly he worked; thus though he earned and charged £2 14s 0d in one week, he received only £2. The other hours he could carry over to the following week so that he could work less hard then.[15]

Thus rates of pay varied according to the nature of the work done in a particular establishment, the ability of the compositor on certain kinds of work, the customs and strength of the individual chapels in implementing the scale, the pressure to maintain traditional rates in changed circumstances, and the ability of the employer to pay these rates.

An interesting procedure developed for settling disputes over the interpretation of the scale. In a disputed charge of work 'the men employed on it endeavoured, as was their duty, to get the opinions of several employers upon the subject'. The men were probably more familiar with details of the scale than the masters were; and generally the verdict was in favour of the journeymen.[16] Yet there were continuous attempts to encroach on the scale and it was complained that 'every opportunity has been taken so to construe the scale as to render the wages of labour less – and every alteration that has been made in the customs of the trade has been to our disadvantage'.

Though it is unreal to estimate the average wages of compositors as if it were a unitary figure changing only over time, it is useful to make an estimate of average wages in order to portray the general trend of wages over the period and to make some comparison with other trades.

Earnings were about 24s weekly up to 1785[17] which indicates that a rise had taken place since earlier in the century when, evidence suggests, weekly earnings were about £1. In 1786 a modification of the existing piece scale took place which gave an average wage of about 27s weekly. Compositors employed on daily newspapers continued to be paid a fixed weekly wage. This was 27s weekly before 1786 and increased to 31s 6d in March of that year. Numerous attempts were made by the compositors to modify the scale as the cost of living increased, and small amendments in the scale were made in 1793 and 1795. In 1800 a further increase in the piece scale from 4½d to 5¼d per 1,000 ens probably enabled the compositor to earn about 5s 3d daily, or nearly 32s weekly;[18] this compares with the non-piecework basic weekly wage of 30s. At this time rates for newspapers advanced to about 37s to 40s.[19]

In 1805 there was another slight advance, and in 1810 the scale was drastically revised. Piece rates up until then meant for the compositor average earnings of about 33s; the 1810 scale increased this by roughly 12½ per cent to approximately 37s.

One factor in the ability to advance wage rates was probably the demand for labour. Printing greatly expanded in the latter part of the eighteenth century and the demand for journeymen at the beginning of expansion probably exceeded the supply. But with the end of the Napoleonic Wars a reduction of ¼d per 1,000 ens was effected which reduced the wage to about 33s. Those compositors on fixed rates appeared to receive similar earnings: 21s to 27s in 1785, 30s in 1793, 33s in 1805 and 36s in 1810. This was reduced to 33s in 1816 and there it remained till the end of the period, though in 1835 it was stated that 'most respectable houses' paid 36s.

An estimate of average earnings in the 1840s[20] gave a minimum wage of 30s rising to £2 2s 0d when work was plentiful. This was fairly representative; and the range of earnings was sufficient to make substantial differences in living standards.

The daily news compositor had received considerable increases since 1786. He received 36s in 1793; 40s in 1801; 42s in 1809, and this was increased to 48s in 1810. An enquiry in 1835 showed that there was a good deal of variety of earnings among newspaper compositors depending on the paper on which he worked. The range was between £2 4s and £3 5s a week.

Living standards and cost of living

It is necessary to try to estimate the importance of these rates in terms of real wages. We saw in the last chapter that up to about 1750 living standards improved; in the second half of the century there were small advances in the cost of living, but the compositor appeared to have more than held his own. Thus the standard of living of the London journeymen seems to have improved during the eighteenth century,[21] despite certain years of high prices; on the evidence of wage rates the compositor was a good deal better off than most journeymen.

But this prosperous condition was not to be maintained for long. Two factors combined to reduce the living standard of compositors; there was first, chronologically, the rising cost of living, and then increasing unemployment.

Silberling's Cost of Living index[22] provides an approximate guide with which the income levels can be compared. It is impossible to construct a wage index for compositors with any precision; but an approximate scale can be made, sufficient to show roughly the relation between cost of living and wages.

	1790	1800	1805	1810	1816	1830	1840	1850
Wages	100	120	122	133	122	122	122/133	122/133
Cost of living	100	170	154	176	135	108	121	83

It will be seen that from the last decade of the eighteenth century to the second decade of the nineteenth century the cost of living was much higher than the increase in incomes. These were difficult years for the compositor. The negotiations of 1793 give the first references by the compositors to the increasing cost of living; again in 1800 and 1805 the 'distresses of the time' are invoked to justify claims, and the master printers also accede 'the extreme and increasing pressure of the times' in agreeing to an increase.

That the situation seemed grave and permanent is shown by a long reasoned attempt made by the compositors to deal with their distressed conditions. In April 1809 they appealed to the master printers for assistance 'to preserve us from the abyss of indigence into which ... we are rapidly sinking, owing to the accumulated enhancement in the price of every article of life; they pleaded that some degree of their previous enjoyment of 'necessities and comforts' should be restored. In the records of the negotiations which lasted one year until April 1810, when the demands were largely granted, a number of references are made to the happier years of the eighteenth century pleading that 'the compositors seek only to be restored, in some degree, to the station they enjoyed'. Comparative prices of certain necessities of life are given in evidence of the rising costs even when compared as recently as 1801, and budgets are also included.

A complete budget is reproduced in Howe. This is a budget for a 'small family of a wife and two children' made in 1810; the small size of the chosen family may be indicative of compositors' way of life. The total expenditure is higher than the average compositor's wage; this was deliberate, the intention being to show the deficiency between need and income, even if the increase in wages asked for were granted. Unforeseen expenses (e.g. medical attention) are excluded.

Something of the material enjoyments of the compositor can be seen from this list, and the final three items in particular reveal aspects of the average compositor's way of life.

To many it was a difficult period; and though these standards must have been fairly good compared with other sections of labour, the compositor felt that his position was declining. From the 1820s the real wages of the compositor increased with the decline of the cost of living, for the wage settlement of 1810, apart from the 1816 reduction and certain other amendments, remained till 1866.

In relation to other craftsmen the average earnings of the compositor was high during the latter part of the eighteenth century. The compositor appears to have been earning between 24s and 30s when the higher paid craftsmen were averaging 19s.[23]

By the end of the period, though, they were said to be the highest paid manual workers whose wages are known,[24] the figures used for this observation are somewhat optimistic, and the compositor's rates appear to be little different from other highly skilled workers; certainly the differential that existed at the end of the eighteenth century had declined considerably.

	£	s	d
Rent		6	0
Bread and flour, five quarters		6	9 ¼
Meat 14 lbs at 9d per lb		10	6
Butter 2lbs at 1s 4d per lb		2	8
Cheese 1lb (average price 11d per lb)			11
Porter, 3 pints a day		4	4 ½
Candles, 1½lb		1	7 ½
Coals (average price) 1 bushel		1	9
Soap, starch and blue			9
Tea, ¼ lb at 7s per lb		1	9
Sugar, 2lbs at 9d		1	6
Vegetables		1	6
Milk			7
Pepper, salt, vinegar, etc.			6
Clothing, shoes and mending		4	0
Schooling, books, etc.		1	6
Benefit society			10
Total	2	7	6 ¼
Average earnings[a]	1	19	2 ½
Deficiency		8	4

a. Including the proposed increase of 6s.

Unemployment

But as wages began to compare more favourably with prices, so it became more difficult to obtain sufficient employment to secure these wages.

It would appear that there was little unemployment during the Napoleonic Wars. One account says there was none.[25] Yet the existence of men ready to work for less than the recognised prices may indicate that employment was not always readily available. A visitor to one printing office in 1806 finds 'a shocking receptacle of blacks and boys'.[26] ('Blacks' refers to black-tailed rats, rats being the name given to those men who are willing to work at less than the recognised rate.)

After the wars, especially, trade was uncertain and employment unsure. The uncertainty of employment continued throughout the period. Each decade had years of severe unemployment which greatly reduced the average income of many compositors. In 1826, 800 London compositors – over a third of the total number – were out of work. Charles Manby Smith, recounting his experiences when unsuccessfully seeking work in London, shows that even compositors resorted to the pawnshop.

In 1830 when attempts were made to reduce wages by sixpence a week the compositors protested at the August meeting of their London General Trade Society: 'Is not the sacrifice of at least three months in one year enough to satisfy the profit-craving appetites of our employers'. This appears to have been typical of the period: in 1834 the average wage received was about 27s weekly because of lack of employment – the rate for a full week at this time was 36s. There were years when wages were much worse. In one particularly bad year, 1841, a thousand compositors were said to be averaging only 15s weekly; in that year, eight printers enlisted and it was said that 15 were in the workhouse.[27]

It seems paradoxical that the great increase in the amount of printing should be accompanied by critical unemployment. The reasons for this are, firstly, that the printing trade fluctuated a good deal until about the mid-nineteenth century: and secondly the expansion of printing brought with it an increase of boys as a source of labour supply. With the breakdown in the control of the Stationers' Company there was no longer any restriction on the number allowed into the trade. The use of boy labour became widespread during the Napoleonic Wars; journeymen were in particularly short supply with the expansion of printing and this, coupled with the need to keep printing fairly cheap at a time of risings costs, led to the employment of boys. Several employers depended almost entirely on the labour of boys, either with or without indentures. These would generally be put on the straightforward work of setting type (which would have been profitable to the journeymen on piecework) and when the boys' apprenticeships expired they in turn would be replaced by other boys. Thus a growing pool of surplus labour came into being as the supply came to exceed the demand.

As early as the 1780s there were attempts by the compositors to restrict employment to those who had been properly indentured. The compositors claimed the right to examine indentures and if these were not properly fulfilled the man 'shall be compelled to quit his employment'.

By the 1790s the compositors were becoming anxious about the growth of boy labour, and in 1794 there was a resolution against the increase of the number of apprentices. A petition was sent to the Stationers'

Company to stop the increase, but this was to no avail, and the first decade of the nineteenth century saw a great increase in the number of apprentices (see Howe Appendix II which doesn't include boys not properly indentured). The compositors were well aware that a large measure of responsibility lay not so much with the master printers, but with the booksellers who were putting pressure on the printers for lower costs – especially after the wage increases of 1801 and 1805. A circular of 1806 in the St Bride Library collection addressed directly to the 'Booksellers of London and Westminster', stated the compositors' line of attack: 'The compositors have not objected to apprentices generally, but only to one species of apprentice; namely, out-door apprentices'. The fact that they no longer lived with their masters, it was asserted, had bad effects on the boys, because they were no longer restrained by living under the master's roof; the very idea of apprenticeship, it was said, was violated when a boy earns a wage and buys his own necessities.

The attack of the compositors was a shrewd one, for they were well aware that the restriction of apprenticeships to those who lived-in only, would have meant, in fact, limiting the number of apprentices; for most employers would not have been able to accommodate a large number of living-in apprentices, though it was not unknown for an employer to have a large number of indoor apprentices.

The attack on the apprentices continued in the monthly, frequently scurrilous, circulars written under pseudonyms in the years 1806–7. These give some indication of the fears of the compositor: 'what a gloomy prospect has a compositor before him by finding those introduced around him who, from their numbers, will in three years deprive him of half his loaf'; the compositor is warned urgently of the 'dangerous precipice you now stand on'. One of the writers, 'Miles' Boy', gives a colourful picture of the effects on the out-door apprentice. 'It would be a good hint to the Society for the Suppression of Vice, that they might, instead of hunting lollypop sellers on a Sunday morning, do their country a service, by preventing any master from having Out-Door Apprentices, who, finding no check, are hurried into every vice, and end their lives "e'en in their teens", on the gallows.'[28]

But within the next decade, the indoor system of apprenticeship had completely broken down. By 1818 it was estimated that only 60 out of 600 apprentices were indoor apprentices. At this time there appears to have been nearly one apprentice to every two journeymen compositors with some offices employing more boys than journeymen.

The contention of Cole and Postgate[29] that the skilled artisans of London were able to preserve their monopoly of labour and their control of the apprenticeship system, despite the repeal of the Elizabethan Statute in 1814, gives an optimistic picture of the time. It was true that in large measure the apprenticeship system was retained, and therefore entry into the occupation was restricted, but the way in which the apprentice system was used meant that in effect the system of preserving a monopoly in the supply of labour had broken down to a large extent.

The large numbers of apprentices continue throughout the period. Indeed in some ways the situation worsened near to mid-century. The reduction from the 1830s of stamp duties on printing, paper, and advertisements, encouraged the introduction into printing of many small printers working as cheaply as possible. The 1840s saw a host of penny Newgate novels such as *The Feast of Blood* and *The Hangman's Daughter*. These were being produced by a good deal of cheap labour: 'There are manufactories in London where hundreds of reams of vile paper and printing issue weekly; where large bodies of children are employed to arrange types, at the wages of shirt makers, from copy furnished by the most ignorant, at the wages of scavengers ... all the garbage that belongs to the history of crime and misery is raked together, to diffuse a moral miasma through the land in the shape of the most vulgar and brutal fiction'.[30]

The uncertainty of employment in a trade which was already rather seasonal (influenced, for example, by the demands for parliamentary printing and the law courts), was aggravated by the number of apprentices, and the employment situation was further worsened by the number of disputes which occurred over apprentice restriction. The attempt to deal with this problem was a major factor in the establishment of a national union, the National Typographical Association (NTA), in 1844. But the disputes which resulted were costly, and in 1846 the compositors of London rejected a stringent policy of apprentice restriction.

Apart from apprentice restriction there were other attempts to deal with the unemployment problem, for example raising funds for relief, and the provision of benefits from the developing union.

One response was the development of the tramping system; men would move over the whole country in search of employment and they would be given aid by the chapels in the firm they called at if they failed to obtain employment. This system already existed early in the eighteenth century.[31] But the growth of the system made the situation rather chaotic – particularly because of the varying amounts that an individual received and because the burden of aid was not carried equally by compositors in different towns. During the nineteenth century the system became much more organized though not without difficulty. Payments became more uniform, being based generally on the number of miles that were tramped, and individual contributions were replaced firstly by payments by the chapel, and then by the local society as a whole. The system was extremely important as a motivator in the attempts to amalgamate the various typographical societies in the 1840s.

The distance covered by many tramps was extensive. Within a few years a man might travel such routes as from London to Glasgow, and then to Manchester; or from Manchester to Glasgow and Dublin; or even from Wales to London, Manchester and Glasgow. The system was useful for finding work up till about 1830, but in the 1840s tramping no longer had this function and it became mainly a means of seeking relief. There were many attacks on the system; tramping meant degradation; also the system made for 'rats', for in desperation men would agree to work for lower wages. The system was gradually used less, though it persisted in London until 1881.

Emigration was also tried late in the period. In 1841, after a bad year of trade it was suggested that emigration schemes should be started. It was argued that such a solution would be preferable to tramping, and the idea was taken up in the provinces. For emigration at that time was not very expensive: for £5 a man could travel to America, and £8 would take him to Australia. Schemes were eventually set up in London but did not have marked success. The reason for their failing, however, does not appear to be, as has been suggested, that loans made by the unions in addition to the fare were not repaid and thus the system broke down; the records of the London Society of Compositors (LSC), at any rate, indicate that most of the loans were repaid in full.[32]

Another attempt to solve the problem of unemployment was made towards the end of the period. This was the formation of groups of journeymen, pledged to help each other in seeking employment. A number of these groups (known as 'gifts'), were formed from the early 1840s and developed later in the century; they are described in the next chapter.

When the employment situation was good, the hours were long. In 1842 the *Compositors' Chronicle* states that the recognised number of hours was 59 weekly.[33] We have seen that this was by no means general, especially where the chapel organisation was weak. Even in large offices pressure of work could greatly increase the weekly stint. A marathon effort is described by Smith, when the production of a blue book necessitated over 50 continuous hours of labour punctuated only by occasional refreshments.

Social status and image of the compositor

The way that an occupation is regarded in society is important in three ways: it is a factor in the level of the aspirations of the occupation; recruitment into the occupation is affected by the image held of it, and this will in turn affect the standing of the occupation; and the image and consequent status affects the satisfaction felt by the member of the occupation.

Throughout the period, despite the feeling of the compositor that his position was declining, his status in the community continued to be high. In 1774 Dr. Johnson thought well enough of the occupation to secure an apprenticeship to the trade of 'a scholar ... [who] has always lived in a clergyman's house'.[34] But their social position was being affected by the influx into the trade from about the middle of the eighteenth century. One employer, William Bowyer, in 1778 wishing to encourage a level of education he considered desirable, provided a legacy to be competed for by compositors with a knowledge of Greek and Latin; many applications were made.[35]

Towards the end of our period a book describing the qualifications necessary for various trades gives some indication of the image held of the compositor. It says that a compositor should be conversant with grammar and punctuation and it would be preferable if he is conversant with the subject he is setting; certain kinds of printing will give a 'young man of taste' scope to display his talents. [36] *The Times* reveals something of the popular image, while dissenting from this view and attacking the union: 'many persons may be disposed to credit compositors with more than an average share of intelligence; but we believe the men belonging to the London Society of Compositors are much the same as in other trades – most of the really good and efficient workmen, even if contributing to the funds, taking no part in its management'.[37] The general image was probably reinforced by the existence of a number of compositors of high literary merit who edited newspapers or journals.[38]

The source of recruitment was affected by the occupation's changing position. There is an important difficulty in using the records of the Stationers' Company as a picture of what was happening to recruitment; increasingly, particularly from the early nineteenth century, boys were not indentured through the Company. But the figures do show a general trend: it is almost certain that they underestimate the increase in recruitment from the lower social groups, for firms which still recognised the Company did so largely for reasons of prestige or tradition, and it is possible that they were more discriminating in recruiting their apprentices.

Table 3 **Source of Recruitment**

	1718–1723		1763–1768		1800–1805		1842–1847	
	%	No.	%	No.	%	No.	%	No.
Above artisan	54	64	37	62	32	75	37	102
Artisan	42	50	59	98	58	132	55	151
Below artisan	4	5	4	7	10	22	8	20
	100	119	100	167	100	229	100	273
Printers	2	3	12	20	16	38	27	74

In Table 3 a comparison is made with 1720: 'above artisan' includes such occupations as 'gentlemen', the professions of medicine, law and the Church, teachers, merchants and shopkeepers, and farmers; 'artisan' includes, in addition to skilled craftsmen, mariners, army NCOs and gardeners; 'below artisan' includes porters, grooms and labourers. Some of the problems involved in classifying these occupations have already been considered in Chapter I. An additional factor, which would further increase the actual proportion of those coming from below the artisan group is that some of the occupations here classified as 'artisan' very possibly became less skilled by the end of the period.

These changes have to be regarded against the background of change in the general occupational structure. There was probably an increase in the number of middle class occupations which were available to be entered; thus the middle classes were less dependent on the artisan occupations as avenues of employment. New skilled occupations were developing for those who wanted to give their sons a skilled trade (e.g. the new engineering and machine tool trades). Also the growth in literacy meant that groups other than the compositors and other artisans were becoming reasonably educated and this gave opportunities for the sons of the less skilled.

Already by the second half of the eighteenth century the social composition of the intake was changing, fewer coming from above the artisan group and more from the artisan class. It will be seen that throughout only a small proportion is recruited from the poorest section. By the end of the period printers form about a half of the recruitment from among artisans and are just above a quarter of the whole; it is possible that recruitment from among printers is somewhat under-estimated because

Table 4 **Payment of Premiums**

	1720s		1760s		1800s		1840s	
	%	No.	%	No.	%	No.	%	No.
Premiums paid	**45**	**53**	**39**	**65**	**34**	**70**	**24**	**65**
Above artisan	53	34	55	34	45	34	34	35
Artisan	36	18	31	30	22	29	16	24
Below artisan	20	1	14	1	32	7	30	6
of whom printers	0	0	10	2	16	6	11	8
Paid by charities	9	5	25	16	39	27	40	26

of the custom of patrimony which enabled the eldest son to learn the trade without indenture; this would be more true of the earlier period. Though the occupation is by no means self-recruited, this source of recruitment greatly increases; this was likely to make stronger the bonds of the occupation and to intensify group-consciousness, and was a possible factor contributing to the establishment of union. The increase in the number of 'below artisan' in the 1800s reflects the large intake – even the selective firms were affected.

Table 4 shows that the proportion paying premiums greatly declined; about half as many paid a premium in the 1840s compared with the 1720s. The decline was greatest among artisans: whereas about a third of the other groups paid a premium; only one in six of artisans did so. As premium paying declined the proportion coming from charities greatly increased. This possibly reflects the growth of institutions to help the needy and the readiness of the needy to appeal to these facilities. The figures are too small to analyse which social groups benefited most from charities.

The amount of premium paid continued to vary widely. In each year the range was from £2 5s to over £100. The mode increased during the period from about £10 to £20 in 1760 compared with £10 in the 1720s, remaining at £20 in the early 1800s and to £25 in the 1840s. The higher social groups paid rather higher premiums: the highest premiums especially were paid by this group, possibly with the intention that the son would learn how to handle his own business. But the lowest social group does not appear to pay lower premiums; this supports the suggestion that they had to make a relatively greater effort to enter the trade; and it was a very selective group from this class that put their sons into printing. Premiums were increasingly paid by charities.

The extent of the need for premiums and the amount required was generally over-estimated. According to Whittock, premiums range from £20–£70 but 'a sum of fifty pounds at least is proper to endow his indentures of apprenticeship, from parents of respectability, to a master who affords him an equally respectable home'.[39] At the time when his book was published in 1842 only four of the recorded premiums paid £50 or more. These were probably for indoor apprentices; but by this time the system had well broken down. The diminishing frequency of premium payments, from nearly 40 per cent in the 1760s to less than a quarter in the 1840s is partly explained by the growth in the number of outdoor apprentices, for premium payments should be seen as a contribution to the cost of keeping the apprentice when he lived in with his master. Another factor was that the occupation was easier to enter; compared with the early eighteenth century the occupation was less attractive to that section which was best able to pay: the higher social group.

We have seen that a fairly high image of the occupation persisted, despite the actual change in circumstances; that is, there was some time lag between the image and the real situation. But the image was not so high as to encourage recruitment from a higher social group at the level it had been in the early eighteenth century. A change in recruitment had taken place; a change that was probably underestimated by the records.

How was the occupation regarded by the compositors themselves? Their feeling of status is important, for it is an expression of their view of their social situation and is, therefore, a motivating factor in any action for changing this situation. Though the statement of individuals cannot be accepted as entirely representative, such expressions are some measure of what is being felt and are particularly important when the individual is speaking on behalf of an organization.

Some indication of the self-image of the compositors can be seen in their circular to the booksellers of London in 1807; this condemns the growing practice of outdoor apprenticeships and decline of premium payment, resulting in a decline in the type of boy entering the occupation. The system, it was claimed, 'has a tendency to introduce those who are the most deficient in education' with the consequence that the compositors are no longer 'the best educated of their rank'.

In 1809 to justify their demands in the negotiations which preceded the 1810 Scale they appealed to Adam Smith's five principal circumstances that 'make up for a small pecuniary gain in some employments and counter-balance a great one in others'.[40] They conclude that these principles do not apply in their case, and again the need for education is emphasized: 'a greater degree of school-learning is necessary than in any other business'. The request to the masters goes on to assert, 'therefore the proximity of the art of composing to the higher professions and liberal arts and science, would seem to entitle it to rank above mechanical and manufacturing employments; and consequently entitle it to a more liberal remuneration'.

In the plan for amalgamating the existing societies in 1834, union was justified in order to 'preserve a station in society above the class of the most ill-used and oppressed of men ... the agricultural labourers and the cotton spinners ... To preserve the respectability of the trade'.

After a period of unemployment in 1838 the union recalls a time 'in living memory when the compositor stood first among the artisans of this great metropolis – courted and respected; his name a passport to credit, and his trade considered to imply a person of intelligence and respectability'.

The need to preserve respectability and the compositor's education are continually stressed. The context in which it was made reveals the feeling of change that was taking place in his material condition, which was, in his view, becoming less appropriate to his social standing.

The development of the union

The attempts to reduce wages were strongly resisted and often led to strikes; yet throughout the years of unemployment the Scale of Prices, drawn up in 1785, was fairly well maintained; this is partly a reflection of the growing strength of the union and also of the acceptance by many masters of a scale which was a useful working guide. By contrast, in the areas without union organization, wages varied from 12s to £1[41] in the 1840s compared, as we saw earlier, with around double this in London.

All the negotiations for revision of the Scale and the endeavours to restrict apprentices show that organization was being developed. 'Miles's Boy' appears to have been an organizer in this early period and adopted the tactic of attacking individuals – probably a useful way of keeping men in check by the occupational community before the union itself was strong enough to function in this way. In a letter dated September 15th, 1806 he refers to a code of laws that some journeymen had been trying to draw up for five years; that is, since the negotiations for an increase in 1801. He reveals a very militant attitude, complaining that so far the constitutions which had been suggested had been too ceremonial: 'it only wanted the insertion ... of a costume for the state officers, to make it completely ridiculous'. He, however, approves of a new constitution that had been drawn up: 'if compositors will suffer themselves to be drilled into the state of discipline required by the accepted code, which is really simple and easy to be understood, the happiest effects may be looked for; the want of discipline having been the ruin of every typographical society from the days of Jacob Iliff to 1801'. The only reference found to anyone bearing a similar name was Jacob Ilive, who died in 1768. He was a printer and typefounder 'Somewhat disordered in his mind' according to Timperley.

The passage is interesting in that it reveals the attempts at organization before the establishment of the Union Society, and shows that it was probable that several formal organizations existed before 1801, the date taken by Richards and Howe as the first evidence of real organization. The meeting place of the Union Society was the public house previously used: 'The Hole in the Wall'. This Society does not appear to have survived very long. It was not until after the Napoleonic Wars, in 1816, that the London Trade Society of Compositors was formed. This was during a bad year for trade when, after a struggle, the compositors had to accept a reduction of wage. This Society was not just an organization for defence: it appeared to accentuate unemployment relief.

But the lack of militancy did not satisfy certain compositors and after ten years a rival organization appeared: the London General Trade Society of Compositors (LTS of C), formed in 1826. This was designed not merely to be a relief society but to protect trade. The new society was financially precarious – the secretary voluntarily went without his salary in 1827. The attempts to make a much firmer organization are shown in 1829 when a committee man was fined for not attending a committee meeting. Even the excuse that he was attending a customary outing, a wayzgoose, was not accepted.

The two societies had formal relations, and an amalgamation of the two organizations was soon attempted. In 1832 a general meeting of both societies was demanded. Eventually in 1834 the two societies combined and formed the London Union of Compositors. The employment situation and the development of tramping influenced the amalgamation of typographical societies into the NTA. This began in January 1845 and was subsequently joined by the London Union, now to be known as the LSC. But the national body was too ambitious in its attempts to deal with problems, and the years 1846-7 saw the collapse of the national body; in 1848 the LSC seceded to become an independent union.[42]

One of the functions of the union was to establish certain legal rights for the compositor, in addition to dealing with the unemployment problem, the provision of friendly society benefits, and the maintenance of the Scale of Prices. In one short period there were seven cases where legal action was taken to establish the right to a fortnight's work or money before a man was dismissed; according to the union's annual reports, all these cases were terminated in favour of the compositor's claim, before London magistrates. The development of the union was also bound up with the provision of friendly society benefits; the function of these benefits was to strengthen the 'bond of union'.

It would appear that even the early unions were supported by a substantial minority. In the 1801 negotiations for a revision of the Scale, the resolutions were signed by nearly 500 compositors. At the inaugural meeting of the LGTS of C in 1826 it was stated that the attendance was 1500. This, however, may not have been due to a strong desire for union, but merely a temporary focus of interest for the large number of unemployed in that year. Only a quarter of the total number of compositors in London was said to be in one of the unions in 1827. After the organizational changes in the 1840s the new LSC emerged with a membership of 1,100, or about one third, in 1848. With the establishment of union on a firm basis, and with good trade conditions, the membership steadily increased to well over 2,000 in the early 1850s.[43]

The occupational community

The occupational community as expressed in the Chapel organization, the existence of which was noted in the previous chapter, remained strong.

Many Chapel customs persisted through the period. For example, the 'bang out' was a frequent activity: everyone would take up any implement connected with printing and would create as loud a noise as he could with it. The din created by the bang out was so great that Hansard tried to prevent it by sacking the person who was the object of the noise. There were also the Chapel fines, some of which were good-humoured. A stranger who called into an office would have to pay a fine for the 'good of the chapel'. This was regarded as a symbolic necessity reflecting a sense of spatial proprietorship. He would have to redress the offence done on entering by 'providing a libation by which the offended workmen may wash away the stain that his misconduct has left on the body at large'.[44]

The custom of paying a 'footing' on joining a Chapel was still recognised according to Manby Smith. This was a monetary payment with which drinks were immediately purchased. Also the more important social events in the life of the individual would be taken as an opportunity for a drink. The compositor concerned would have to buy beer for his fellow workers, and there would possibly be a ceremony, too. One compositor avoided all this by keeping his marriage a secret and congratulates himself on his prudence when he relates a mock wedding ceremony on the occasion of the marriage of another compositor in his firm. In addition there was the annual wayzgoose, or outing, an occasion, it has been alleged, for much hypocrisy by occasioning false 'bon homie'.

The Chapel then, continued as a social organization. It not only regulated the behaviour and various tempers of the men, but was also a mutual charity – to which even the master often regularly added his contribution.[45]

But its character was changing. In this period the general social character was being paralleled by a specific purpose: as a nucleus of the union[46] and the means for stimulating union growth. Chapels began to put pressure on their members to join, and it began to be responsible to the union for ensuring that work was done in the firm according to union rules.

One employer protested that the Chapel no longer had the function of bringing 'good understanding between journeyman and employer'.[47] The Chapel was being perverted, it was alleged, to evil purpose – combination. A journeyman could not claim relief from Chapel funds unless he was loyal to 'the Committee' (i.e. the Union Committee). Chapels became arbiters of who worked on what – of price, quality and time worked. The picture this writer paints was probably exaggerated as was his claim that the Chapels were abolished by the masters in answer to their tyranny, yet the changing character of the Chapel was probably true.

Working class identification

The period to about mid-nineteenth century is one of transition for the compositor. His declining material position, particularly during the early part of the nineteenth century, combined with the influx of more working class boys of a different culture, fostered the extension of sympathy towards other working class groups.

In the early nineteenth century the compositor still stood aloof as a separate group and was quick to point out that he was not to be confused with the pressman. Indeed he showed little solidarity, being willing to work at press if need be; also men in the machine room were regarded as inferior by the typographical societies. While the compositor was developing his own form of combination he often disparaged the methods of other unions. The attitude of the emerging union though militant was not aggressive. 'We desire peace not war' claimed the union committee in the 1843 annual report; the history of trade societies, they said, teaches that 'associations of workmen must be employed not as organs of aggression but for defence'. Gradually, however, the compositor's economic condition became little different from other working class groups; and he became increasingly aware of this through wage disputes and the uncertainty of employment.

It is not suggested that all compositors were alike in their growing sympathy. There were the conservative as well as the militant groups. Also status differentials divided the compositors themselves. But the changing position of the occupation is reflected when the voice of the militants becomes stronger. We have seen how the compositor became subjected to conditions more like those of the rest of the skilled working class. It is important to emphasize that when reference is made to the 'working class' what is meant is the skilled, i.e. 'the trades'. The gap between the compositors and the other skilled which existed during the eighteenth century grew narrower and the compositor became more willing to associate with them.

At first this association was rather tentative. Records of financial aid to other groups exist in the 1830s. The LTS of C in conjunction with the LGTS of C gave aid to the Tinplate Workers who had formerly 'assisted the trade'. In the annual report of 1835 it is noted that aid of £65 10s 0d had been given to the Operative Builders. But the compositors' unions kept apart from the general working class movements: in granting aid to the builders it was emphasized that there was a 'wish to dispel any suggestion that the LUC are connected with the Consolidated Trades' Union', they were unconnected with the movement and had no interest in the cause of other societies 'except that which a hatred of oppression ought ever to create'.

Sympathy and identification with the trades became clearer and less need was felt to excuse the giving of financial aid. The 1830s saw the beginning of a strong sense of awareness that the compositors were just one section of the working classes, and the willingness to express in a material way their support of other similar groups of skilled workers.

In the 1837 annual report of the LUC the need for working class solidarity is expressed. 'The great question is, how are the working classes to be made sensible of their condition? We answer by communion with each other; by association; by the establishment of unions like that of the compositors of London; it is this alone which will show them their wants, and the power they possess to secure the supply of those wants'.

By the end of the period a dispute arose which showed clearly the kind of sentiments which were developing. In this dispute the printers appealed for help from other trades. But it should be noted that the appeal specifically disclaims financial aid.

The dispute was with the *Sun* newspaper which in 1852 had tried to reduce the scale of prices on which piece rates were based. A Defence Committee was set up which appealed to other trades for help, and many other occupations responded to the call (see posters overleaf). Offers of financial help were made but declined: 'we are not in need of pecuniary assistance'. What was requested was a boycott of those places where the paper was taken: coffee shops, public houses and other places of entertainment.

What is interesting in this dispute is the strength of the solidarity of a certain section of the working class: the majority of those giving support were skilled, for these were the only groups that were really organized. It is no doubt true that many compositors identified themselves with the working class long before this, and struggles with the employer were noted in chapter I. But now the identification was beginning to widen and is given formal expression through the organization which the occupation erected. This formal expression was likely to make the attitudes of the members more conscious and structured.

Working class and political activity

The fact that the union largely stood aloof from political activity cannot be supported merely on the grounds that the union wished to be free from politics. For the union was vociferous in the repeal of the Corn Laws, in the hope of lower costs of living; and more particularly in the agitation for the repeal of the various duties on paper, advertisements and newspapers. This agitation was not merely against the 'taxes on knowledge', for the abolition of taxes on foreign books was not sought, and the Copyright Bills between 1836 and 1844 were opposed because they thought they would reduce employment. The repeals were demanded simply in the hope that this would increase the amount of printing. Indeed, contrary to the spirit of avoiding politics, the request to repeal the stamp duties – in an 'address to the Throne' – is preceded by an eloquent testimony of the approval of the conduct of His Majesty's Ministers: 'That this meeting: viewing with alarm and regret the late decision of the peers of the realm on the Reform Bill; and fearful lest the decision should induce a

TO ALL THE

CARPENTERS AND JOINERS

OF

LONDON AND THE SUBURBS.

MEN AND BRETHREN,

It is with the profoundest feelings of respect for humanity that we appeal to the noble-minded, to the magnanimous, to the free and independent who are amongst us, to lend a helping hand in wresting the scourge from the oppressor, in putting an iron foot on the neck of tyranny, and, with one combined effort, to hurl back the wheel of oppression on the head of the despot.

We have only to call your attention to the attempt of the Proprietor of the

"SUN" NEWSPAPER

TO REDUCE THE COMPOSITORS' SCALE OF PRICES

(ESTABLISHED IN 1810).

to rouse up every inherent feeling of protection within you to vindicate the cause of the oppressed, and free all from the shackles of the "SUN'S" inquisitor.

As far back as last October the Proprietor of the "SUN" commenced a system which would, if allowed to go on, strike at the very core of the best-regulated system of labour, provided the employer were base enough for the action. Yes, brethren, not only have a set of unprincipled individuals been hired to take the situations of men (some of whom had been upwards of thirty years in the establishment) who would rather submit to be paid off than accept the terms of an unfeeling employer, but attempts have been made to induce others to countenance this base effort to starve working men; thanks, however, to Christianity, there are gentlemen who spurn the proposal, and the base example has not been followed.

Fellow Men, before we can succumb to this, every feeling that is ennobling in man, everything that is upward and onward in progression and development must be shut out, and give place to the grinding principle of living upon death, of capital riding rampant over the gory field of its own victims, and committing sacrilege with the golden rule of doing as you would be done by.

By the exertions of all the Trades, the circulation of the Paper has been

REDUCED NEARLY 1,000!

and, with a full determination on our part not to countenance any coffee-house, public-house, or any other place where it is taken in, we will frustrate the design of the Proprietor, we will protect the industry of the country, and establish on a more permanent basis the claims of Toiling Humanity!

Signed on behalf of the Members of the Friendly Society of Carpenters and Joiners, held at the George IV., Leicester-street, Regent-street.

J. LITTLE,   ⎱
A. J. BLACK, > *Committee.*
J. COX,   ⎰

TO THE MEMBERS

OF THE OPERATIVE

STONEMASONS'

SOCIETY

IN LONDON AND ITS VICINITY.

FELLOW WORKMEN,

You cannot but have learnt with the deepest indignation the late base attempt of the proprietors of the "SUN" Newspaper to reduce the Compositors in their employment to the starvation point, by reducing the scale of prices that has been in existence for more than forty years.

Is it not a monstrous disgrace that labour's sons should always be the sport of a base and selfish oligarchy of mad and grinding capitalists, and that ever and anon the infernal screw should be sought to be imposed upon the toiling millions! The case of the Compositors is no new phase in the grinding curse of rampant capital; yet does it not demand, as in a voice like thunder—O ye toiling millions, come to the rescue!

And will not the members of the Operative Stonemasons' Society—nay, every Mason in the land—respond with a willing heart and leaping soul to that call, and declare, by every means in their power, that toiling humanity shall not be crushed, that labour's sons shall not be oppressed, that they will not stand quietly by and see their fellow-toilers impaled on the iron spear of a heartless cruelty and soulless despotism. Have not the Compositors for months been battling with their oppressors? Has not the warm blood leaped through your veins, and has not every swelling pulsation of your souls said—Go on, ye brave ones, and beard the lion in his den; clip the claws, nay, pull them up by the roots, that for ages have lacerated the hapless sons of toil.

If we had acted as we ought to have done, long ere this the struggle would have been at an end. Is not, then, the case of the Compositors ours? If it is, support no house of whatever kind, whether public-house or coffee-house, where the infamous "SUN" is taken in; but banish, we say, the vile thing from your presence wherever you go. By this means we shall teach our oppressors it is a rather dangerous game to attempt to infringe on the just and legitimate rights of the sons of toil; and the press will learn, too, that their prosperity and chief honour does not lie in clipping down the wages of the working man, but on all suitable occasions vindicating the inalienable claims of the toilers. Long live that press, we say, that honours the toiling millions by advocating their rights! and perish right quickly that paper that would dare to oppress them.

In conclusion, we would say, never rest till the oppressed are free—until might gives place to right—until oppression gives place to justice—and not until the banner of freedom waves gloriously o'er the sons of toil.

Signed on behalf of the Operative Stonemasons' Society.

	J. WOOD.	**G. SCOTT.**
Committee Rooms,	**J. TURNER.**	**G. ALLANSON.**
Paviour's Arms, Johnston Street, Westminster.		

Elliot, Printer, Tottenham Court Road

belief that His Majesty's Ministers have lost the confidence of the people, and thus cause a change in His Majesty's Councils, consider their duty to come forward at this crisis and declare that they place the fullest reliance on the benevolence, the wisdom and the patriotism of His Majesty's Ministers, and earnestly hope that they will not quit the posts they have so beneficially filled, but will continue their endeavour to ameliorate the condition of the people, and thus secure to the nation the blessing of peace and prosperity'. Then followed an appeal by the union committee in 1831 to repeal the Stamp Duties 'which limit the diffusion of knowledge, depress and impoverish the printing business, and are a disgrace to the present civilized era'.[48] It is fair to point out that there was a good deal of controversy over this affair from members who did not agree with the testimony to the Ministers; it appears that this was because it involved politics. As far as the union was concerned political interest was restricted to self-interest.

Though the union refused to participate in radical movements as such, several individuals gave their enthusiastic support. It is perhaps hardly surprising that the compositor figured prominently in certain movements, for he had the educational ability to express himself and was also familiar with the means of widely communicating his sentiments through printing. Coming simultaneously with his loss of material position, it was likely that the compositor was to be found in some of the social movements of the first half of the nineteenth century.

The views of Robert Owen and the success of the New Lanark venture inspired the attempt by a group of printers in 1821 to form a residential community. Though the community was to consist of individuals from every class, the initial meeting consisted in the main of journeymen printers. These men visualised a community of consumers, who retained their ordinary work in London but whose families lived communally.[49] There were a number of printers in the community when it was eventually established, for in addition to printing and publishing *The Economist* the community was also prepared to 'execute orders in...Bookselling, Bookbinding and Stationery'.[50]

Another Owenite Society, the London Co-operative Society, came into existence in 1824 with James Watson as one of the leading figures.[51] Watson, though not originally a compositor, learnt the art of composing in the printing office where Richard Carlile's *Republican* was printed, and he eventually became a printer.[52]

Further suggestions to set up a co-operative printing office came in the 1840s. The idea received considerable interest, not so much due to the ideals of co-operation but as a means of finding work for the unemployed.

The idea was put into practice when the *People's Newspaper*, called 'the Herald of the Co-operative Printing Press',[53] was founded. In addition to finding work for the unemployed, the aim of this paper was to raise reading standards and create a cheap press. Started under the auspices of the NTA, the paper – a weekly – soon ran into financial difficulties.

The paper was very radical. There were demands for the abolition of capital punishment and in a republican spirit it questioned the necessity of the Monarchy. Appeals were made to its readers to read Comte and Mill; though apparently either the latter was not read thoroughly or there was disagreement with him over his perception of women, for it was only sufficiently radical to demand universal male suffrage.

Several individuals were active Chartists though the union completely ignored this important social movement. There were several reasons for this. The compositors were probably divided in their views of the movement. Also there was the union policy of confining their funds entirely for trade purposes as did other skilled trades, and would not want to be in a position of having to support the movement financially, even if it were sympathetic. They were probably out of sympathy with Chartism in its later period, and O'Connor, especially, was attacked for employing boys on his *Northern Star*.[54]

Recognition of the role of printers in the Chartist movement has already been made. Cole gives the printers as an example of the relatively prosperous skilled artisan who initiated the People's Charter.[55] Printers played an important part in the establishment in 1836 of the London Working Men's Association, which drew up the main points of the Charter and was the precursor of Chartism in London. There were 14 active leaders.[56] Out of the 11 of these whose occupations can be traced,[57] seven were printers or connected with printing and at least five of these had worked as compositors. When the Chartist resolutions were forwarded to the House of Commons in 1837, it was signed by 12 men; six MPs and six workmen.[58] Of the latter six, at least three had worked as compositors.

Some of the men involved in the movement were not originally compositors; it was the need to communicate their ideas that attracted them to printing; but this does give some indication of the kind of man who was engaged in the occupation. Such men rebelled against the condition of the working classes and saw that the only hope lay in certain political reforms. Their interest was wider than the confines of their own occupational group. It is significant that these leaders of working class radicalism did not take a leading part in the development of unions in their own occupations. The vision of these men was towards a different society. In this they differed from those prominent in the organisation of occupational unions who were more concerned with maintaining the social condition of their members within the existing organization of society. The words of the compositor, Hetherington, in his last will and testament reveal the attitude of the radical interest in the working classes as a whole. 'While the land, machines, tools, implements of production, and the produce of man's toil, are exclusively in possession of the do-nothings; and labour is the sole possession of the wealth producers – a marketable commodity, bought up and directed by wealthy idlers – never-ending misery must be their inevitable lot'.[59]

The mood of the union, however, was changing as it became apparent that the condition of the compositor had become permanently worse off, relatively. It was not enough to try to maintain the superiority and respectability of the compositor. His economic condition became little different from the other trades, and with growing literacy generally and the decline in the source of recruitment, the compositor no longer had a monopoly of those qualities which had given him a higher social status. As we have seen, the awareness of this change in social condition was reflected by the changing attitude of the union towards identification with the skilled working class.

Woodcut of a printing office signed Thomas Kelly of Paternoster Row circa 1825. It shows composition and press work at a Columbian press.

Conclusion

In summary, this period is essentially one of transition from an occupational or group consciousness towards class consciousness. The causes for this change are to be found in the worsening situation of the compositor. Though it is true that employment was probably always uncertain, unemployment appears to have become much more endemic. Though there is evidence that the social standing of the compositor was still high, that the occupation still attracted a fair proportion of recruits from the higher social groups, and that the position was not entirely depressed (and this depression was temporary except for a minority), wages were relatively less high than they had been at the middle of the eighteenth century.

The occupation became more formally organized. The impetus to this was the persistence of unemployment, and the worsening condition which made friendly society benefits more necessary – particularly those for unemployment and strike pay. With the development of the Union, there is a growing identification with the working class especially those sections which were also organized i.e. the skilled working class.

It must be emphasized that no rigid date line can be fixed for the changed situation. Apart from individual idiosyncrasies of personalities in the occupation and the union, different economic situations in different years vary the intensity of the identification. Further, the extent of the widening sympathy should not be exaggerated: the status of the compositor probably reinforced the reticence of the majority to be drawn into militant working class movements in the period. What is important is that there was a greater receptivity towards identification with other trades.

Notes

1 See Webb, *British Working Class Reader.*
2 Knight, *Old Printer*, p. 261; Howe and Waite, *London Society of Compositors*, p. 155.
3 Knight, p. 248.
4 LSC Pocket Guide (1855) quoted in Howe and Waite, p. 147. This possibly omits a number of very small offices outside the central area.
5 Plant, *English Book Trade*, p. 88.
6 Nichols, *Literary Anecdotes*, v. 4, p. 589.
7 Howe, *From Craft to Industry*, p. 5.
8 Howe and Waite, *London Society of Compositors*, p. 24, 148.
9 Howe, *London Compositor*, p. 73n, 372–4.
10 In the provinces, where most towns had only small printing firms, the union embraces both compositors and machinemen. In London there were separate unions until 1955 when the LSC and the PMMTS amalgamated into the London Typographical Society (LTS).
11 The earliest reference to a sick benefit club is the Phoenix in 1792 (Howe, *London Compositor*, p. 84n). See also Richards, 'Social and Economic Aspects of Combination in the Printing Trade before 1875', p. 22.
12 Pendred's list in Howe, *London Compositor*, p. 41–50.
13 Howe and Waite, *London Society of Compositors*, p. 26.
14 LSC Pocket Guide (1855) in Howe and Waite, p. 147.
15 Smith, *Working Man's Way in the World*, p. 169–70, 184–5.
16 London Trade Society of Compositors, *Annual Report*, 11th, London, 1828, p. 7; London Union of Compositors, *Report of the General Trade Committee to the Compositors of London*, 1834, p. 8–10.
17 Many of the wage figures are taken from Howe, *London Compositor*, e.g. from the historical introduction to the London Scale of Prices written about 1835 (see Howe, p. 71); see also Howe and Waite, p. 125. It may be noted here that neither the estimates made by Bowley (in *Wages and Income*, p. 9, 20, 21) nor those of Francis Place (in 'Journeyman Printers', *Gorgon*, 28 November 1818, p. 220) are reliable. The piece rate for 1805 is one put forward as an average by the master printers. The compositors suggested 30s as being nearer, but were ready to discuss 33s. The 1847 figures are also in Howe, p. 281.
18 London School of Economics library, Webb Trade Union Collection, v. A30, f. 8. An 'en' is roughly equivalent to the thickness of an average letter. The speed of setting had to be about 1500 an hour in order to effect an average of 1000 ens an hour because time had to be allowed for correcting and distributing the type. (Howe, *London Compositor*, p. 59).

19 Richards, 'Social and Economic Aspects of Combination in the Printing Trade before 1875', p. 30.

20 Whittock, *Complete Book of Trades*, p. 391.

21 Gilboy, *Wages in Eighteenth Century England*, p. 37.

22 Clapham, *Economic History of Modern Britain*, v. 1, p. 601–2.

23 Gilboy, p. 19.

24 Cole and Postgate, *Common People*, p. 206.

25 Richards, p. 34, 45, gives the figure for 1826.

26 Howe, *London Compositor*, p. 119.

27 *Compositors' Chronicle*, June 1841, p. 77.

28 Howe, *London Compositor*, p. 118–22; quotation from p. 119.

29 Cole and Postgate, *Common People*, p. 206–7.

30 Knight, *Old Printer*, p. 280.

31 Richards, 'Social and Economic Aspects of Combination in the Printing Trade before 1875', p. 63; there is an excellent account of the whole tramping system between p. 63 and p. 323.

32 See the LSC Emigration Aid Committee minute book of monthly meetings, which covers the period from 9 February 1853 to 18 July 1857 (MRC, MSS.28/CO/1/2/1/1).

33 *Compositors' Chronicle*, Oct. 1842, p. 211.

34 Austen-Leigh, *Story of a Printing House*, p. 26.

35 *Printer*, Apr. 1845, p. 188.

36 Whittock, *Complete Book of Trades*, p. 389–90.

37 'Rattening in the Printing Trade' [Letter to *The Times*, signed] O. and Co., *The Times*, 12 August 1868, p. 10, col. 5.

38 Timperley, *Encyclopaedia of Literary and Typographical Anecdote*; also the *Compositors' Chronicle* and the *People's Newspaper*, both of which were produced in the 1840s.

39 Whittock, *Complete Book of Trades*, p. 494; quotation from p. 390.

40 Howe, *London Compositor*, p. 141–4.

41 LUC annual report 1840–1 (MRC, MSS.28/CO/1/8/1/1 or CO/4/1/1/11).

42 For the history of this see Richards, 'Social and Economic Aspects of Combination in the Printing Trade before 1875', p. 348–56, 372–3, 448.

43 Howe and Waite, *London Society of Compositors*, p. 338.

44 Hansard, *Typographia*, p. 308–9.

45 Hansard, p. 309.

46 This is the function emphasized by the Webbs when they saw the Chapel as the earliest form of combination, *History of Trade Unionism*, p. 27–8.

47 Hansard, p. 308–9. His picture is far too militant for the period, though no doubt the signs were there and indeed bore fruit in certain offices.

48 Union Committee of the two London Trade Societies of Compositors, minutes of meeting of 13 October 1831 (MRC, MSS.28/CO/1/1/3).

49 *Report of the Committee appointed at a Meeting of Journeymen, chiefly Printers, to take into consideration certain propositions submitted to them by Mr George Mudie.*

50 Co-operative and Economical Society, 'The Society's Circular', *Economist*, 9 March 1822, p. 409–10.

51 Cole and Postgate, *Common People*, p. 242.

52 Linton, *James Watson*, p. 21.

53 'Address to the People', by 'Silverpen', *People's Newspaper*, 30 May 1847, p. 1, col. 2; see also the issues of August and September 1847.

54 *Typographical Gazette*, June 1846, p. 42–3.

55 Cole, *Chartist Portraits*, p. 6.

56 Linton, *James Watson*, p. 44.

57 A number of other sources were also used: *Memories* by W.J. Linton, *The Chartist Challenge* by A.R. Schoyen, and *The Chartist Movement* by M. Hovell.

58 Linton, *James Watson*, p. 46.

59 Holyoake, *Life of Henry Hetherington*, p. 9; his 'Last Will and Testament' was written about January 1848.

III

The Growth of Class Consciousness: Mid-Nineteenth Century to 1914

The expansion of printing

In the second half of the nineteenth century the expansion of the printing industry continued. A number of factors contributed to this: the use of printing in different forms by expanding trade and organizations; the repeal of the paper, advertisement and newspapers taxes, which stimulated demand by cheapening the cost of printing; the increase in the scope of government and the extension of the franchise resulted in printing of various kinds (e.g. royal commissions, committees of enquiry, legislation and voters' lists); and, most important, the increased demand for reading matter by a population increasingly exposed to education led to demands for reading, serious and light, and especially stimulated the growth of magazines and a popular press.[1] Developments in transport and communications further encouraged the expansion of printing. Railways aided national distribution, important for the newspaper industry, and long and comparatively smooth-running journeys encouraged a demand for reading, leading to the setting up of bookstalls on the main line stations. This expansion was reflected in the number engaged in the industry: in 1851 there were about 23,000 employed in the letter-press printing industry in England and Wales; by the time of the 1911 Census this had grown to over 138,000.

In London printing expanded, but at a rate rather less than that for the provinces. In 1851 the number of letterpress printers in London was 10,000 and by 1911 43,000. Thus, though the rate of expansion in England and Wales was six-fold, that for London was little more than four-fold. The explanation for this lies partly in the demand for printing in the growing number of large towns as a result of commercial and industrial expansion, and partly in the movement from London of printing, especially of books, to areas where printing could be produced more cheaply.

Similarly, the number of compositors in London expanded less than that of printing as a whole in London; though census figures do not distinguish compositors until 1911, fairly reliable estimates of the number of compositors have been made. In the 1850s there were about 4,500 compositors and apprentices, this had grown to about 12,000 in 1885 according to the LSC's annual report, and remained at roughly this level until the end of the period, when there was a total of 12,150 compositors in London at the of 1911 Census.

This lack of growth in the number of compositors towards the end of the century requires explanation. Part of the difference is due to the different geographic base of enumeration: the number in 1885 is based on the union's area which was larger than the area of the administrative county of London, used for the 1911 Census; for a 15 mile radius from the General Post Office was becoming the geographical extent of the LSC's authority. Thus the numbers within the administrative county would have been rather smaller at that date, though it is true that the major part of the printing in the area would be done within the County of London. Other factors were also operating: first, it is possible that the attempts to limit the number of apprentices were beginning to have some effect; secondly, there was the introduction of composing machines, particularly during the 1890s; this was probably the most important factor for the failure of the number of compositors to expand with the expansion of the industry in general.

The social condition of the compositor

Wages

Composing is an occupation in which wide differences in earnings existed, and estimates of these earnings can only be formulated with the proviso that the variations referred to earlier largely continued, and that wage rates can only be used as a very rough guide to what compositors actually earned. Bearing this in mind, it can be said that wage rates moved upwards very slowly over the period.

Two kinds of payment need to be considered: the fluctuating wage based on piece work, and the fixed weekly wage for a definite number of hours. Men engaged on the latter basis were regarded as working 'on the establishment' and were known as 'stab hands. It would appear that though a compositor on piece work had the possibility of substantial earnings, on average the earnings of the piece hand were not greatly different from the 'stab hand, the reason being that the flow of work for the man on piece work was not regular. A rough guide to earnings can thus be obtained by considering the changes in the 'stab rate. It must be pointed out, however, that though the two rates were on average roughly parallel, some compositors earned wages well above the 'stab rate.

The minimum 'stab rate recognized by the men was 33s a week at mid century and had been at a similar level since the reduction of 1816. From 1845 the compositor was becoming concerned about this and there were protests that the wages, that had remained much the same for 30 years, 'but barely procure for the compositor sufficient means to sustain a respectable position in society'.[2] By an agreement in 1866 there was an advance to 36s; it became 38s in 1891; this was increased to 39s in 1901, where it remained until the First World War.[3]

There was considerable variation on these rates. In the early part of the period it would appear that when the general establishment rate was 36s, compositors on bookwork received only 33s.[4] Also, not all men in the same firm would necessarily receive the same 'stab rate: in 1889, for example, it was stated that 'although 36s is the lowest wage, the cases are numerous in which the same roof covers men receiving, as abler journeymen, 38s, 40s or 42s'.[5]

Piece rates had changed little since 1810, when the piece scale had been completely revised. Since then, technical changes, difficulties of interpretation, and anomalies of various kinds had led to certain amendments; the major ones being the modifications of 1836 and 1847. More important changes came with increases in the rates in the second half of the century. The scales are extremely complex and it would be impossible to assess the effects of all the changes on the compositors' earnings; only the most important features can be presented here. In 1866 the rate had advanced by ½d per 1,000 ens; which probably increased earnings by about 2s a week. The agreement contained the important principle that overtime be paid at 3d per hour. In 1872 there was a further increase of ½d per thousand, and in 1891 another rise of ½d per thousand was achieved. The 1891 scale was a complete revision of the 1810 scale, taking into account all the amendments made during the previous 81 years.[6]

At that time the daily newspaper compositor earned about £2 15s 0d a week.[7] A few years later, after an increase in wages, it was reported that the book compositor averaged between 27s and 33s; this branch was subjected to great fluctuations, and while a man earned £2 to £3 one week, he might get as little as 10s to 15s the next. The jobbing compositor had somewhat steadier earnings of about 36s weekly. The compositor on a weekly newspaper received between 36s and 40s, while the daily newspaper compositor was the highest paid of all. Sometimes a newspaper compositor was paid a 'stab rate of 48s, but generally he was on piece work, and such compositors averaged between £2 10s 0d and £3 10s 0d and even occasionally earning as much as £4 10s 0d. These high earnings were received for night work.

Some estimate can thus be formed of the range of wages being paid at the early part of the period. At mid century the range was very wide in London: from 33s to 48s weekly. In an enquiry into health in 1863[8], the medical officer of the Privy Council found that though the weekly establishment wage was 33s, the average was somewhat higher, between 33s and 38s. The piece worker's had a greater range from 24s to 44s, with an average from 30s to 36s.

Until the third quarter of the century the majority of compositors were paid by piece work, but the system of paying a fixed weekly sum was becoming widespread. The compositors were continuously hostile to the breakdown of the piecework system. There were two basic reasons for this attitude; first, a source of possible high earnings was eliminated; and secondly, the trend was seen as unjust as the 'stab hand earned more than they received.

The men complained of other attempts to avoid the piece scale. For example, founts of type were introduced which did not conform to the traditional widths and depths. The use of these condensed types meant that the compositor had to work harder for the same wages, for the compositors' charges were based on standard type sizes which were accepted at the time of the 1810 agreement. Other technical innovations also tended to reduce the scale, and the compositors tried to maintain their position by claiming extras when the innovations were made.

Towards the end of the century various composing machines were becoming a practical and economic possibility and were being introduced in certain offices;[9] the advent of these machines almost eliminated the hand compositor on piece work. At first the new machines were worked at 'stab rates, but this did not reveal what the machine could actually produce, and soon the employers themselves were demanding that a piece scale for composing machines should be formulated. The LSC eventually agreed to a machine scale in 1894, which enabled very high earnings to be made.[10] This was not so much due to the profitability of the machine, as to the uncertainty of the machine's capabilities. The uncertainty of how in fact the scales would work out is indicated by the clause that the rules with regard to type-composing machines should remain in force only till the end of 1895. By then the high earnings possible on the scale was obvious: evidence was given by the masters that machine operators earned from £3 10s 0d to £4 5s 0d a week. A general reduction in the machine scale was proposed by the employers and lengthy negotiations ensued. The members of the Society refused to vote in favour of a proposed agreement: the operators wanted to maintain their high earnings; also, no doubt, the fact that the earnings of the machine operators were vastly in excess of those earned by the hand compositors was probably seen as a means of restraining the adoption of the machine. The LSC executive appealed to a delegate meeting to accept the agreement and not to regard composing machinery 'as some plaything to be toyed or trifled with' and not to place themselves in the 'undesirable position of attempting to fight machinery'.

Eventually, in 1896, a new scale was signed which gave guaranteed minimum weekly earnings of the piece operator equal to the minimum 'stab rate. With the introduction of composing machines in general printing offices at the beginning of the twentieth century, operators were generally paid at 'stab rates slightly higher than those paid to the hand compositor.

It should be emphasized that the union was concerned that only men who had been compositors should operate the machines for though the Linotype Machinery Company soon claimed that they always drew their operators from existing printers this was not originally their intention. In 1889 they distributed a circular[11] to people outside the trade which invited 'applications from 500 intelligent, educated young men of good character who are willing to learn the manipulation of Linotype Machines, and so become "operators" in newspaper and printing offices (an occupation analogous to that of a compositor under the old hand typesetting system) and be able to earn regular wages of from £2 up to £5 per week according to efficiency, when vacancies occur'. A school was to be established in London where the machine could be easily learned (like a typewriter) in from one to six weeks (no wages being paid); it was stated that an operator could learn in one week to operate as fast as a hand compositor. The union insisted that 'if machinery is to be introduced, we claim a right to benefit by its introduction; but if it can only be made to pay at the expense of those who have served an apprenticeship to a trade, we submit that in such an event no real advantage is to be derived'. This was in 1892; by 1893 negotiations were satisfactorily completed with the Linotype Company.

The introduction of machinery was an additional factor in making an advance of wages difficult. The only increase between 1891 and 1914 was one of 1s in 1901 and this was brought about only when the Board of Trade intervened at the request of the employers after strike action had been decided on by the union. Some firms refused to accept the arbitrator's award even though this fell far short of the demands of the compositors.

The effect of these changes on the actual earning of compositors is revealed by a Board of Trade enquiry in 1906.[12] The enquiry covered about 40 per cent of the printing industry, and shows the average weekly earnings taken over a year. It is probably a fairly reliable account of wages at this time, but any bias would arise from understating the number of employees in very small firms who were likely to be paid below the minimum union rate of 39s. The given proportions of compositors earning the amounts refer to the figures in the enquiry and not to the total number of compositors in London.

The average weekly earnings of a 'stab hand compositor working full-time, other than those engaged on daily newspapers, were 39s 11d; whereas 40s 9d were the average earnings of all those at work irrespective of whether they worked less or more than full-time. The higher rate would indicate that on balance more was earned by over-time than was lost by unemployment. But these were not the same people, and the average earnings of a certain number of compositors was below the general rate; the figures would indicate that these formed about nine per cent of the total and the majority of them earned between 30s to 35s weekly. About half of the men earned between 40s to 45s and approximately six per cent earned over 50s a week.

The proportion of men engaged on piece work in these general printing houses was about one quarter. If engaged full-time, a hand compositor on piece work averaged 43s 7d, rather above the general rate. But while good earnings could be achieved (about 14 per cent averaged over 50s a week), the average earnings of those on piecework, taking into account working less or more than full-time, averaged 37s 8d; over one third of the total on piece earned less than 35s and about 17 per cent earned less than 25s a week. About five per cent of all hand compositors in general printing firms, time and piece, averaged less than 25s.

Machine compositors numbered about 11 per cent of all compositors.[13] They earned rather higher wages than hand compositors, but there were considerable differences among them. Those in general printing were mainly engaged on time work – over 80 per cent; these had average earnings of 52s 1d whereas those engaged on piece averaged 69s 6d. The machine operators on daily newspapers were among the highest paid manual occupations – certainly the highest in the printing industry. About half of the machine operators, according to the enquiry, were engaged on daily newspaper production, and these had average earnings of 78s 5d. All were piece hands and some earned very high wages, the upper quartile being 87s 6d (the lower quartile was 70s 6d).

Thus basic wage rates did not improve greatly during the period: from about 35s in mid nineteenth century to 39s by 1914, that is by about 11 per cent. At the same time great variations in pay continued throughout the period, and lack of employment continued to make for considerable fluctuation in earnings over the year. It must be emphasized, however, that certain sections did rather well, periodically at least. Machine operators had rather better earnings than the ordinary hand compositor, the newspaper compositor earned consistently high wages, and even the compositor in a general printing office had opportunities for overtime, and the possibility of 'grassing', i.e. doing extra work for another employer.[14]

The cost of living

Some comparison with the cost of living can be made. The decline in living costs was halted about mid century, and the trend after this was upwards, with fluctuations, to the early 1870s. From the 1870s the cost of living fell greatly, and for 20 years the real value of wages continually increased. From the mid 1890s the cost of living rose steadily again, increasing by 25 per cent from about 1895 to the First World War.[15] Thus taking the basic rates there was a real rise in living standards over the whole period if 1914 is compared with 1850, but there is actual decline towards the end of the period, particularly in the early twentieth century.

But comparing the whole period gives a false picture of the effect of changes in the cost of living. Few men experienced the position as a journeyman at mid century *and* at 1914: that is, the effects of wages increasing by about 11 per cent while the cost of living increased just over six per cent: different generations of compositors had different experiences.

The young journeymen in 1850 would have experienced, by the time their working lives were drawing to a close in 1880, a cost of living increase of eight per cent balanced by an increase in wages of nine per cent. The young journeymen, coming out of their time in the decade 1860–1870, just prior to the great fall in the cost of living, would have experienced, towards the end of their working life around the end of the century, a fall in the cost of living of something over 25 per cent, and an increase of wages of over five per cent. But the young journeymen of the early 1890s would have had an entirely different experience by the eve of the First World War: the cost of living having increased nearly 25 per cent, but wages only two and a half per cent.

Relative position of the compositor

In relation to other trades the position of the compositor grew less favourable over the period. Printing as a whole was a well paid industry; 65 per cent earned over 35s a week, compared with 33 per cent of that part of the population designated by Booth as the 'central classes'.

The compositor was well within this wage group. Compared with the majority of other trades the wage rate of the compositor was high for most of the period. For some time, the compositor continued to be among the labour aristocracy – defined as those earning 30s or more weekly between 1840 and 1890.[16] But his relative position was declining. The general increase in wages of something like 80 per cent between 1850 and 1900[17] was by no means paralleled in the case of the compositor, whose 'stab rate increased in the same period by a little over 15 per cent.

The compositors were aware quite early in the period that their relative position was declining. As already noted, around mid century references were made to wages barely procuring means to sustain a respectable position. In justifying their proposal for an advance of wage in 1866, the union pointed to 'the very general advance which has taken place in the wages of almost all classes of working men during the last 30 years, amounting on average to 20 per cent'.

In an address to the employers in 1890 the Secretary of the LSC stated that 'it cannot possibly be said that the London compositor has been extravagant in his demands – on the contrary, it is quite clear that he has not kept pace with the times, for while other trades have improved their position, he has looked on and contented himself with subscribing towards their support.'[18] A table was appended showing that many trades in London had minimum time rates ranging from 33s 6d to about 48s a week, and up to about 60s for piece work – comparing with the 36s minimum paid to compositors at that period.

At the beginning of the twentieth century Hobsbawm includes in the labour aristocracy those earning 40s a week. The compositor is not among the 15 occupations in this group.[19] The emphasis was going towards the new metal industry, and the old established labour aristocracy were, as Hobsbawm points out, beginning to feel the threat of downgrading.

There were a number of factors for the inability of the compositor to maintain his differential earnings in relation to other trades. It was not simply, as is suggested by Hobsbawm, the result of the introduction of machinery. The differential was being closed, as other sections of the working class advanced their wages, well before composing machinery was widely used, and there are a number of reasons for this. The years immediately after mid century were relatively prosperous and the compositors did not see any need to ask for an increase – especially as there was probably still a certain number of unemployed. Compared with the previous 30 years they were better off and were enjoying the improved employment situation and were also concentrating on building up the union. By the time they tried to advance wages their position was more vulnerable. Apprentices had continued to pour into the trade and there were renewed attempts at the end of the 1860s to deal with this problem, which was helping to increase unemployment, and was a further difficulty in improving wages. Another important factor was the increasing bitter competition between employers in London;[20] as printing expanded outside London, attempts to raise wages were met with the argument that this would further intensify the drift of work from London to other areas and even to the Continent. Competition became increasingly keen towards the end of the century when a meeting was organized by the master printers of London to prevent the 'cut-throat competition'. This led to movements throughout the 1890s to improve methods of costing and estimating printing work.[21] The introduction of the composing machines was only another factor, albeit an important one, in aggravating these conditions.

Unemployment

A persistent problem confronting the compositor throughout the period was the prospect of unemployment. Three main kinds of unemployment could be broadly distinguished, though it is difficult to estimate the relative contribution of each of them. There was the kind of unemployment which resulted from a particular job being completed, the slack period after a periodical had been set up would mean reduced earnings for the piece hand; secondly, unemployment resulted from varying demands for printing at different times of the year, this would particularly affect those men engaged on jobbing or parliamentary work; finally, and most important of all, there was the unemployment which was fairly endemic in composing over the whole period.

Employment in the late 1860s has been described as 'normal', while the early 1870s were 'exceptionally good'. The late 1870s were considered normal, though one year (1879) was very bad. The 1880s were below average[22] when about one compositor in five was unemployed. Unemployment continued for the rest of the period, reaching very high figures in the six years prior to the First World War, yet compared to other industries the situation in printing was fairly favourable and had become less of a problem. In 1909 for example, unemployment in printing was about 5.4 per cent whereas it was about 7.7 per cent for all the organized trades.[23] The swings of industrial activity were less extreme in printing, which was hardly tied to the capital industries where dependence on exports made for great fluctuations.

It may be expected that this increase in unemployment was due to the introduction of composing machines, especially the Linotype; but this is not a sufficient explanation. Fairly efficient composing machines were not used in the country until the late 1860s and then only a few were in use. But they could only be used economically with the aid of cheap labour to distribute the type, and even in the late 1870s the trade was uncertain of the economic advantages of these machines. In 1894 there were only six Linotype machines in London,[24] though by the following year they were being widely used in newspaper printing and from 1900 in general printing.

Unemployment as we have seen was a persistent feature of the occupation long before this. Even during a very bad period of unemployment the Secretary of the LSC asserted that the displacement of labour through the introduction of the Linotype had not been appreciable.[25] This was contrary to a widely held view at the time. Another machine, the Monotype, was also in existence having been introduced in the States towards the end of the nineteenth century, but it was not widely used in the UK until the first decade of the twentieth century when it was used in book and commercial printing.

Composing machines were not without their beneficial effects – in fact they eventually aided the employment situation, for their high outputs made it less necessary to use boy labour; certainly they obviated the need to introduce a large number of boys that would otherwise have been necessary to cope with the continued expansion in the demand for printing, and which could have possibly had a further depressing effect on the compositor's condition. There was also less need to use casual labour, otherwise useful when work was urgently needed and for press days. The introduction of the machine led to agreements which embodied the permitted ratio of apprentices to journeymen operators who could learn the machine. Such agreements foreshadowed the ratio of apprentices to journeymen throughout the trade. In addition the machines improved working conditions in printing firms.

Thus the reason for unemployment cannot be related merely to the introduction of machines. Though it was an important factor in unemployment, especially from the 1890s, a more valid view would be that machinery only aggravated an existing condition. There were other forces behind the amount of unemployment that need to be considered.

A fundamental cause of the problem had been operating throughout the century: the inability to control entry into the occupation and the consequent widespread use of boy labour. This boy labour would be replaced as the boy became a journeyman thus adding to the numbers of men on the labour market. It is not surprising that many boys left the trade when they reached manhood. Two firms gave particulars of 18 boys who entered the trade 'of these, three afterwards emigrated, two became soldiers, one a milkman, one a ship's steward, one a school board visitor, one an insurance agent, one a photographer, two reporters, one a reader and five remained printers'.[26]

An additional factor causing unemployment in printing was, as already mentioned, the fluctuating nature of the work. Though some years were worse than others there would be regular fluctuations within the course of each year. These would be in addition to the temporary slack period after a periodical had gone to press. In a comprehensive survey of several industries the seasonal fluctuation in printing was found to be a 'prominent and regular phenomenon' of the industry.[27] In the period 1897 to 1906 a seasonal pattern throughout the year was found: the slackest month was August, followed by improvements to the busiest month of November, and then a decline followed by a further improvement in February.

Attempts to solve unemployment

Several solutions were attempted by the compositors and in particular by the union. One obvious solution was to try to restrict the number of apprentices. Throughout the period it would appear that a seven year indentureship was generally observed. More difficult than maintaining the institution of apprenticeship was the problem of controlling numbers. Here there was not only the problem of enforcing a ratio of apprentices to journeymen; there was much uncertainty about what actual ratio was desirable or practicable, and by the end of the period there was still no specific agreed rule between employer and union on the ratio for hand compositors. This was not agreed until 1922 when the ratio was fixed at one apprentice to four compositors.

Another solution to the problem was to ensure better training provisions for apprentices. This would slow down the productive output of the apprentices and would minimise the extent to which they were employed on the more profitable work to the detriment of journeymen; there were increasing demands by compositors for the proper training of apprentices.[28]

Some compositors found it preferable to leave the country and seek their fortunes abroad, and emigration increased at the end of the period from about 30 a year in the 1880s to 70 a year in the years immediately preceding the First World War. We saw that earlier internal migration, tramping from one town to another in search of work, was another possibility for the unemployed; this became less resorted to during the period as a means of relieving unemployment. Tramping still existed, and was often a means of searching for work; but it was often resorted to by the young man without ties, as an experience for its own sake.

The fact of unemployment was given expression in a system which, though eventually coming under attack from the union, did reflect the existence of the occupational community. This was the 'Gift System'.[29] A 'gift' was an informal organization of men (which appears to have been limited to 100) who pledged to assist each other in finding jobs. They also paid a low subscription, and a benefit was received during unemployment. Gifts became the vogue in London between the late 1850s to 1870s; they appear to have been derived from similar organizations among the pressmen, but were probably a development of an earlier custom of a group meeting in public houses and forming an aid club.[30] The names of many of the gifts were taken from the public house they met in. The gift system began with the LTS of C, an unemployment society. By around 1890 there were ten gifts with a membership of nearly 1,000; therefore roughly one eighth of the union was in a gift, for no-one was in two gifts. The system provoked a great deal of controversy, because the Society clashed with the gifts as a means of obtaining employment; for the gifts kept their own 'call book' for employment which existed alongside that of the Society.[31] After an enquiry in 1892 the gifts were reconstituted so that they were no longer inimical to the principle of the Society and their call book was abolished.

Hours and conditions

The compositors' working day was very long at mid century. Generally he worked a 12 hour day, usually from 8 am to 8 pm,[32] with one and a half hours for refreshment for six days a week; so that the actual working hours were ten and a half a day or 63 a week. It appears that some offices already stopped work on Saturday at 2 pm. On morning papers the hours for night work were shorter – about eight to ten a night, starting some time between 5 p.m. and 9 p.m. to between 3 a.m. and 5 a.m. according to the newspaper schedule.

In 1866 came the first demand for shorter hours, a 58 hour week. The needs of health was the explicit motive 'hardly a trade which exercises so great a strain upon the system, both mentally and physically, as that of an operative printer';[33] eventually a 60 hour week was agreed.

In 1872 another reduction was requested. This time the reason for the request was that there was a general movement by other trades – the Nine Hours Movement – which was being achieved: 'in all directions and in all sorts of trades, the limitation of the week's work to 54 hours, or nine per day, has become an accepted creed with the great mass of skilled workmen'.[34] Further justification was found in the influence of unhealthy offices, 'over 50 per cent of our members dying from diseases of the air passages' because of the 'vitiated atmosphere' they worked in. In addition another justification for reduction of hours is advanced: the 'increasing cost of rent in central London compels us to make our homes at a considerable distance from our various places of employment, and hence a further necessity exists for restricting the hours of labour within such limits as will enable us to spend some little time with our families and to obtain the relaxation which is so essential in sustaining bodily health'.[35] The master printers did not readily agree to the adoption of a 54 hour week, but the compositors were adamant knowing that they formed part of a national movement and the 54 hour week was gained.

As well as affording more leisure, the major impetus behind the eight hour day movement at the end of the century was the hope that unemployment would be reduced by distributing the hours of work more equally. It was not until the early twentieth century that the eight hour question was taken up with enthusiasm. But trade conditions were not good. The dispute was sent to arbitration in 1901 and a mere one and a half hour reduction was secured, making a 52½ hour week. With increasing unemployment, the eight hour day was becoming an important objective for the compositors, as it was for the trade union movement in general, and the hours question became the centre of a bitter dispute. The majority of the members supported the hours movement,[36] the plan being to reduce the existing hours of 52½ to 50 by January, 1911 and to a 48 hour week a year later.

The masters' association did not agree to the plan though many were in favour of the reduction, and a strike took place. It became the largest widespread strike that the industry had known,[37] lasting several months. Several other London unions followed the lead of the LSC and tendered notices. Strike action was strongly supported by the compositors and a substantial levy of 5s per week had been agreed to by an overwhelming majority. Continental printing unions were appealed to not to engage in work diverted because of the strike; and messages of support came in. By the end of the year, though the masters' association refused to acknowledge any agreement to the effect, the 50 hour week was generally recognised. The eight hour day, however had to wait until 1919 when the First World War was over.

The actual number of hours worked was often considerably more than the agreed working week, for overtime continued to be an important feature of the industry. Part of the reason lay in the seasonal nature of the trade. Slack periods were often followed by long bouts of overtime, for once a customer decides to buy printing he usually wants it in a hurry. But much of the overtime was continual; even while there was unemployment, certain sections of the trade were working many hours overtime on work which had to be completed by a definite time.

Holiday with pay was not a recognised custom of the trade, and the compositor had to lose earnings if he took any time off. But the movement for a recognised holiday with pay began in the latter part of the nineteenth century and in 1885 it was observed 'with considerable pleasure' that many Chapels had been able 'to secure a few days' holiday in the summer months at the expense of their employers!'[38]

Social status and image of the compositor

We have already observed that one of the important aspects of the social situation of an occupation is in the social ranking it receives in the society in which it forms a part; this depends on the 'image' held of the occupation by the general public. This image depends not only on the actual material condition of the occupation, but on the real or imagined ability required for the occupation, the training necessary, and partly by the social section it is recruited from. Something of the social standing of the compositor in the second half of the nineteenth century can be seen from the fact that composing was one of the occupations which received attention from those agitating for women's rights.

Composing was seen as a desirable occupation when suitable employment for women was being sought. It was stressed by those concerned in this endeavour that they were not speaking for the wives and daughters of labourers, but for middle class women, who had too much leisure on their hands. It was insisted that it was not true that work other than teaching and governess work would spoil their gentility.[39] Composing was an occupation suited to women, for 'setting of type, called composing, which is the higher branch of the trade' would enable such women to use their 'superior delicacy of touch' and the occupation would also enable them to 'exercise the feminine quality of taste' in layout.[40]

A visitor to the Victoria Press which had been established in 1860 as a means of providing employment for educated ladies, found rooms full of girls. It was noted that order, industry, kindness and good manners prevailed. The writer went on to claim that 'The compositors' trade should be in the hands of women only. They are eminently suited to it, and it is eminently suited to them'. Composing was much 'better than the tedious stitch, stitch, stitch, of the poor seamstress, better for health and mind and body, and far better paid'.[41]

Some years afterwards in 1874 the Women's Printing Society (WPS) was formed. Picking up type was considered to be a 'light and genteel' occupation, and a female compositor urged her sisters who spent their time idling and reading periodicals to become useful artisans.[42] The following advice was given: 'this work is much more remunerative and far less toilsome and irritating than the occupation of the average nursery governess.'[43]

In 1885 it was estimated by the LSC that there were about 50 female compositors in London.[44] This is probably an underestimate; other evidence suggests that in the 1890s there were 100 to 200 women employed. These were paid about 18s 6d weekly, (at the WPS the older girls received

Frontispiece to 'Printing at Home' marketing a home press, showing printing as a socially acceptable hobby in a gentleman's household. It lends support to the view that composing could be a suitable occupation for women.

24s weekly). A few women were admitted to the LSC, the first in 1893. It should be noted that these women were not being introduced in order to operate the composing machines. In the 1911 Census when the Linotype was fairly well established, there were only 11 women machine operators in London; the number of female hand compositors at this time was 138, a small fraction of the total of over 12,000 compositors in London.

The educational, literary and artistic associations of the occupation were important contributions to the image of the compositor. The occupation itself had a strong educational effect on the follower of the trade. Even where education was lacking when he entered the trade, within a few years of continually setting possibly 2,000 words a day, a young man was likely to be familiar with punctuation, spelling and the rudiments of grammar. It would be to his own advantage to acquire this knowledge especially when he was on piece work, because it would mean that less time would have to be spent on correcting errors. Nor did the education stop there. Latin and Greek quotations were frequently used at the time and most printing offices had a case of Greek type, so that it was desirable that the compositor was familiar with the Greek alphabet at least. The more curious compositor was likely to find out the meanings of the phrases. This educational function of the occupation was recognised by another author. Arnold Bennett observed that 'one cannot be a compositor for a quarter of a century without insensibly acquiring an education and a store of knowledge far excelling the ordinary.'[45]

There were many printer-editors, and a country printer would often decide to issue a local paper and frequently wrote the copy himself. Several journals also appeared which were produced for and by printers themselves,[46] and for most of these the copy was provided entirely by compositors; it was amongst compositors that the first Labour daily newspaper, the *Daily Herald*, originated. In addition to trade items in the journals there were frequent articles on English grammar and punctuation in these publications. Many compositors were indeed highly literate and were proud of their knowledge of the English language.[47]

A high standard of literacy is also revealed by the reports of the early compositors' societies. The Webbs commented on the moderation, formality, almost stateliness of their proceedings; the constant investigation of disputes instead of rhetorical abuse is similarly indicative. Though later compositors' reports are less detailed they also maintain these standards; for example, the 'strong and excellent attack' on current economic theory in the May 1906 journal included historical references to activities of the clergy in order to provide comparative material.

The association of the compositor with literacy and with literary acquaintance was an important contribution to this image. Literary aspirations would be fostered by his intimate contact with writing; for example, by seeing the written copy before printing (particularly before the advent of the typewriter). Where the compositor himself had no such aspiration (and this was probably the majority) the contact with editors and authors was a possible factor in producing an image of the compositor which had these literary associations. Though the compositor no longer had a virtual monopoly of education (and the education of other artisans in earlier periods must not be understated), and though the quality of the lad attracted to the trade was declining, this image regarding the occupation appeared to remain throughout the period.

Despite the persistence of a high image of the occupation, the actual condition of the compositor was reflected in the source of recruitment and there were constant statements that the class of boy was deteriorating. A speaker at a meeting of Printers' Managers and Overseers Association said 'we seem now to get the failures at school, the riff-raff of the streets, the rejects of other trades. I can remember when printing was an occupation to which the lower middle class and the upper lower class were glad to put their sons, when the printer ranked as being a grade higher than the joiner, the brick-setter, and the fitter ... we ought to get the pick of the lads bred by our working class and the cream of the day schools. A business like ours ... ought to attract the brighter boys of the artisan class, to say the least'.[48]

Complaints about the decline in the kind of boy entering the trade were not merely the exaggerated grouse about the younger generation which is so frequently expressed. The view that the kind of boy entering the trade was coming from a lower class than hitherto is given some support by the records of the Stationers' Company. In Chapter II it was seen that the social group from which compositors were recruited had declined with changing social conditions. Table 5 shows that this process continued to the end of the period.

It must be emphasized that the Stationers' Company records may not be typical and can only be taken as a trend, for the proportion of composing apprentices indentured in the Company was certainly less than ten per cent in the latter years analyzed. In all probability (for reasons given in the previous chapter), they are likely to over-estimate the numbers recruited from the higher social group.

Composing was certainly an occupation in which changes in social recruitment were taking place. The occupation was attracting fewer boys

Table 5 **Source of Recruitment**

Social group of fathers	1840s[a] %	1878–1880[a] %	comps. %	1900–1902[a] %	comps. %
Above skilled & non manual	37	20	23	21	25
Skilled	55	69	66	62	58
Below skilled	8	11	11	17	17
	100	100	100	100	100
Printers	27	28	28	26	21

a. In the 1840s boys were recorded as being apprenticed to printers. In the later years they were recorded in specific occupations. The first column in each period includes the occupations covered by 'printers' in 1840 and earlier years, and is thus comparable with the earlier figures. The second column for 1878–1880 and 1900–1902 also gives the percentage for compositor apprentices only.

from the class above that of the artisan and more from the ranks of the less skilled.

To state the causes for this with any finality would be difficult. The obvious explanation seems to be that as the social condition of the occupation grew relatively worse, so middle-class parents became less willing to enter their sons into the trade, despite the status which it conferred. On the other hand, it could be argued that the decreasing proportion of boys from the 'above the artisan' group reflected the growing opportunities of more desirable occupations for the children of this group, particularly around mid century. Support for this second argument can be given by the fact that the image of the occupation still remained high during the period.[49]

Similarly, the larger proportion from the less skilled would reflect the greater opportunities of education for this group by 1900: the sons of the less skilled were having more opportunities to rise and enter more skilled occupations.

Both arguments could be supported by the recruitment into the trade from the sons of printers. The earlier trend for an increasing proportion of the boys entering the trade to be sons of printers did not continue. This could be explained by the fact that as the social condition was relatively worse, printers were less willing to put their sons to the trade. On the other hand, the declining proportion of sons of printers could well reflect a situation in which the aspirations of printers for their son's employ-ment were higher than that of compositor, and were being realised. The real level of decline in the sons of printers is possibly understated. For it is possible that printers were more likely to put their sons to better firms, who were likely to be members of the Stationers' Company. Those with traditions were likely to maintain the older attitude to apprentices and to give a better training.

The two arguments are not mutually exclusive. In a situation where social mobility is a possibility it is likely to take place within those occupa-tions which are undergoing change. Despite a high image of the occupa-tion, the contact with the trade which is occasioned by, or indeed makes possible an apprenticeship, is likely to reveal the actual social condition of the trade. Thus it is suggested that just as an occupation that is declining is the first to be left by those interested in maintaining, if not improving their position, so these occupations are the first to be entered by those who are rising in the occupational hierarchy. The declining demand for the occupation by higher social groups makes it possible for those worse off to enter the occupation.

The changing amount of recruitment of composing apprentices from among sons of printers is suggestive of their condition. Between the 1840s and the 1870s the percentage hardly changes, but between the latter period and 1900 there is a decline from 28 per cent to 21 per cent. It is significant that the proportion of those whose fathers were printers was the same for compositors as for 'printers' as a whole in the 1870s, whereas the proportion was falling more for compositors during the last quarter of the century than it was for 'printers' as a whole. By 1900 the Linotype machine was becoming established and with the advent of machinery there was probably some anxiety about the compositors' future. This sug-gestion is reinforced by the Board of Trade enquiry in 1915 which stated that there was no evidence that boys were mainly recruited from print-ers; this may be partly due to some fear about the impact of machinery.

Premium payments became extremely rare during the period. There were only three cases of premium payments for printers in the Stationers' Company records in the late 1870s, and none in the 1900s. However, in the years immediately prior to the First World War there appears to have been some attempt to revive the system of premiums. The attempt was opposed by the journeymen compositors. In reporting several recent instances, it was stated that 'the system is a bad one from every point of view.' The attempt was not successful.

The development of the union

During the period the compositors' union, the LSC, which had been reformed in 1848, became firmly established. As the 1885 annual report shows membership had increased gradually and about half the London compositors were members (6,435 out of about 12,000 compositors). Membership then rapidly increased after a recruitment campaign which commenced in 1884, with a circular to the trade showing the attractions of joining the union. In it the LSC claimed to be the largest centralised trade society in the Kingdom; it is pointed out that it was distinguished from many other societies in that meetings did not take place in public houses, all business being transacted in their own premises at Racquet Court.

Growth was especially rapid between 1880 and 1893 when membership almost doubled,[50] and the number of Chapels covered by the LSC rose to well over 500. The success of the campaign was no doubt partly because it came at a time of unemployment, when it was necessary for a compositor to try every means of securing work, for the union acted as an employment exchange. It was probably true that unemployment was especially heavy among non-union labour, which, though cheaper to employ, tended to be less well-trained. In addition working in a union shop meant getting the full rate. However, there were still about 3,500 men outside the union in 1897. This would represent about 70 per cent unionization, and by the end of the period the proportion was even higher.

The attraction of friendly society benefits was an important incentive to join the union. At a time when subscriptions were 8d weekly, the benefits were very attractive.[51] Unemployment benefit had been established in 1861 and the benefit in the 1880s was 12s weekly for 16 weeks in a year. Strike benefit was very high at 25s a week because of the need to encourage men to fight to maintain the scale. A union superannuation scheme had been established in 1877 and gave a pension of 4s to 6s weekly, and the funeral benefit begun in 1868 gave between £4 and £15 depending on the length of membership. These benefits increased by the end of the period and must have done a good deal to alleviate the compositor's condition when his income from work was depleted.

A variety of problems had to be faced by the union during the period: boy labour, maintaining the piece scale, advancing wages and reducing hours have already been referred to; so has the need to deal with technical innovations, such as the effects of stereotyping and the regulations over the introduction of composing machinery. In addition pressure was brought on the government, municipalities and other organizations, to ensure that printing orders were placed with firms recognised by the union as 'fair' houses; and local 'advisory' groups, based on the residential areas of the compositors, were set up to further this.

Working class identification

With the relative decline materially and especially with the growth of the union, there was an increasing identification with the working class. It was noted earlier that by the middle of the nineteenth century, this identification was becoming crystallized. However, the working class militancy felt by the compositor was not very strong at first and the sympathy shown to other working class groups was rather detached or of a temporary nature.

In 1863 one working class journal complained that the compositors were largely aristocratic and conservative, and that the LSC was rarely represented at general delegate meetings of the London trades, 'studiously keeping aloof from their movements.'[52] Later in the same decade they again protested that the compositors were isolated and conservative and were not displaying identity of interest with the working class. Yet delegates were sent to the International Working Men's Association in 1866. In 1874 the LSC connected itself with the Trade Union Congress (TUC), having previously been associated with the Conference of Amalgamated Trades which had been dissolved about 1871,[53] but the union was not very active at this time.

Stronger feeling of solidarity developed towards the end of the century with the relative decline in the condition of the compositor. Within the union itself it was insisted that the society was for protection of trade, rather than a benefit society, and the growth of militancy was extended to other working class groups.

When the idea of a federation of trade unions developed, the LSC gave its support, though at first its reception to the idea was cautious. In 1897 LSC's delegates to the London Trades Council (LTC) stressed that though such a federation may be advisable, it must be remembered that the primary object of trade unions was to obtain and retain members. Soon, however, the scheme was winning the sympathy of the LSC: 'No subject at the present moment', it was asserted in the annual report for 1898, 'possesses more importance to the workers than that of Federation, and the scheme recently formulated will assuredly receive the careful and earnest consideration of members of this as of all other trades.' The extent to which the members approved of the scheme of the General Federation of Trade Unions (GTFU) is indicated by the large majority who were in favour of affiliation: over 6,000 in favour and less than 1,000 against; the LSC actually affiliated in 1900. The early ideas of the Federation typified the mood of the LSC: while the capitalist system was accepted and the aim was to promote industrial peace, the trades were prepared to show their solidarity by presenting a common front to the employers through financial aid during disputes. It may be noted that the Federation was not supported by all printing unions; for example, the provincial compositors' union, the Typographical Association (TA) decided against affiliation.

The LSC also became more active in the TUC during the early twentieth century.[54] At the TUC of 1913 the LSC delegates demanded that the TUC be reorganized and the suggestion reflected the ideas of industrial unionism which were prominent at that time. It was urged that in order to produce more effective policy each industry should be represented in the TUC, instead of separate unions. A fund should be established to help the industry as whole and fight for its demands; this, it was asserted, was not mere 'syndicalist theory'. This demand is somewhat surprising as the LSC had always been wary of action which could lead to losing its identity and this had been a stumbling block to amalgamation in the printing trade which had been often attempted. It was possible that the great 1911 strike had created a more receptive atmosphere, though the delegates may not have been typical of the membership.

Almost every year there were examples of financial aid to other groups of workers in dispute, and nearly £17,000 was contributed over the period. When large grants were to be given they were decided by ballot and the record of votes indicates that relatively few compositors displayed their lack of solidarity towards other workers. For example, only 118 voted against granting a loan to the shoemakers' society in 1884 whilst 3,600 voted in favour. A grant of £70 to London carpenters in 1891 was decided by over 4,500 votes for and about 450 against. Nor was this willingness to help others confined to skilled workers: in the great dockworkers' dispute of 1889 over 5,500 voted that a £500 grant be made (about 190 voting against), and substantial grants were made to the transport workers. Individual members were also prepared to make contributions: when the Amalgamated Society of Engineers were fighting for an eight hour day in 1897, the men were levied in addition to a grant by the LSC; a total of over £3,000 was paid by the Society and its members. Workers in other countries, in Austria, Germany and Denmark, were also voted grants by substantial majorities.

Many compositors took part in working class demonstrations, for which the LSC had a banner made. An old compositor recalls a May Day procession in the early 1890s: 'We assembled on the Embankment with our new banner, blue with gilt wording. It was a great procession, Jack Ward heading it on horseback, the streets all the way crowded with spectators, nearly all the bands playing "The Marseilles" at intervals, for we were nearer revolution in those days than ever we have been since'.[55] It must be stressed, however, that this enthusiastic expression of working class identification was by no means true of all compositors: in one ballot, in 1893, there was a majority of over 500 against the active participation in a demonstration in Hyde Park for the eight-hour day; the voting was 2,340 for, 2,857 against.

One outcome of the conflict over hours of 1911 was the publication of a strike sheet which eventually became Labour's first daily paper. Demands for a daily paper devoted to the Labour movement had been increasing during the early twentieth century and steps had been taken in this direction, without success. The LSC had always supported the idea, not the least reason being the employment it would produce. As it was thought that the national press had not given a full picture of the negotiations between the masters and the men in the dispute, the LSC decided to publish a strike sheet, which was also a link between the Strike Committee and the Chapels: this was the *Daily Herald*. Though a strike sheet, it was soon hoped that it would become a newspaper. The first issue proclaimed 'We have arrived. At last we have a daily paper of our own'. Soon the *Daily Herald* was being described as the basis for a real Labour daily. From 25th January to 13 April 1911, it was published by the LSC. Early in April a meeting was held which decided that it should continue as a Labour daily newspaper but it ceased publication on 28 April, 1911. After much agitation it was restarted in April 1912 by George Lansbury and others, and had strong support among LSC members.

The 1911 dispute could be seen as the culmination of a developing feeling of resentment from the end of the nineteenth century about the compositor's declining condition. A master printer suggests that the dispute had a long history and dates 1901 as the beginning of the dissatisfaction, when there was great disappointment with the arbitration award.[56] From then on there was mounting tension expressed in the restrictions on overtime and the 1911 strike. In the general trade union legislative background there was the Taff Vale case and the Osbourne judgment as well as the fears about composing machinery. At a time when the condition of the compositor was in absolute as well as relative decline, the 1911 dispute could be seen as a major expression of discontent by the compositor.

Politically the compositor was mixed in his allegiance. Neither of the political parties in the nineteenth century represented the working man specifically, and the compositor, as with other sections of the working class who had the vote, had no party which he could support as clearly representing his own interests.

Any tendency for working class movements to become politically active was regarded with deep suspicion and hostility by union members. It was desired that any activity should be confined to the industrial field, and unions were discouraged from becoming involved in party politics. The only political activity permitted, especially in the early part of the period, was agitation and representation of views to secure certain benefits only; there was no identification with either of the main parties. Thus, printers were exhorted to support political action which in general would tend to increase the demand for printing. Later, political activity was more concerned to direct specific policy on printing – on fair wages and hours, government printing contracts, and pressure for a government press.

The attitude toward politics of the LSC was evident in a report made by delegates to the 1875 Trades Union Congress. They admitted that the TUC had given 'infinite service to the cause of labour' in bringing about the repeal of legislation which had restricted trade union activity. But now that the chief difficulties had been removed they were 'not impressed with a conviction that their continuance in the future, at least at such frequent intervals, is desirable'. This idea of associating with other unions for specific purposes only, was paralleled by a horror of the introduction of 'politics' into the proceedings, for it was evident that some delegates desired to 'adopt class legislation'. This occasioned some comment on behaviour within the LSC itself. A tendency to make the society a medium 'for discussing and agitating on political questions ... should be carefully watched'. For, it was pointed out, over general political questions working men 'disagree as widely as any other portion of our fellow-countrymen'.

In common with other working class groups, there was a greater readiness to engage in political activity towards the end of the century. Trade unions, it was asserted, should not hold aloof from politics; beneficial legislation had been secured from parliament because of trade union political action. The idea of the LSC having its own parliamentary representative was suggested as early as 1885, but nearly two decades were to pass before such a suggestion was seriously considered. When the Labour Representation Committee (LRC) was established, the LSC affiliated very early, in 1900. In this respect the compositors were in advance of other trade unions, who were sceptical of the LRC.[57]

In 1902, it was decided that a shilling a year levy should be imposed in order to have a Member of Parliament to 'represent working men, trade unions and compositors'. Despite the recognition and emphasis by the union that direct representation was essential to preserve the efficacy of trade unionism, political activity was still regarded with suspicion by a considerable number of compositors, and a substantial minority opposed this decision to enter directly into politics. About seven-eighths of the eligible membership voted – over 4,200 for, but nearly 3,000 against the proposal. Though many voted against because of their political allegiance to other parties, the size of the opposition may reflect continued suspicion of political activity. One of the reasons for running their own candidate was that it was considered desirable to have somebody in the House to represent the printing industry in the interest of the workers. After a close contest with four candidates expounding their political views, Bowerman, the secretary, was chosen. He was accepted as the candidate for Deptford and won the seat at the 1906 General Election; shortly afterwards the political section of the LSC was formed.

In order to get the members to support the Labour Party it was deemed to be necessary to appeal to those who were rather wary of political activity, and to those who were politically conservative. An article in the union journal on 'The LSC and the Labour Party' suggested that the new Labour Party represented an interest rather than a political party, and was certainly not merely socialist. The special attention of Conservatives was drawn to the fact that the Labour interest is outside the purely political: 'our Parliamentary Secretary is the Labour Member for Deptford. He has plainly avowed himself not to be a socialist. In his constituency the support he obtains is many-sided. Socialists support him as a member of the Labour Party, Liberals as a Liberal, trade unionists as a trade unionist, Non-Conformists and Social Reformers as being favourable to causes which they consider supremely important … So far as our Society is concerned, we send him to Parliament to look after the interests of Labour, of trade unionism, and of the LSC. We have decided that he can do this most effectively as a member of the Labour Party; and so long as he looks after those interests he is serving us all, whatever our politics may be.'[58] The article stressed that support for the Labour Party was not a political issue, pointing out that much of the work of Parliament was quite apart from party issues and on which the parties collaborated. As various interests were represented in Parliament, so what was required was a representative of the wage-earner: 'It is essential that we as wage-earners should have a corrective in the form of a party whose members are united in watching over the interests of labour, independent of capitalist influence or middle class prejudice. The members of the LSC may be church-men or agnostics or non-conformists, they may be Liberal or Socialists or Conservatives, but so far as they are trade unionists they must be Labour men'. One wonders how far the members agreed with these distinctions.

When the major restrictions on political activities were removed in 1913 the Society decided not to take advantage of the new Act. The LSC committee recommended to the August 1913 delegate meeting: 'That the society take no action in regard to the powers conferred by the Trade Union Act, 1913; and that the Voluntary Parliamentary Association be asked to continue as at present constituted.' That the proposal was agreed to almost unanimously reflected the lack of any widespread desire to sup-port political activity or strong support for the Labour Party. In fact the only criticism of the proposal in the discussion reported in the *London Typographical Journal* (LTJ) for August 1913 was that the second part of the recommendation should be deleted as 'the Labour Party in the House was held in contempt by the great majority of workers in the country.' Not until 1916 were the provisions of the Act adopted by the union; and this appears to have been brought about by strong pressure from the Labour Party. In July 1915, the Parliamentary Committee was invited to a meeting by the LSC Executive to consider taking a ballot of the Society on the Trade Union Act of 1913. It was disclosed at this meeting that representatives of the Labour Party had met the executive and had urged that the LSC should adopt the Act, contending that 'abstention from that course would possibly place Mr Bowerman in an awkward position if the Labour Party found itself compelled to withhold support from him during a General Election';[59] this was the motivation for taking the ballot, 'anxious that Mr Bowerman's position should not suffer by this attitude of the Labour Party, the Parliamentary Committee expressed to the LSC Executive the hope that a ballot would be taken on the Trade Union Act.'

The ballot, taken in March 1916, 'approving the furtherance of Political objects, as an objective of the LSC' was in favour of the resolution, but only by a narrow majority on a rather small vote. Already by the end of the year, 1,610, one-fifth of the working membership had contracted out, making a total membership of the political section of 6,437 (after deducting members on national service, superannuitants and apprentice members).

This evidence of political activity shows the reticence with which the early Labour Party was regarded by one section of the working class, and that many of the appeals to support it had to be made on the grounds of industrial self-interest rather than political idealism.

Socialist ideas were not responded to, generally, with any warmth. As with other skilled workers, socialism was treated cautiously if not with indifference by the majority of compositors. It might have been expected that the ideas of socialism would have appealed to a group of workers who were comparatively well-equipped intellectually, and whose economic position was in decline. One explanation may be that their situation, though in decline, was not depressed, and the image of the compositor was such as to give him considerable status. While other groups were improving their position, an association with socialism would have been an expression of identification with that depressed section of the working classes who found socialism attractive. By not embracing socialism, the compositor could cling to a status which the egalitarianism of a socialist society may have denied him.

The compositor's attitude to socialism, expressed in a paper devoted to chronicling the affairs of the LSC, reveals a mixture of scornfulness towards socialism and feelings of patriotism. A suggestion had been made that there were a large number of compositors in socialistic movements abroad. The paper was quick to deny that the same was true in England. 'We suppose the pestilent rubbish they are daily engaged in setting-up gets into their heads. An English compositor generally has the sense to see through it, and either laughs at the writer for a fool, or curses him for a villain'.[60] Such a view did not exclude a working-class consciousnesses, for the writer agrees with the need for working class members in parliament.

Such anti-socialist views were somewhat modified when the wave of socialistic sympathy in the nineties and the feelings of working class solidarity carried a considerable number towards socialism. In 1894 the TUC had passed the resolution 'to nationalise the land and the whole of the means of production, distribution and exchange, and that the parliamentary committee be instructed to promote and support legislation with the above object'. This resolution was rejected by the London compositors, but the voting is revealing. Over a quarter of those eligible to vote were in favour of the resolution, and about one-third failed to vote at all. It is not suggested that those in favour of the resolution were convinced socialists; they may have just had a general sympathy to the ideas and were willing to show their sympathy in this way. Such sympathy made possible grants to socialist bodies – as that of £5 towards the expenses of the International Congress of Socialist Workers and Trade Unions in 1895; the Society was also represented at the International Workers Congress in 1896.

However, socialists were in a minority, and the earlier view of socialism as being utopian was still widespread. Compositors preferred to deal with the present fact of capitalism and work to better their position within it, rather that to see socialism as the inevitable result of the progress of society. The general attitude to socialists at the beginning of the twentieth century is perhaps best summed up by an ex-compositor, himself a socialist sympathiser. 'Socialist compositors', he said, 'were regarded by the majority of the men with a good-humoured tolerance; just as if they had been members of the Salvation Army'.[61]

Certainly the socialist attitude to imperialism and war was not held by the majority of compositors. The LSC's annual report at the time of the Boer War gave the information that 20 members were serving in South Africa and expressed a sympathy hardly in keeping with socialist sentiments: 'It is hoped [that they] return safe and sound, and with all the honours that active military service can confer upon them'. Similarly, the outbreak of the First World War did not arouse strong anti-war feelings – the attitude being similar to that of the trade union movement in general. In the LSC journal covering the first month of the war it was stated that 'the trade unions, realising the gravity of the situation, did their best to adjust matters in the common interest'. The LSC's annual report for 1914 was evidently concerned with the war's effects on unions and appealed to the trade unions to be vigilant to preserve their position: 'History teaches us that organized capital is ready to take advantage of labour ... the trade union must preserve its defences in order that their members shall not suffer unduly from the reaction that will inevitably follow the war.'

Conclusion

Certain trends during the period can be summarized. Before doing so it must be stressed that there is danger in summarization because of over-simplification. There was a good deal of variation in the condition of the compositor, depending on where he worked, and what kind of work he was engaged on. Earnings, for example, could vary considerably according to the nature of the work and opportunities for overtime.

In certain respects, the position of the compositor was advantageous. The status of the compositor continued to be fairly high, and the compositor reflected the general image held of him, by his own feelings of status consciousness. A compositor in steady employment was likely to live fairly comfortably and respectably. On the other hand, the position of the compositor in relation to other sections of the working class was not maintained. He was losing his position among the aristocracy of labour: other occupations were rivalling him or were well in advance of his earnings – even within printing: for example the machine minders and bookbinders. Also the unskilled were reducing the differentials that had obtained in the past. Employment prospects throughout the period were uncertain. No longer had he such a monopoly of education as in earlier years, though probably a higher proportion of literary-minded men were to be found in the ranks of the occupation. The social origin of the boy entering the trade declined, and this may have been a factor in the growing willingness to identify with the working class.

Under these conditions, and in the wave of working class feeling towards the end of the nineteenth century, there was a gradual identification by the compositor with the working class in general.[62] This can be seen by the amount of aid given to other workers' organisations and by the growing willingness to participate in organizations of the trade union movement. Though the material position of the compositor was not such as to make him a strong socialist, he became increasingly willing, though grudgingly and to a limited extent, to participate in politics. With the general support for the growing Labour Party, the expressions of other political sympathies were heard less, though there was a considerable section of London compositors who were Liberal, and many even Conservative. Class consciousness was becoming fairly strongly developed, especially with the real decline in the condition of the compositor in the early years of the twentieth century. This expressed itself in support of that body which represented the labour interest, the Labour Party. But the expression of working class solidarity was less strong in the political field than in the industrial. What political activity there was, centred less on the wider issues of changing society, than on the limited needs of the trade; it was more important to be a good union man than it was to be Labour.

The movement towards class consciousness should not be overstressed: status consciousness inhibited full identification with the working class. Yet it can be said that in this period an ethos was beginning to emerge of the compositor being a strong union man, of identifying with the working class, and because of this that he ought to support the growing Labour Party.

Notes

1 Knight, *Old Printer*, and Webb, *British Working Class Reader*, describe the situation to the middle of the century; for the later period see Lee, *Origins of the Popular Press*.

2 Howe, *London Compositor*, p. 260, quoting the LSC annual report for 1845.

3 Howe and Waite, *London Society of Compositors*, p. 291.

4 *Print*, September 1896, p. 2.

5 Howe, *London Compositor*, p. 291, quoting from a letter from William Blades to the members of the London School Board.

6 The revised scale and the amendments of the previous years are clearly set out in Howe, *London Compositor*, p. 327–55.

7 'The London Society of Compositors' by 'Scourge', *Bee-hive Newspaper*, 10 October 1863, p. 1, col. 1.

8 'Report by Dr Edward Smith on the Sanitary Circumstances of Printers in London', *Sixth Report of the Medical Officer of the Privy Council, 1863*, p. 397.

9 Howe, *London Compositor*, p. 490.

10 Webb, *Industrial Democracy*, p. 407.

11 'To Unemployed Young Men' (St Bride Library).

12 Great Britain, Board of Trade, *Report ... into the Earnings and Hours ... of Workpeople ... in 1906*, p. 8, p. xviii–xxii, 1–84.

13 This is about twice the number indicated by the 1911 Census, which gave about 5.4 per cent machine compositors. It would appear that newspaper offices were over-represented in the sample.

14 McAra, 'Reminiscences of Print and Fleet Street', p. 22.

15 Cole and Postgate, p. 441.

16 Hobsbawm, 'Labour Aristocracy', p. 278–84.

17 Cole and Postgate, p. 445.

18 Howe, *London Compositor*, p. 319.

19 Hobsbawm, p. 281, 288 (His figures are based on the 1906 Wage Census).

20 *Printing News*, January 1893, p. 8.

21 Sessions, *Federation of Master Printers*, p. 40–1.

22 Evidence of the LSC to the Royal Commission on Depression of Trade and Industry, *Second Report, Appendix, Pt. II*, p. 78.

23 *Conference between representatives of the Federation of Master Printers ... and ... the Printing and Kindred Trades Federation* [on the 48-hour week] ... *1911*, p. 8, col. 2.

24 Howe and Waite, p. 228–30. For a fuller account of the historical development of composing machinery see Howe, *London Compositor*, p. 490–509.

25 *Print*, October 1896, p. 11.

26 Booth, *Life and Labour, Second Series, Industry*, v. 2, p. 189.

27 Webb and Freeman, *Seasonal Trades*, p. 5.

28 See for example *Print, Fleet Street Gazette* and the *Printer* (1883–8).

29 Richards, 'Social and Economic Aspects of Combination in the Printing Trade before 1875', p. 358–63.

30 Howe, *London Compositor*, p. 308n.

31 London School of Economics library, Webb Trade Union Collection, v. A31, f. 295–6. Webb says 'Perhaps not over one fifth of Soc^y now in Gifts', but union membership around 1890 was over 8000, suggesting nearer one-eighth.

32 Howe, p. 230; there was no accepted rule about hours: some offices worked from 7 a.m. to 8 p.m.; some from 8 a.m. to 8 p.m.; and others from 8.30 a.m. to 8 p.m.

33 Howe, p. 268–82; quotation from p. 270.

34 Howe, p. 283–9.

35 Howe, p. 284.

36 Howe and Waite, *London Society of Compositors*, p. 292–6.

37 *LTJ*, March 1948, p. 8. An historical review is given here by T.E. Naylor, Secretary of the LSC at the time of the struggle.

38 The one week's holiday with pay was not generally recognised in the printing industry until 1919; see Howe and Waite, p. 194.

39 A.R.L., 'Tuition or Trade?', *English Woman's Journal*, May 1860, p. 179.

40 'Society for Promoting the Employment of Women', *English Woman's Journal*, August 1860, p. 391–2.

41 M.M.H., 'A Ramble with Mrs Grundy', *English Woman's Journal*, June 1860, p. 270–1.

42 Gillespie, *Hundred Years of Progress*, p. 103.

43 'Women and Work', *Victoria Magazine*, November 1879, p. 90.

44 LSC *Annual Report*, 1885, p. 24.

45 Bennett, *Clayhanger*, p. 83.

46 See the chronological list of these journals at the beginning of the Bibliography.

47 Clowes, *Family Business*, p. 48.

48 *LTJ*, May 1906, p. 5.

49 Also among letterpress occupations it would appear that compositors attracted a larger proportion of the 'above the skilled' group.

50 Howe and Waite, *London Society of Compositors*, p. 338.

51 A prospectus 'To the Non-Society Compositors of London and its Vicinity', dated January 1884.

52 'The London Society of Compositors', by 'Scourge', *Bee-hive Newspaper*, 10 October 1863, p. 1, col. 1.

53 Richards, 'Social and Economic Aspects of Combination in the Printing Trade before 1875', p. 453. A similar reticence was true of the provinces, though

individual leaders were significantly involved in the formation of the TUC, see Musson, *The Congress of 1868*, p. 17.

54 The LSC's secretary, Bowerman, held several positions in the TUC (Howe and Waite, p. 326).

55 'Memories and Impressions of Fifty & Sixty Years Ago', p. 18.

56 *London Strike*, by a Master Printer, p. 1.

57 Halévy, *History of the English People*, v. 5, p. 211–46.

58 *LTJ*, February 1909, p. 2.

59 LSC Parliamentary Labour Association, *A Retrospect*, p. 5.

60 *Printer*, May 1886, p. 82.

61 Conversation with George Rowles, printer and journalist.

62 The age factor here is important – it is probably significant that those who experienced a decline in the real wages were most active in the union.

IV

The Inter-War Years

The expansion of the industry

Between the two wars the printing industry continued to expand. Books and periodicals were being read widely in a period of social and political controversy. Light reading, such as magazines and newspapers was also heavily in demand with the existence of an adult population which, no doubt, had benefited from the Education Acts of 1901 and 1918. In addition there was a growth in bureaucratic activity as a result of the pre-war social legislation of the Liberals, an extension of centralized government activity of the war years, and an increase in the scope of local government. The development of various kinds of trade organizations resulted in the production of trade journals. All this activity helped to stimulate the demand for printing.

From 1911 to 1931, the numbers engaged in the printing industry rose by nearly 68 per cent: from 138,000 in England and Wales in 1911, to the 233,000 who were engaged in producing newspapers, periodicals, books and in general printing in 1931.

The numbers engaged in composing however, did not expand in the same way. This was due to the effects of the increased adoption of composing machines[1] and the development of printing processes other than letterpress printing, which required less handling in the composing department. Even in letterpress printing typographical styles reduced the amount of work done by the compositor: illustrations were used more widely; also, improvements in typographical layout gave a greater ratio of space to type, this was particularly apparent in advertising which was greatly expanding.

Thus, despite the great increase in printing there was an actual decline in the overall number of hand and machine compositors, from about 42,000 in 1911 to less than 39,000 in 1931.

In London, the trend during the previous period, when the provinces expanded at a greater rate was reversed: in London the printing industry expanded from 43,000 in 1911 to nearly 95,000 in 1931. The number of compositors engaged in London over the period was in sharp contrast with this expansion of the industry as a whole. Here, the Census figures are particularly unreliable as evidence: they show an increase in the number of compositors in Greater London to 1931, but in the figure for that year they include 6,600 composing machine operators. This is probably at least 4,000 too high; it gives a proportion of hand to machine compositors which is obviously inaccurate, being over double that at the present day.

The pattern of change is more accurately reflected in union statistics. These figures are a fairly reliable guide, for comparison with other data indicates that the proportion of compositors who were members of the LSC rose to over 90 per cent. In 1914, the first year in which the union membership is broken down for journeymen, apprentices and old age pensioners, the number at the trade was 11,195. This figure grew after the First World War, and in 1920 the highest figure of journeymen at the trade is recorded: 14,153. From 1920 until 1939 there is an almost successive decline each year: by 1930 there are about 12,000 and by 1939 the figure had dropped to about 10,700. Thus in 20 years the number of compositors in London had fallen by nearly 25 per cent. Apart from the technical causes outlined above, the decline also reflected the union's strict control over the recruitment of apprentices into the trade. Such control prevented the overstocking of the trade by boy labour and was an important factor in advancing the relative material condition of the compositor.

The social condition of the compositor

Wages

During the First World War wages rapidly increased. The basic minimum of 39s for the hand compositor, which had existed since 1901, was increased to 41s in October 1915, and to 42s in April 1916. In October of that year a further increase of 3s was to 'continue for the period of the war and for six months after peace has been signed',[2] but the increase in the cost of living nullified this intention. Five further increases, culminated in a basic rate of £3 12s 6d in September 1918. The immediate post-war increases in the cost of living led to four further increases, until, in November 1920, the London compositor's basic rate rose to £5, the highest peak for the period between the wars.

In the early twentieth century, in common with other occupations, a number of wage reductions were imposed. An important feature in these reductions is the way in which they were opposed by the LSC. The strength of the opposition by the union and the compositors, enabled the

extent of the reduction to be restrained. A proposal in 1921 for a reduction of 10s in the basic rate was opposed by an overwhelming majority of
the members of the LSC. These members, in similar proportions, voted
in favour of a weekly levy of 7s 6d until the wages question was settled.
Later in the year, a proposal for a reduction of 7s 6d was also opposed
by a substantial majority. Finally, in September 1921, a 5s reduction
was accepted, though a quarter of those eligible to vote still opposed the
reduction. During 1922, a wage reduction was again resisted at a time of
substantial unemployment. This time the proposed reduction was higher.
In May there was a proposal to reduce the minimum rate by 15s which
was met by a determined refusal. A compromise reduction of 7s was also
opposed in October, though the membership was less unanimous in its
opposition. Finally in November, a 6s reduction was accepted; even then
about a quarter of the membership were obdurate. The reduction was
in two stages: 4s in December 1922, and a further 2s in January 1923.
Thus, by the beginning of 1923, the basic rate for the hand compositor
was £4 9s 0d. Attempts to further depress wages in the printing industry
were successfully resisted by the unions,[3] and this rate remained until the
Second World War. It should be noted that in addition to the strength of
the union, a further source of the ability to resist reductions was the fact
that the employers, not needing to face overseas competition, together
with their ability to restrain price cutting attempts by their members,
were not so compelled to enforce reductions.

As in previous periods, wide differences in earnings existed for different kinds of work. The minimum rate for hand compositors in general printing was 89s. A compositor in a firm that did a high proportion
of periodical work was likely to receive the periodical rate, which was
96s. If a man had responsibility for a particular job, he would probably
have a small differential: as little as 2s 6d perhaps, or 5s more generally.
Occasionally a firm would pay 2s 6d over the rate to a hand compositor
who was considered particularly able and who also had long service with
the firm. The Linotype machine compositor in general printing had a
basic rate of 96s, whilst the operator on evening newspapers had a basic
rate as high as 155s and the morning newspaper operator's basic rate was
160s. These rates were minimum. Earnings were in some cases very much
higher if a man was on piece work. For example, the *LTJ* reported that
when a group of printers on newspapers were summoned in 1926 for not
paying income tax, they were said to earn between £10 and £18 weekly.

Such higher earnings were obtained by only a minority of compositors. Yet the number earning in excess of the minimum rate must have
been fairly considerable. For the increase in the number of machine com-

positors meant that a higher proportion of compositors were receiving wages above the basic. It is significant that when a levy was applied, a distinction in the amount to be paid was made according to whether a man earned under or over £6 a week, excluding overtime. However, the majority of compositors were probably 'eighty-nine bobbers'.

The London compositor also advanced his relative position within the printing industry. Compared with certain other trades within the industry, the London compositor improved his position as reductions were enforced more successfully on other unions. The bookbinders were particularly resentful that 'they had lost their proudly held position of parity with the LSC';[4] at the end of 1921 the London bookbinder's wage was 2s 6d less than that of the compositor, by the end of 1922 it was 6s less, and by mid-1923 the gap had increased to 9s. Even in the same occupation the differential increased, for the compositor's union in the provinces, the TA, accepted greater reductions than did the London union; the differential of 2s 6d between the London rate and the highest grade of pay in the provinces increased to 11s 6d in 1922.

Time constraints were high in printing with work often demanded quickly. Aiding the union were publication dates of newspapers and periodicals – a major pressure on publishers to reach resolution in disputes.

Other conditions also improved. By 1914, a 50 hour week was general in the industry, and after the end of the war a series of friendly conferences between the Printing and Kindred Trades Federation (PKTF) and the British Federation of Master Printers (BFMP) concluded in a new agreement which gave the industry a 48 hour week from March 1919. The same agreement laid down one week's holiday with pay. In 1920 there was an attempt by the unions to introduce a 44 hour week, but the attempt was not very strong and the matter was dropped. The movement for shorter hours in the late 1930s, when the 40-hour-week was being demanded, had its counterpart in the printing industry. In 1937 the 1919 agreement was revised and a 45 hour week was introduced.

Compared with other industries, wages in the printing industry had recovered from their position in the earlier period, and between the wars printing was the highest paid industry. Likewise the position of the compositor, in terms of wage rates greatly improved in relation to other trades. Comparison will be made here with the wage rates of the skilled worker in the building industry, whose rates were, in general, among the highest of the skilled trades.[5] The compositor's rate taken is the weekly minimum rate of the hand compositor.

In 1914 the rate of the building craftsman, at 40.6s, was a little above that of the compositor at 39s. By 1920, the year which was the peak year for wage rates between the wars for both groups of workers, there was even less difference between them. The builder's rate was 100.8s and that of the compositor, 100s. From then on the relative position of the compositor improved considerably: by 1928 the builder had dropped to 72.5s, but the compositor only to 89s; five years later, in 1933, the builder's rates had been reduced still further to 65.4s, whereas the compositor remained at the same rate; by 1938 the builder had improved his rate to 73.1s, but was still considerably below the compositor at 89s.

Compared with the skilled worker as a whole the compositor was in an even better position. A comparison with wage rates in general show the compositor to be in an equally favourable position despite the higher increases of the less skilled. Taking 1914 as 100, a general wage index advanced in the same period to 187 in 1939.[6] An index for the compositor would have advanced in the same period to 228. A small relative decline took place towards the end of the period, for after 1933 the wage index advanced from 162 to 187 in 1939 or 15 per cent, whilst the compositor's rate remained the same.

Cost of living

The ability to resist wage reductions made it possible for the compositor in full employment to enjoy the benefits of the falling cost of living. From 1914 to 1920 the cost of living increased from an index of 100 to 265 and the compositor's wages approximately kept pace, rising from an index of 100 to 256. When the steep decline in the cost of living in 1921 reduced the index from 265 to 192, and by the end of 1922 to 178, the compositor's index of wages fell to only 228. From then until 1932 to 1933 the cost of living index fell gradually to 142, whilst the compositor's rate remained at the same level. For those in employment the gain was substantial, and it was in this period that a number of compositors raised mortgages to purchase their own homes. It was only after 1933 that the stability of the compositor's wage rates was at a disadvantage, as the cost of living index moved from 142 in that year to 174 at the end of 1939. For those compositors who experienced the early period the improvement in their position was very evident. The compositor who entered the trade as a journeyman in the early 1930s may well have felt the effects of a rising cost of living of nearly 23 per cent whilst his own wages remained the same. Yet during the period the compositor had regained his position among the financial aristocracy of the working class, and even the younger compositor must have been aware of his favourable position compared with other occupations.

Unemployment

Unemployment was a problem, to a varying degree, almost throughout the period. The causes of unemployment were rather different from those operating before the First World War. Then the major cause had been boy labour. In the inter-war period this was no longer a problem, though the effects of the overstocking before the war were still apparent. Boy labour was much less attractive to employers, for the strict regulation over entry by the unions was paralleled by a growing concern by the union over the welfare of the apprentice and there was strong pressure on the employer to release boys for a half or a full day each week in order to attend technical classes; thus apprentice labour became rather more expensive.

Unemployment in the inter-war period was due to a number of other factors: the increase in machinery for composing; other forms of rationalization that speeded up production; the movement of printing, particularly during the 1920s, to the Home Counties and beyond; general slump conditions; and to some extent, the changing nature of the demand for printing which encouraged fewer words in relation to the total output as noted earlier: larger type, more space in relation to the type, and more illustrations.

There was also the temporary unemployment due to the war. Partly to escape the difficulties in the printing trade compositors had flocked to the colours in 1914. Then, during the First World War, the employment situation changed; from one of instability due to the general fall-off in trade, to one of shortage of labour as the services and the armament industry attracted labour. The number of individual members of the LSC who had experienced unemployment some time during the year was over 2,400 in 1915. During 1916 and 1917 there were no claimants for unemployment benefit, but by 1920 the figure rose again to 1,450.

From the early 1920s until the slump the unemployment problem improved. The average weekly number of recipients declined from 1,156 in 1922 to 460 in 1925; this figure increased to 727 in the year of the General Strike, mainly as a result of certain firms turning non-union, but in 1927 the figure, at 652, was again declining.

A number of factors had contributed to this improvement. A major cause was the introduction of a new superannuation scheme in 1923 which gave a pension of £2 a week to men over 60 who had 35 years consecutive membership; this scheme encouraged retirement among members, and the number of LSC pensions rose 50 per cent over one year in 1923. Secondly, in 1922 a policy to restrict membership was introduced and it became very difficult for non-unionists to join the union, and difficult even for members of the trade union for compositors in the provinces. Thirdly, the supply of apprentices was reduced by an agreement which took effect in January 1923, this restricted the proportion of apprentices to journeymen to one in four.

Any suggestion that the unemployed were a hard core of unemployables would be false. As figures in the *LTJ* reveal, a larger proportion of the membership experienced unemployment than the figures of averages show. For example in 1925 when the average weekly number of recipients was 460, the number of different compositors who received benefit during the year was over 1,700; in 1930 the figure was nearly 1,800, and by 1935 it was over 2,300. Indeed, our contemporary survey reveals that over 50 per cent of the journeymen between the wars experienced some unemployment – mainly in the 1930s, and excluding those experiencing unemployment in 1939 because of the war. As one informant said, though he wasn't unemployed himself, 'many good tradesmen were out'.

A frequent employment pattern at this time was that a man would obtain employment for a short period which was followed by another period without work: 'on and off for a couple of years' was a typical remark by those who were interviewed in the survey. Some of the men experienced very long spells of unemployment, sometimes out of work for months at a stretch; but the on/off pattern of short alternating periods of work and unemployment was more frequent. To the young man living at home and without responsibilities the position was not critical. Indeed one man, in his early twenties when he was unemployed, recalled his four months out of work as the 'happiest days of my life with plenty of unemployment pay'.[7] It was a different story for the man with responsibilities, and some single men volunteered to become unemployed rather than allow a married man to be placed in this critical situation.

Whether unemployment really had a beneficial effect on craftsmanship, as alleged by one compositor, is questionable: he asserted that one 'had to be good to keep a job' (he himself experienced unemployment!). More likely, it had a different effect: the man who was 'in and out for two years, after falling out with the "O" [overseer]' was yet to learn the lesson of prudence; as one compositor put it, the fact of being 'pushed and shoved around, teaches you to hold your tongue and do as you're told'.

Unemployment greatly increased in 1932, the worst year of the slump for compositors. Every month in that year between about 1300 and 1600 union compositors were out of work. This compares with a figure varying between 500 and 800 per month for the period 1933 to 1939. In addition to this, many firms engaged their compositors on short time, for example three days work a week during the slump. Though the amount of unemployment in 1932 was lower among compositors than it was in many trades,[8] the compositor's unemployment rate at 11.6 per cent was somewhat higher than the rate of 10.3 per cent for the printing, publishing and bookbinding industry, which was still expanding, as a whole.

Overtime was still worked considerably during the period, and consequently there were numerous attempts to redistribute the work more equitably. For example, in 1926 there was an unsuccessful attempt to reduce the overtime limit to 16 hours a month instead of 24. The continual working of overtime in some firms was also attacked on behalf of the working member himself, for it was alleged at a Quarterly Delegate Meeting for that year that 'in such offices members at present find it difficult to make sure of more than one free evening in a week, and even that may sometimes be denied them'. One argument adduced in favour of overtime was that seasonal fluctuations in the work meant that if high amounts of overtime were not worked at peak periods, then extra men would be required and this would exacerbate the unemployment problem in slack periods. This argument was not very strong, for seasonal variations in the printing industry were shown to be not so marked as before the war: unemployment fluctuated between six per cent in February to 4.6 per cent in June and July.[9] The decline in seasonal fluctuations had no doubt been largely due to the increase in the number of regular periodicals and trade journals. Apart from one or two months, a substantial amount of overtime was worked throughout the year. Even during the particularly difficult year of 1932, a good deal of overtime was worked by those compositors who were fortunate enough to be in employment: in every month in that year, an average of over 5,000 men worked overtime to the extent of ten hours each per month, and was particularly high in news and periodical offices because of press nights.

From 1933 to 1939 unemployment declined. On the eve of the Second World War the number of unemployed was about 400. Within a fortnight after the outbreak of war, however, the demand for printing contracted and the figure rose to over 1,100; in November it reached a peak of 2,300 – higher than at the worst of the slump.

Emigration was not seen as a possible escape from these employment conditions, and did not take place on the scale of the period before the First World War. This trend was in keeping with the general trend of declining movement out of the UK, especially with the general condition of world depression; the movement became almost non-existent during the 1930s.

Status and social origins

The general improvement in the compositor's material well-being, despite unemployment, was reflected in the fact that his status and the image held of the compositor was maintained. It would seem that when his material condition was declining, the compositor was concerned to hang on to his feelings of status and emphasized this; when, however, his position improved there was less need to express his status, nor did movements for wage advances take place which needed to be justified in terms of maintaining status differentials.

It was likely that as jobs became more difficult to obtain, a skilled occupation in an industry which was relatively favourably placed was an attraction to those parents who were willing to allow their sons to embark on a long apprenticeship. Referring to both masters and craftsmen, John Johnson, Printer to the University of Oxford stated in a Dent lecture in 1933 that for the previous two decades 'the printer had moved up the social scale', and he mentions 'the change in the quality of the boys who are recruited to the craft'.

One expression of the competition for entry to the trade was the attempt to revive premium payments. This revival, though on a very small scale, was condemned in the November 1927 Stationers Craft Lecture by J.R. Riddell, Principal of the London School of Printing (LSP), who stated that the premiums were mainly being requested by small printing offices giving an inadequate training. The figures involved were given in a

Aristocrats of labour celebrating a wayzegoose (annual outing) in style in the 1930s.

Ministry of Labour Report on an enquiry that took place in 1925–1926.[10] It was found that 2.7 per cent of apprentices in the printing industry paid premiums, the number being greatest for compositors (though the highest proportion was for lithographic printers). The amounts ranged from £1 to £100, the most common being £10.

In the 1930s there were again complaints about premium paying, particularly in non-union firms, where, it was asserted, amounts of £5 to £50 were being paid. It was complained that these shops gave low wages and no security of work, and parents were warned against being attracted by an occupation which was regarded as 'genteel'.

Further evidence of the increase in premium payments between the wars is shown by the contemporary survey. 12 of the 84 compositors in the sample who entered the trade between the wars paid a premium, that is, about 14 per cent. Several of the payments were made by charities; some of these had sums of money which could only be used for the purpose of procuring apprenticeships; and firms who had particular connections with such charities could apply for a grant when an apprentice was indentured. Thus premium payments increased between the wars as the occupation became more desirable.

According to one report, a high degree of literacy was still regarded as desirable for entrants to composing, despite the increased use of machinery: they should be able to speak, read and spell well, have a good sight and write a neat hand; also a knowledge of drawing and design was considered desirable for display work.[11]

Evidently these standards were not always fulfilled, and in the mid-thirties there were protests about proficiency in English. It was also urged that in the existing conditions of competition for jobs it should be possible to attract lads with a better education; that is, lads who left school at 15 instead of 14.

With the improvement in the material condition of the occupation, there was a realistic basis for the existence of a fairly high public image. It was likely that this image would affect recruitment into the trade. Another compositor confirmed this: 'In my experience the apprentices who came to us between the wars were better spoken, better dressed, and in the main eager to take advantage of the half day ... at a printing school ... I am of the opinion that the lads entering the trade between the wars were of a better quality than prior to World War One'.[12]

Statistical evidence that compositors were being attracted from higher social origins, as indicated by their father's occupation is available from the contemporary survey (Table 6); this source of information is certainly more reliable than that used for previous periods, namely the records of

Table 6 **Social origin of Compositors**

Father's occupational grade when entered	1918–1945		1900–1902	Premiums paid for 1918–1945 intake
	No.	%	%	No.
Managerial, professional & supervisory	21	28	21	2
Other non-manual	8	11		
Skilled	31	42	62	6
Semi or unskilled	14	19	17	1
	74			
Father not alive	10			3
Total intake 1918–1945	84			
Of whom:				
Compositors	18	21	–	3
Other printing	8	10	–	
% of fathers in printing		31	21	

the Stationers' Company, for the Company was now rarely used for the purpose of recording apprenticeships.

The sample reveals that the proportion of boys who came from families in a higher social group than skilled workers had considerably increased. However, two countervailing factors need to be considered. On one hand, these figures may slightly exaggerate the increase: for they contain fathers who originally were manual workers, but who had achieved supervisory status. In the analysis they would be included above skilled workers, whereas the figures for earlier periods may not always reveal any supervisory status. On the other hand, these figures apply retrospectively to the intake between the wars, thus they do not include men who had left the occupation, either leaving the industry or achieving higher positions; it may well be that the more mobile originated in higher social groups, and to this extent the intake from higher social groups may be under-represented.

It can be seen that nearly 40 per cent came from what may be regarded as middle class backgrounds, compared with about 20 per cent before the First World War. The figures suggest that composing increased its attraction for the downwardly mobile, and was also seen as a means of improvement by the less skilled (12 of the 14 were semi-skilled and two were unskilled). Among the less skilled it was possible that the parents were better educated, and therefore had some aspiration for their children. One son of a dock labourer, for example, sketched his father as a man of considerable talent: with the ability to speak foreign languages and play musical instruments.

It is also significant that a larger proportion of entrants than before the First World War were the sons of compositors and other printers. This in particular reflects the improved position of the compositor in relation to other trades. It should be noticed, however, that the legend that composing was a father-to-son occupation was by no means accurate. Certainly there were families in which the occupation was traditional. There were occasional references in the *LTJ* to 'records' of years in the trade, one example quoted in January 1939 was the Archer family: James Archer entered the LSC in 1853 and had six sons apprenticed to the trade, as well as other members of the family. But such family traditions were exceptional: four out of five entrants between the wars had fathers in occupations other than composing, and under one-third had fathers engaged in some section of the printing industry.

Thus, with their high pay and relative stability, reinforced by the literacy with which the compositor was doubtless associated by the public, the status of the compositor in the inter-war period was high. The extremely high pay of a minority, particularly those engaged in the newspaper section, heightened this image. In a period when jobs were difficult to obtain, composing was regarded as a desirable occupation for one's sons, and the literary association with which the occupation was linked helped to isolate composing from other manual work. Consequently recruitment took place from a higher social level. It should be noted that there was a general upgrading of the social structure during the period with an increase in the non-manual occupations. It is difficult to know what effect this would have on the recruitment of the compositor: there were more in the middle class for the compositor to be recruited from but also there were more such jobs for the entrants to be placed in; thus the number of non-manual sons available for skilled work is likely to have decreased. On this interpretation the increase in the proportion of compositors recruited from non-manual occupations is even more significant.

Working class consciousness

We have seen that the identification of the compositor with the working class was being established prior to the First World War. Yet though the majority of compositors would probably have identified themselves with the working class, militancy did not intensify. The inter-war period for the working class was far from smooth: there were the immediate post-war industrial struggles, the General Strike, the depression and the political controversies of the 1930s. These were issues likely to arouse fervour, yet apart from a minority, there is little sign of militant involvement by compositors. The impression is rather that the compositor whilst sympathetic to the movement, tended to stand on the fringe of working class activity. It is as if as his material well-being improved and he had regained his position among the upper crust of the working class, the compositor wished to preserve this position by not becoming too involved in working class struggles.

The extent of the militancy of the compositor during this period can be seen in two fields: industrial solidarity and political participation.

Industrial solidarity

There was no lack of sympathy by the compositor for less fortunate workers. For example, in 1921 a grant of £1,000 to the miners was agreed to by an overwhelming majority of LSC members, though it is worth pointing out that nearly 2,000, or over one in five of those voting, were against the grant being made. In another example, in 1930, when industrial solidarity was likely to have been heightened, fewer were willing to express disapproval of aid to the textile workers in dispute, even though in this case a £1,000 grant was to be supplemented by the proceeds of a 3d a week levy for eight weeks.

The most important evidence of class feeling was the attitude to the General Strike of 1926. Gone was the appeal to class solidarity that was expressed in a leaflet issued by the LSC in 1915 exhorting non-unionists to join the LSC. Then, trade unionism was presented as necessary 'because it is your class organisation. Your interests as a seller of labour are the interests of your class'.[13] By 1926, the class struggle was played down so far as the compositor was concerned.

Already, in 1925, the official attitude of the LSC to the proposed General Strike was, seemingly from the annual report, lukewarm; whilst being prepared to support the strike, the struggle was not seen as essential: 'whilst refusing to believe that there must of necessity be a general fight between Capital and Labour in May next, or at any other particular time, and whilst deprecating the spirit animating those who are urging the workers to bring about a violent clash of forces, we recognize the need of preparing for emergencies'.

When the national strike, in support of the miners' refusal to accept a reduction in wages, was eventually called by the General Council of the TUC, most of the printing unions came out immediately. The compositors' union was more reticent. At the meeting of the General Council of Trade Unions on the Saturday prior to the strike the Secretary of the LSC was asked whether he was prepared to hand over his powers to the General Council. He replied that he could not do so until the members, who were meeting the following Wednesday, could be consulted; the action was endorsed by the LSC Committee. This delay might well be more realistically interpreted as lack of enthusiasm, rather than concern for democratic procedure, especially as an emergency delegate meeting could probably have been arranged when the date of the strike was first known.[14]

The compositors eventually entered the General Strike three days late. The lack of enthusiasm felt was revealed by the way in which the resolution was moved that strike action be taken. The executive had decided that the TUC policy was mistaken, especially as the strike could become 'political'; also, the strike was regarded as unlikely to succeed as the force of the Government was against it. However, once the General Strike had started, the LSC was faced with the fact that its members were working in the same office where fellow trade unionists were out on strike. Therefore the executive decided 'driven by the irresistible logic of events, to advise the delegates, owing to the untenable position created by the cessation of all the vital industries, including the means of getting to and from work, to agree to a general cessation of work.' No discussion took place on this decision, based on expediency, rather than militancy, and the resolution of the Committee was carried unanimously.

It might be argued that the LSC officials were less enthusiastic than the members. It is true that once called out most of the members refrained from working. It is also true that among the members there were those who felt a stronger solidarity than the executive cared to show. According to the *LTJ* of January 1936 many ceased work before awaiting official instructions. A union official related to me that compositors were to be found among strike organization committees; these did work such as organizing the distribution of essential services in their areas of residence and putting pressure on local tradesmen not to increase prices.

However, the majority of the members probably felt they could not help the miners by the strike. Yet it is rather surprising that the occasion should evoke such a negative attitude. No letters regarding the strike appeared in the *LTJ* and the event, from reading the minutes of two fair-sized chapels, occasioned little discussion in Chapel meetings. It is also significant that it was members of the National Society of Operative Printers and Assistants (NATSOPA) who, on the night before the General Strike, had refused to print the editorial of the *Daily Mail*, and not the compositors who would have been the first of the manual workers to have seen the leader and set it up. Similarly, when the *Evening News* tried to quote that editorial, it was again the NATSOPA members who refused to print it.

The eventual general acceptance of participation in the strike was considered by an observer to be the result of some sense of loyalty to the working class. However, this was not strong. A delegate to the LSC meeting on Wednesday, May 4 wrote: 'There was, so far as I recall now, no criticism of the reasons for the strike, neither was there any great enthusiasm. I think we must have been a trifle overawed by the immensity of the movement. It was in no sense a political effort. The compositors I knew were willing to join an industrial effort to help the miners gain a decent wage. We knew we had no quarrel with the master printers and therefore the urge to fight and win was absent. There might have been more excitement had the dispute related to our own wages. Hence it seems to me it was a deep sense of loyalty to the workers as a class and to the TUC as the leaders, that brought out the compositors'.[15]

One of the reasons for the lack of enthusiasm was financial. Union benefits for the compositor during the strike was £3 a week, and this could have placed a heavy strain on resources had the strike continued longer. Pleasure was expressed when the members returned to work and thereby reopened the main source of revenue. In addition, there was the lack of feeling in support of a conflict which could only damage the industrial harmony which was being built, to some extent, in the printing trade in contrast with the heavy industries. There was also, perhaps, the fear of some firms turning non-union. But it is likely that a major cause of this lack of militancy was the relatively high position of the compositor at the time.

Political participation

Some indication of the political allegiance of compositors is given by the extent to which they contributed to the political fund of the LSC. It must be stressed that this is only a rough indication of allegiance: some Liberal or Conservatives might continue to pay into the fund because of a real or imagined feeling that they would otherwise be scorned by their fellow workers; a number of left-wing sympathisers might not be included if they didn't wish to support the Labour Party; others might feel that trade unions should not become politically involved.

The Trade Union Act of 1913 provided the legal basis for a trade union to set up a political fund, but as we saw in the last chapter it was not until 1916 that a ballot took place on the lines laid down by this Act. Though there was a majority in favour of a fund for 'the furtherance of political objects', it would appear that a large portion of the membership was opposed to the establishment of a political fund, for 45 per cent of the votes were against the fund. It must be remembered, however, that this was war-time, and the voters contained a large proportion of older men who may still have been committed to their early political allegiances. Even so, when it was proposed in 1921 to increase the amount of a member's subscription that was 'set off' to the political fund, from 1s a year to 2s a year, roughly half the membership were against the increase; there was only a very narrow majority in favour and many abstentions. This would indicate that there was not an over-readiness to identify with the Labour Party, despite the fact that the ballot took place in a year when wage reductions were attempted. The majority was too small for the increase to be introduced, and it was not until another ballot took place in 1923, when more members were persuaded to vote, that the two-thirds majority, which was necessary for the change, was obtained. Even then, there were fewer than 60 per cent of those eligible to vote who were in favour of increasing contributions.

Once the fund was established, the proportion of members who paid the political levy was maintained at a very high level. The exact proportion of journeymen who contributed to the fund, in relation to total journeymen is difficult to determine because the number of contributors can be related to different 'universes'. If the number of contributors is related to the number of working journeymen then the proportion will be too high, because the contributors will include an indeterminate number of superannuitants who continue to pay their political subscription. On the other hand, if the number is related to the number of working journeymen together with the superannuitants, then the proportion will be too low, because a large proportion of the less politically committed pensioners give up paying the political subscription when they retire. The fact that a smaller proportion of superannuitants paid political contributions is shown by the fact that the gap between the two sets of figures increases as the number of superannuitants increases. The following table constructed from the annual reports which show political balance sheets gives percentages in each group; the true proportion of working journeymen who paid their political subscription will be somewhere between the

Table 7 **Contributions to the Political Fund**

Year	Journeymen at the trade %	Journeymen at the trade plus the number of superannuitants %
1920	82	79
1923	78	72
1924	95	86
1926	93	84
1927	99	88
1928	89	78
1932	84	71
1935	79	67
1936	79	66
1939	83	67

two sets of percentages, but nearer the first set than the second, because the proportion of those who do not pay is higher among the superannuitants. Only those years which show changes are included.

These figures give some indication of the political climate among London compositors. There is a small initial decline in 1923 following the decision to increase the political contribution. In 1924, a year of heightened interest with the general election and the formation of a Labour Government, the proportion of contributors rose considerably. This heightened political atmosphere, which probably reflected a combination of increased individual political interest and the pressure of the occupational group, was maintained through the following years of industrial conflict. In 1927 a very high proportion was contributing, probably over 90 per cent of members in the trade. After the Trade Union Act of that year, which laid the responsibility on the member to contract in, the proportion fell immediately by about 10 per cent. This was still high: higher than for example, the 65 per cent who continued to contract into the political fund of the TA, the union to which the provincial compositors belonged.

The reduction would no doubt have been greater had the union not exhorted the members to contract into the fund, so that the high percentage should not be regarded as necessarily reflecting a strong political iden-tification of the members. After the Act was passed, the union urged that members should strive to achieve a 100 per cent return otherwise it would seem, it was asserted, that previously there had been coercion! Appeals were made to Chapel Officers to encourage contracting in, and a special souvenir card of membership was to be issued to all who did so. With the Chapel appeals, and the mechanism of the procedure to contract in simpli-fied through the Chapels, the pressure would have been difficult to resist.

However, the short decline after 1927 was not arrested as, as might be expected, more members contracted in. A gradual decline of approx-imately a further 10 per cent took place until the mid 1930s. Initially, no doubt, Conservatives and Liberals had dropped out of the fund, but the continued fall might have reflected the unfavourable attitude to the Labour Party after its period in office from 1929 to 1931. The decline ceased during the mid 1930s, and from then until the Second World War the proportion of journeymen who contracted in actually increased slightly. This may be due to concern over the international situation, and members might have become more sympathetic to the Labour Party as it abandoned its anti-war attitude in favour of rearmament; the campaign in Abyssinia and the Spanish Civil War also probably helped to stimulate left-wing sympathy. At the same time, the economic position of the com-positor also slightly declined relatively. Younger journeymen members might well have been more politically interested in this period of agita-tion and activity.

Contributions to the political fund among compositors were main-tained at a much higher level than was true for most trade unionists. It is probably true that the political view-point of the majority of compositors was Labour in varying degrees; but the extent of that identification as revealed by contributions into the political fund, is probably exaggerated by the strength of influence by the union and chapels.

A number of compositors were active in local politics. The rule under which financial assistance was given to members standing as candidates ensured that municipal election grants could only be made if the candi-date was under the auspices of the Labour Party. In 1926, 19 compositors received such grants; this number was particularly high. An example of a more average year during the period is 1931 when there were nine candidates. This would suggest that in proportion to their number there were a considerable number of compositors who were politically active. It is likely that the occupation contained a higher number of intelligent and literate members than was true of most manual occupations. In local affairs (trade councils and local politics), such men were recognised as being familiar with the language and with the means of propagation through printing, and were likely to participate to a greater degree than members of other working class occupations.

Conclusion

In the inter-war period the trend of a declining material position of the compositor was halted and indeed reversed. The most important factor in this was the ability of the Union to resist, in the main, the imposition of wage reductions after the advances in wages of the war and immediate post-war period; at a time of decreasing prices, the relative position of the compositor greatly improved. This situation continued until the last four years of the period when there was a slight decline in the relative position of the compositor.

Other conditions that had led to the compositor's declining position had also changed. The harmful effect of the increased use of composing machinery was mitigated, though the number of compositors declined. Recruitment into the trade was, in the main, strictly regulated by a union that had consolidated its strength. Relations with the employers had considerably improved with the agreements that had been made during the war years and the setting up of a Joint Industrial Council (JIC) after the war; this recognition had helped to further strengthen the union. With the regulation of recruitment, severe unemployment was no longer endemic. During the worst period of the slump, unemployment was heavy, but the fact that the industry was also sheltered from foreign competition protected the employees from the severity of unemployment experienced in other industries.

This improvement in the relative position of the London compositor was reflected in the high image that was held of him by the public, and affected the source of recruitment: boys from higher social origins than in the previous period were attracted into composing, and compositors and other printers were more willing to allow their sons into the trade. It was in this period that the occupation was seen as well paid, fairly secure and well protected by a strong union.

The rise in the compositor's position tended to restrain the growing class consciousness of the previous period. Evidence of the decline in militancy should not be exaggerated: there is no doubt that a not inconsiderable minority of the compositors were militant, and certainly the tradition of association with the working class that had been more explicitly established in the preceding period had been maintained. But for the large majority, the association was sympathetic rather than militant: the improvement in their economic position had lifted the compositors more clearly into the ranks of the upper working class, and the compositor was likely to wish to preserve his distinction from the rest of the working class by not becoming too involved in class movements.

Politically, support for the Labour Party continued and possibly grew over the period as a whole, though the high proportion of compositors contracting into the political fund of the union exaggerated the amount of real support, for some of this contribution was due to conformity to the attitudes of the occupational community. Temporary high feeling, after the General Strike and the introduction of the 1927 Trade Union Act, was modified and more members were prepared to show that they did not identify themselves with the policies of the Labour Party.

Some changes in this decline in class and political militancy became apparent in the mid 1930s with the experience of unemployment, and the small decline in the relative position of the compositor. Political controversy and anxiety led to a growing political interest and involvement, and the hardening of political identification; it is significant that the proportion of union members who contracted into the political fund did show a small increase. This may well be attributed not to members changing their attitudes, but the greater willingness of the new, younger journeymen to adopt the growing radical spirit of the period.

Notes

1 Further discussion of census and union statistics is to be found in the original notes to the Thesis.

2 Howe and Waite, *London Society of Compositors*, p. 288.

3 Howe, *British Federation of Master Printers*, p. 115–17.

4 Howe and Child, *Society of London Bookbinders*, p. 251.

5 Bowley, *Wages and Income*, p. 51.

6 The figure of 188 derived from the table of wage rates in Knowles and Robertson, 'Differences', p. 126.

7 Unemployment pay in the LSC was 28s a week in 1931 plus 8s supplementary benefit if eligible; state benefit was in addition to this (Howe and Waite, *London Society of Compositors*, p. 258).

8 Beveridge, *Full Employment*, Table 33 at p. 317.

9 *New Survey of London Life and Labour*, v. 5, p. 288.

10 Ministry of Labour, *Report of an enquiry into Apprenticeship*. p. 14.

11 Ministry of Labour, *Report*, p. 47.

12 Quoted from a letter to the author from H.E. Waite.

13 *Invitation to join the London Society of Compositors*, p. [7].

14 *LTJ*, June 1926, p. 4.

15 Letter to the author from H.E. Waite.

Part Two

The Present-Day Compositor

*Social and Ideological Situation and the
Role of his Occupational Community*

V

The Social Condition of the Compositor

The printing industry

The industry as a whole has expanded since 1931: then, less than a quarter of a million people were engaged in the industry, today the industry contains about 300,000 people.[1] The rate of change has not been the same for all the processes: lithography and photogravure have expanded but the size of the letterpress section, where the compositor works, appears to have remained about the same. However, this does not mean that the output of letterpress has remained static. On the contrary, part of the explanation for the little change in the numbers employed has been the increased mechanization and the use of methods requiring fewer men. It should be added that there has been a shortage of labour in most sections of the industry since the Second World War.

Though the printing industry as a whole has expanded somewhat, the number of compositors employed has continued to decline. The reasons for this are rather similar to the previous period; in particular it has been due to the increased use of machinery, the changing nature of the work, and the expansion in the use of other processes. The censuses of production show that in 1951 there were about 34,600 compositors in England and Wales, compared with nearly 38,000 in 1931. Thus though the total number engaged in the printing industry increased, the number of compositors declined by about nine per cent. In London the decline has been even greater. The Census, which enumerates about 15,000 compositors in the Greater London area in 1931 and 11,000 in 1951, exaggerates the extent of the decline at 25 per cent; for, as suggested in Chapter IV the 1931 assessment was too high, and a more accurate indication of the trend is shown by membership of the London Society of Compositors. The number of members working at the trade was nearly 11,800 in 1931, by 1951 the number had fallen to nearly 9,550, so that the amount of decline was still substantial at nearly 20 per cent.

The greater decline in London than in England and Wales as whole is due to a number of special factors. In the first place, there was the upheaval of the Second World War. The bombing of central London had a very disturbing effect on the highly localized industry and encouraged some movement of printing to the home counties. Many compositors were out of the trade during the war, either serving with the forces or working in munitions: from nearly 10,700, the union membership had dwindled to about 6,500 in 1945. The reduction in the number of men reduced the intake of apprentices, because of the fixed ratio of journeymen to compositors; in addition the intake of apprentices was further restricted by the PKTF–BFMP agreement which allowed apprentices in the forces to be included as apprentices in calculating the number of apprentices to be permitted by the ratio. This is likely to have been more strictly enforced in London than in the provinces where the level of unionization was less. Another reason is that a greater proportion of work in London is done at speed which necessitates composing machinery, and there is a higher proportion of larger firms which are able to introduce machinery.

Since the war the number of union compositors working at the trade has increased, and appears to be still increasing slightly each year, standing at 9,821 in 1959, though the number of compositors today in London is still below the 1939 level of 10,682. Technically, the period since the war has been an exciting one in printing. The development of processes that can by-pass the traditional compositor, though not yet a real challenge, do present a danger to the existence of the occupation in its present form. Various kinds of office machinery and the attempts at using photocomposition commercially are likely to undergo considerable improvement. In these circumstances, though at present there is a demand for men to compose and arrange metal for printing[2] it is unlikely to expand much further.

The unions

In England and Wales, three separate unions cater for the compositor: the Typographical Association which covers the area outside London; the Printing Trades Alliance which theoretically is not geographically limited but in practice draws its members from the London area; and the London Typographical Society whose area extends 15 miles from the General Post Office. Probably over 90 per cent of the 35,000 hand and machine compositors are in unions; but it is difficult to estimate accurately because the TA does not give any breakdown of its membership into occupations; possibly over 95 per cent are unionized in the Greater London conurbation.

The TA is the largest of the unions with a total membership of over 54,000. This includes a large number of printing occupations besides those in the composing department. The union is an association of a large number of branches, which are fairly autonomous administratively, but bargain nationally on important issues. Its headquarters are in Manchester.

The PTA is an interesting group, rather different from the other unions. It was formed in 1918 and contains employers and employees among its members and its keynote is co-operation. Strikes, lock-outs and the closed shop principle, are opposed and it depends only on round-the-table negotiations.

The LTS was formed in 1955 by an amalgamation of the Printing Machine Managers' Trade Society and the London Society of Compositors. The membership of the LTS in 1959 was over 20,000. Of this total rather less than 14,000 were in the composing department and over 6,000 were machine managers (including nearly 600 apprentices). The number of compositors in the LTS is about 9,800 at the trade, just over 1,000 apprentices, about 2,200 superannuitants, over 400 working outside London, and less than 200 members not in the trade. Union subscriptions are high. They are graded on earnings, but the majority of members working at the trade pay the maximum rate of 9s 6d a week. About two-thirds of this amount is for superannuation; the rest covers benefits such as unemployment, strike pay and administration. The union also acts as an employment agency. All these benefits are a strong incentive for staying in the union, especially as the closed shop principle is widely maintained, and it would be difficult to obtain work without a union card.

Wages

Since the war, the compositor, like other skilled workers, has been bemoaning the loss of his position in the hierarchy of working-class wage rates. The war has largely been blamed for this, for compositors lost their differential position as other skilled and less skilled occupations were heavily in demand; in addition it is alleged that the members left in the occupation during the war were older, many having come back into the trade after retirement, and therefore were less militant or concerned about maintaining the wage level.

During the war a series of three increases brought the minimum wage in London from £4 9s 0d in 1939 to £5 6s 6d in November 1943.[3] No further rise came until after the war when, with the return of many compositors to civilian life, there was deep concern among them to re-establish their pre-war position. In November 1945, a leader in the *LTJ* called for a remedy of the situation whereby, it was alleged, the printing trades were the lowest paid of all industrial groups. After considerable agitation two increases of 8s 6d and 10s during 1946 brought the compositors' minimum to £6 5s 0d.

Reports of very high earning in certain industries gave the compositor the impression that he had fallen well below his position before the war. By the summer of 1947 resolutions were sent by a number of Chapels demanding wage increases to a varying degree (one of them demanding a minimum of £10 10s 0d). Eventually, after a National Arbitration Tribunal in January 1948 the basic rate increased to £7 a week. The compositors' attitude to wages at this time set the pattern for the series of disputes that followed the 1948 settlement. The London compositor, looking back to the inter-war situation, was concerned with regaining his position among the financial elite of the working class: the author recalls that a recurring theme among them was that before the war the compositor was at the top of the list for wage rates and that now he was near the bottom. The 'traditional differential' was the characteristic appeal in the immediate post-war period.

In 1950, after a bitter dispute, a Court of Inquiry made an award which brought the basic rate to £7 15s 0d. In addition, it was agreed that a cost-of-living bonus be introduced, giving 1s increase for every point rise in the official index; to reduce the labour shortage the LSC agreed to increase the ratio of apprentices from one-in-four to one-in-three, and a reduction from seven to a six-year apprenticeship. A five year stabilization period was agreed upon.

In 1955 the newly amalgamated LTS was demanding a basic rate of £12 a week. The increase from £7 15s 0d though substantial, was not as extraordinary as it might appear. Increases in the cost of living were already giving the compositor 33s a week extra, and in addition firms were paying 'merit money' (a pseudonym for shortage money) of about 30s a week or more. The LTS wanted a minimum that would approximate to the 1938 differential; to this the BFMP replied that a minimum of £12 would place the compositor well above other craftsmen and would have an adverse effect on the rest of industry. But the traditional differential was only one argument in the union's case. The secretary of the new union was concerned with the possibility of unemployment in the near future, and wanted to ensure a rate from which extras, such as 'merit money' could not easily be taken. Indeed, the appeal to traditional differentials began to be emphasized less as the argument lost some of its strength. The emphasis on keeping a differential in relation to the union in the provinces also changed: in the immediate post-war period there was some concern with maintaining the differential; later there was a demand for greater uniformity of wage rates, especially as the low-rate areas were attracting printing firms.

Skill rather than traditional differentials was the major emphasis: 'this Society never has based its wage claims upon what other unions may secure. Our claims are related to the varying skills of our members. For too long has quality and craftsmanship been ignored and the unreal values of manpower shortage superseded those based on skill and craft knowledge.'[4] After the dispute it was emphasized that 'the Society has never attempted to suggest that craftsmen in other trades unions should receive less than the amount accorded to the compositors and machine managers'.[5] Part of this change of emphasis was due to the need to give a sense of unity to all the craft unions in the printing industry: in view of the hopes for amalgamation, especially of the craft unions, it was no longer desirable that 'traditional differentials' be emphasized.

After a lengthy dispute agreement was eventually reached that gave a minimum rate of £11 to the compositor – £1 lower than that demanded by the union. But in the agreement the employers undertook to recommend to their member firms that whatever rate of pay a compositor was getting he should receive a flat rate increase of 27s 6d; this in effect meant that most compositors would receive rates above the £11 basic. The agreement provided for stabilization for three years.

The changing arguments in the justification of wage advances – from traditional differentials to emphasis on skill – took on a new character at the end of 1958, when the 1959 dispute was anticipated. The keynote of this appeal was 'the just rewards to which our members are entitled for the skill with which they help to contribute to production within the printing industry'.[6] The change was partly due to the fact that differentials were no longer a strong argument, partly because it would have been unwise to have stressed this aspect when most of the unions were making a joint approach for increases in wages, and partly because amalgamations were still being considered. The major tenor in 1959 was that the large profits being made in the printing industry warranted a more equitable distribution. 'Great play has been made by the BFMP,' wrote the secretary of the LTS in an editorial, 'on the average earnings of printers ... whether this is so or not, it is irrelevant, the point to be made is, are printers receiving a reasonable share of the product?'[7]

Take-over bids were receiving unfavourable publicity and workers were strongly impressed by the vast sums of money that were involved and the resultant tax-free gains. When similar activities became apparent in printing, they were regarded as some justification for the union's claims. One large bid attracted particular attention: 'At the same moment in time [as this] is deemed practicable... the members of the union employed by this great firm are being refused, through the employer's association, a reduction of hours to forty, and an increase of wages by ten per cent... In varying degrees this prosperity is reflected throughout the printing industry.'[8]

An important factor in the 1959 dispute which had been absent from the previous ones since 1946 was the question of the reduction of hours. The union's demand for a 40-hour week (from 43½ hours) was seen as a vanguard battle for industry in general; if the reduction could be secured for the printing industry, there would be an important argument for the attempt to gain a 40-hour week throughout all industry.

The dispute was a particularly bitter one, and the men were out of work for six weeks. Though there was a large majority in favour of a strong policy over the issue there was also criticism over the fact that the whole industry could be brought to a standstill, for it was widely felt by compositors in the survey that a settlement could have been reached by more peaceful negotiation. Negotiations under an independent chairman resulted in an agreement on an increase of four and a half per cent on wages, and a reduction of one and a half hours to make a 42-hour week. The settlement was to be regarded as an interim one, and in 1961 the situation was to be reviewed again in the light of attempts to increase productivity (the employers had suggested a number of basic requirements on manpower and methods of working which the union, after modification, agreed to try to implement). The settlement brought the basic wage of the London compositor to £11 10s 0d, plus the cost of living bonus of 12s; this was agreed to on ballot by a large majority.

Thus, since the war until 1959, the compositor has achieved an increase of 156 per cent on the 1938 rate (116 per cent on 1945 rates), a reduction of three hours in the working week, and a fortnight holiday with pay since 1946. This outline of the course of wages since the Second World War has been presented partly in order to indicate the changing rationale given to justify the increases, and partly in order to emphasize that each successive dispute was prolonged and bitter; it is in such conditions that a mood of militancy is fostered.

The following is a list of basic rates:

Basic Wage Rates

	£	s	d
General printing			
Hand compositors	11	10	0
Machine compositors[a]	12	0	6
Periodical houses			
Hand compositors	12	0	0
Machine compositors	12	15	6
Advertisement setters[9]			
Hand compositors	13	10	0
Machine compositors	14	0	6
Newspapers			
Time hand compositors[b]			
Mornings	18	1	0
Evenings	17	13	6
Sundays	16	1	6

a. Machine operators includes Linotype, Monotype, and Intertype operators.
b. Piece rates enable much higher earnings to be made; most newspaper machine operators are engaged on piece-work.

Earnings of the compositor

So far we have been concerned with basic wage rates; but throughout the period the majority of compositors earned more than the minimum. For in practice, some of the differentials laid down for different sections of the industry and for different kinds of work may not be reflected in actual earnings. Apart from the different rates for compositors engaged in different sections of the trade, on different work, and for responsibility, compositors in most sections of the industry receive more than the basic because of extra bonuses and 'house rates' paid mainly in order to attract labour, but also to encourage productivity; wages are also supplemented by the opportunity to work overtime. Night work is done by about ten per cent of the general trade, that is apart from the newspaper section; this work is paid at one and a half times the day rate for the number of hours actually worked; this is 40½ on nights, instead of 42 hours a week on days. The lowest rate for a hand compositor on night work is £16 12s 5d and £17 7s 7½d for machine operators.

It is evident from the above that the basic rate gives a false impression of compositors' wages and the kind of earnings actually received by them. Some indication of these earnings is possible from information collected during the contemporary survey of compositors. 27 of the 28 firms in the sample supplied information on wages. These firms are fairly representative of the letterpress printing industry in terms of size range and the kind of work done, and thus a fairly reliable picture can be obtained of the distribution of actual earnings of the London compositor engaged in periodical and general printing houses (the sample excludes newspapers, where earnings are much higher). The earnings presented are those paid to the majority of hand compositors in the firms, without special responsibility.

It has already been observed that the shortage of labour has encouraged firms to attract men by offering extra payments in the form of 'merit money', 'house rates', and bonus schemes. Thus, though the basic rate is £11 10s 0d with an additional cost of living bonus of 14s as from 1 January, 1960, no firm had men working at that rate. Wage rates, inclusive of cost of living bonus but excluding overtime, ranged from the lowest wage (earned by one man only) of £12 10s 0d to over £15, and the majority were getting £14 a week or more. It is worth noting that both of the firms in the sample who were not on the LTS 'fair list' (i.e. they were 'open' houses, employing non-union labour), were to be found amongst the three firms paying the lowest rates – this would suggest that despite full employment there still tends to be a lag between rates of pay in union and non-union firms.

Many compositors receive higher rates than these, for in most firms there are men who have special responsibility. There are no standard scales for these extras and similar work may be paid for at different rates in different firms. In some firms the men in charge of jobs (known as 'clickers') receive as little as 5s a week extra, in others the extra payment may be considerable: the highest rate mentioned was nearly £4 above the usual rate paid to compositors in that firm. Men operating typesetting machines receive additional payments. It is here that the largest differences occur. In some of the firms, monotype operators received 10s more than that received by hand compositors in the firm; some firms paid £1 or 30s above the hand compositors. Where, however, piece work was in operation very high earnings were possible: £25 a week was not unusual for mono and linotype operators, and in one firm night operators were receiving up to £35 a week.

Considerable additions to wages can be made by working overtime. Because of date lines on printed matter overtime has always been a feature of the industry. This fact, combined with the shortage of men since the war, has made overtime particularly important. The words 'guaranteed overtime' frequently appear in advertisements for vacancies. Employers mentioned that one of the first questions a man asks when he applied for a job is 'How much overtime is available?' Sometimes overtime is laid on in firms even when it is not strictly necessary 'because the men need the money and it helps to keep them happy.' Certainly overtime earnings are generally regarded as part of one's regular income and contribute considerably to the compositors' level of living.

Though not all men work overtime, it is done by the majority of compositors. In most months throughout the year about 70 per cent of compositor members of the LTS worked overtime; the figure is probably an under-estimate as it is based on returns from Chapels which are not always complete. Payment is paid on a rather complex scale. On a weekday, overtime is paid at time and a quarter for the first two hours (i.e. one and a quarter times the usual hourly rate the man is paid), time and a half for the next three hours, and double time after that. Overtime on Saturdays is paid at time and a half for the first four hours (i.e. up to 12 mid-day), and double time after that. On Sundays the rate is double time all day. Various privileges have become traditional in some firms, and extra payments are made for working certain lengths of time.

Earnings of compositors are rather difficult to estimate because the amount of overtime worked by different numbers of compositors is unknown. Also, because of the different hourly rates that are paid for overtime it is impossible to compute the actual payments received even if the number of hours worked were known. However, a crude estimate of earnings can be given by taking the average number of hours that the men work overtime and multiplying this by the lowest hourly rate for overtime, based on the minimum wage rate. If this is added to the usual basic rate in the firms, it gives some idea of the minimum gross earnings for the majority of compositors. This would show that about half the men receive between £16 and £17 a week and a further third obtain over £18 a week gross. A few firms indicated that the majority of their compositors earned over £20 a week. To obtain earnings of this order a very high level of overtime would have to be worked; five hours for each of two nights plus four hours on Saturday morning.

Comparison with other occupations

Compared with the rates of pay of workers in general, compositors' wage rates to date have not maintained their pre-war level. Whereas the general wages index shows an increase from 100 in 1938 to 274 in 1956,[10] an index of compositors' wages would show an increase in the same period from 100 to 236. The difference is largely due to the relative decline that took place during the war. However, in making this comparison there are three points that need to be considered. Firstly, the comparison has been made between compositors and a general wage index, and wages among the less skilled have increased faster than those for skilled workers; had the comparison been made for skilled workers only the picture for compositors is likely to have been less unfavourable. Secondly, it must be remembered that a comparison is made with the pre-war period, when the rates for the compositor were very high relative to other occupations. Thirdly, it must be emphasized that wage rates not earnings, have been compared: the gross earnings of compositors, including bonuses, house rates and overtime, are, on average, higher than obtains in other occupations.

Status and image

The image of the compositor

We have already noted in earlier chapters the important effects of the kind of image of the occupation held by the public. This image is related to the status accorded to the occupation which in turn affects recruitment, work satisfaction, and expected (and even accorded) rewards.

Technically, the occupation of composing has undergone a number of changes since the beginning of the century. Typesetting by machinery has expanded considerably and has virtually replaced hand setting, except for the setting of occasional lines, such as headlines, captions, and advertisements. Consequently, knowledge of the language by hand compositors, though important, is less essential than it was when continual hand setting placed valuation on knowledge of spelling, punctuation and grammar. Changes in typographic design, with its reduction of ornamentation, together with the use of mechanical aids, have speeded up the work process and have fostered standardization and precision; consequently less ingenuity is, in general, demanded of the compositor's skill (see Appendix A).

Yet the image that is held of the compositor does not appear to have drastically declined: literacy, intelligence, and artistic sense are seen to be required to a greater extent than for other skilled occupations. Publications offering guidance on careers list the qualities that the compositor should have. He should be good at English, sufficiently intelligent to make sense of bad writing and untidy alterations, and accurate. The occupation requires clear thinking in order to make up pages without bad breaks that would confuse the reader. Emphasis is laid upon the interest that the work provides, and upon the fact that it presents opportunities for exercising artistic abilities. A similar image is provided by an outside observer, discussing printers as a whole: 'they are above the average in intelligence, are more intellectual than other workers, and have more artistic interests.'[11]

The layman probably thinks in terms of the industry as a whole in his image of printing, rather than specific occupations within it. Boys leaving school often think of getting into 'the print' and are less concerned with what the different occupations offer. They accept the image presented by other adults who lay emphasis on the high wages and security of employment believed to be offered in the printing industry. Such aspects are expressed by the characters in a novel which has a compositor as one of its central figures: 'there's always good money to be earned in printing' says the compositor's mother; and another character asserts: 'the wages are fantastically high... and the numbers are deliberately kept down so that there's never any danger of unemployment'.[12]

Though average earnings are higher than most manual occupations the level of material rewards tends to be exaggerated by the general public. This is also reflected in the novel quoted, which gives earnings for the compositor in the immediate post-war period as £15 a week including overtime; yet the rate of pay in the kind of area referred to in the novel at that time was less than £6 a week – a compositor would have had to maintain an extremely high level of overtime to achieve earnings of the order stated. Such exaggeration by laymen of the likely earnings is often keenly felt: one young apprentice spoke with feeling about the difference between what people expect him to earn and the actual earnings that he knew were being received in the firm where he worked: 'they almost give me a guilty conscience,' was his unexpected comment, greeted enthusiastically by his fellow apprentices. Another comment was 'they got me in under false pretences.' This over-estimate of earnings is largely due to the existence of certain sections in the industry which are highly paid. Frequently compositors in commenting on the fact that they are 'thought well off', added that people regard them as being highly paid because they have in mind the national newspaper compositor, who does receive very high earnings.

It would seem that when people think about printing in more detail than the industry as a whole, the compositor comes into especial prominence. This may be because people tend to think initially of the person who sets up the type, and though they have little clearer idea than this of the functions of the compositor, they seem to stress not only the rewards of the occupation but also the requirements – especially knowledge of the English language. This is reinforced by writers who have had happy associations with compositors: a letter in the *Daily Telegraph* (31/12/58), for example, relates a story revealing the ability of compositors to interpret bad handwriting, and continues 'When you don't know how to spell, leave it to the comps.'

The public image of the occupation is given expression in the status level that it is accorded among manual occupations. Some indication of this status can be given from the results of a small enquiry that was conducted. A class of Workers Educational Association students were asked by the author in 1960 to arrange a series of occupations in order of prestige. The following is the rank order which resulted, and as can be seen the compositor is highly placed.

1 Dentist
2 Teacher (secondary modern)
3 Librarian (assistant)
4 Compositor
5 Small shopkeeper
6 Office clerk (routine)
7 Sales representative (door-to-door)
8 Carpenter
9 Shop assistant
10 Lorry driver

Part of the explanation for the high status accorded to the compositor is probably the lack of knowledge about the occupation. A much clearer idea is probably held about the demands of those occupations that were placed below the compositor. Justification for the relatively high placing given to him was in terms of skill, literacy, and high pay – reflecting the popular image.

When the students were asked to place the occupations into class divisions using any method of classification that they wanted to use, the nomenclature most frequently accorded the compositor was either 'lower middle class' or 'upper working class'. A skilled manual trade that would be classified by most class investigators as similar to that of the compositor, that of the carpenter, was more frequently given a social class ranking lower than the compositor.

Classification	Compositor	Carpenter
	No.	No.
Middle class	3	0
Lower middle class	5	2
Upper working class	5	3
Working class or similar	5	13
	18	18

It should be said, however, that when obliged to use a specific termi-nology, 'upper', 'middle' and 'working' class, for the ten occupations, the compositor was regarded as belonging to the working class rather than to the middle class.

Recruitment

In previous chapters we have seen that recruitment into the trade was related to the public image of the occupation and its material condition in different periods. According to the Glass study of Social Mobility present-day British society is characterized by a substantial amount of upward and downward mobility. It would be interesting to know from which social groups the compositors are being recruited, for their social condition is comparatively good in terms of material rewards and status and the occupation can be considered fairly borderline between the classes. Is the occupation consequently attracting boys from relatively high social origins, or is the upgrading of the occupational structure that is taking place increasing the outlets for boys in these groups, and there-fore encouraging an increasing proportion of boys into composing from skilled and less skilled fathers?

Whether or not the social origins of compositors are changing can be seen by comparing the origins of the present journeymen with those of boys coming into the trade today. The social origins of present day journeymen are shown in Table 8. The numbers are based on those 88 compositors in the contemporary survey whose fathers were alive when they entered the occupation. Fathers from all kinds of non-manual occu-pations are grouped together.

Table 8 **Social Origin of Journeymen Compositors, 1959**

| Origin | Compositors | | Skilled workers | |
	No.	%	% (A)[13]	% (B)[14]
Non-manual	34	39	16	28
Skilled	36	41	54	50
Semi-skilled	15	17	14	12
Unskilled	3	3	13	10
Don't know	0	0	3	0
	88	100	100	100

A substantial proportion of compositors, about 40 per cent, come from non-manual backgrounds and about three quarters of these were higher than routine non-manual. The proportion is similar for sons of skilled workers, and of the remainder the majority are from semi-skilled backgrounds. It should be noted that of the latter a large proportion came from other printing occupations, especially from the warehouse. Only three per cent were the sons of unskilled workers.

Comparison can be made with the social origins of skilled workers in general, this is derived from two sources: the first is from a 1957 study and the second is from a study in the early 1950s which show different levels of recruitment from the non-manual group. A more realistic figure for comparison is likely to lie somewhere between the two columns. It will be seen that even compared with the figures in Column B, there is a high degree of recruitment from the non-manual group among compositors, with fewer recruited from skilled fathers. It will also be seen that the proportion of compositors recruited from unskilled fathers is much lower than it is for skilled workers in general.

Mention should be made of the educational background of the compositor. 82 per cent went to elementary school, eight per cent to central, five per cent to technical, and five per cent to grammar school. Though material to compare them with the education of similar manual workers is not satisfactory, it would appear that the educational background of compositors differs little from that of other skilled workers.[15] This does not mean that their education was of the same level, it might well be that the occupation attracts the better educated of those in elementary schools. For this educational experience refers to the period before the

Table 9 **Social Origin of Apprentices**

Origin	No.	%
Non-manual	44	32
Skilled	65	48
Semi-skilled	22	16
Unskilled	6	4
	137	100

1944 Education Act and it is likely that many compositors before this date had the ability for an education higher than that of elementary school.

It will thus be seen that, as expected from their high status, the social origins of compositors are higher than those of other skilled workers, in terms of father's occupation at least, if not in terms of educational background. But this recruitment largely took place between the wars when the occupation was relatively attractive. Has the degree of high social origin of entrants been maintained?

Fairly reliable evidence of the social origins of present apprentices was provided from a survey of composing apprentices. Of the 137 apprentices analysed in Table 9, 64 were first year and 73 were fifth year students on day-release courses. Little difference was found between the two groups so they were combined to make a larger figure for analysis. There may, however, be some bias as a number of apprentices who started at the printing school did not stay to complete the five-year course, and this wastage may well be associated with social class. If this is so, then the fifth year may have originally contained a higher proportion of lower social groups, and thus the present first year could show an increase in the number of apprentices from higher social origins.

Compared with the journeymen, it will be seen that there has been a slight decline in recruitment from non-manual sources, from 39 to 32 per cent, despite the increase in this category in the population as a whole.[16] An increase has taken place amongst those coming from skilled backgrounds; the less skilled contribute a similar proportion as they did for the journeymen. It might well be that this picture under-estimates the extent of the decline: a number who entered the trade at the same time as the present journeymen have since left, possibly moving to higher social groups inside or outside the industry, and it is possible that these men tended to come from higher social groups. The decline is not unexpected:

Table 10 **Education of Apprentices**

Type of School	First year		Fifth year	
	No.	%	No.	%
Secondary modern	35	54	42	55
Central and technical	9	14	13	17
Comprehensive	9	14	1	1
Grammar	11	17	21	27
Private	1	1	0	0
	65	100	77	100

for the material position of the compositor before the war was materially higher than it is today in relation to other manual occupations; in addition, the expansion of non-manual occupations has possibly helped to provide other opportunities for boys from these groups.

The decline in the extent of self-recruitment into the occupation is noteworthy. Composing is far from being the father-to-son occupation that it is often envisaged to be. Between the wars 21 per cent of the intake were the sons of compositors. Today it would seem that compositors are less willing to put their sons into the occupation: less that eight per cent of first year apprentices had fathers from the composing department. Yet the attraction of composing for boys whose fathers are in other printing occupations seems to have increased: whereas ten per cent of the inter-war intake had fathers in printing occupations other than composing, 14 per cent of the fifth year and 20 per cent of the first year apprentices had fathers in such occupations, many from less skilled occupations. The family does not seem to be all-important as a means of entry into the trade: nearly 60 per cent of the apprentices stated that they had no family at all in any branch of the printing industry.

Educational experience of the present entrants to composing is, expectedly in view of the 1944 Act, more varied than the journeymen. This is shown in Table 10, where the type of school attended by the apprentice is given; the first and fifth years are shown separately so that any changes between the two can be seen.

A considerable number of boys, nearly half, receive an education above that provided by secondary modern schools. This is true for both the years, but between the years the content of the non-secondary modern group has undergone some change. A sharp increase has taken place in the proportion of boys from comprehensive schools; this rise being at the cost of the proportion of boys from grammar schools. Part of the explanation for the loss from the grammar schools may be that many of those who might otherwise have gone to grammar schools were border-line anyway. Certainly it is true that a number of boys who had attended comprehensive schools stated that they were in higher streams.

Adequate comparative material is lacking, yet it would seem that this degree of educational experience from non-secondary modern schools is somewhat higher than for other skilled workers.[17] It supports the conclu-sion that composing is continuing to recruit from higher social groups than are other skilled workers. The high status of the occupation and the association with literacy is likely to make composing more attractive than other manual occupations. Choice of occupation is not entirely for-tuitous: there is an occupational sieve of images of occupations which is receptive to the suitability of some occupations and rejects others. To the non-manual father of a possibly downwardly mobile son, the peripheral position socially of the compositor, is likely to be more attractive than other working class manual occupations. It is interesting to note, however, that there is some evidence to suggest that within the printing industry itself, composing no longer has a monopoly of the better educated. A survey of apprentices at the London School of Printing (Apprentices in the London Printing Industry May 1957) showed that in 1957 compos-ing students ranked second of six occupations in the proportion of boys who had stayed at school until 16 or over; by 1959 they had dropped to third place. In 1957 8.3 per cent of composing students had one or more subjects in G.C.E. being second to lithography and photogravure students who had 8.8 per cent; by 1959 they had fallen to fourth place with only 5.4 per cent with at least one G.C.E. subject.

Conclusion

Since the war, the compositor has been struggling to regain the position among the working classes that he held between the wars. During these struggles a mood of militancy has been fostered which has probably tended to reinforce the compositors' association with the union and also with the working class, though the earlier emphasis on the need to main-tain differentials might have tended to weaken this identification. At the same time the improvements that are taking place are reaching a level where militancy, it may be thought, will have less appeal. The possibility of fairly high earnings may be making them rather less dissatisfied with their pay: 50% of the sample of compositors regarded their pay as good or excellent. Though it is true that dissatisfaction may arise with the very multiplication of wants, there may be less readiness to jeopardise regular income by resort to the strike; many compositors were certainly critical of the lengthy dispute in 1959.

The compositor continues to enjoy a high status, and though the social origins of compositors seem to be lower than before the war, the occupation is obviously still invested with some prestige. Thus the compositor's position is high among working class occupations, and his social origins, status, and material condition combine to place him rather ambiguously in the class structure. We now need to consider in what ways this is reflected in his actual way of life, and the effect this is having on his class and political affiliations.

Trade card from the author's collection

Notes

1 The 1931 Census of Population enumerated 253,458 persons in the printing industry, while the 1954 Census of Production indicated 304.0 thousands. (*Census of England and Wales 1931, Industry tables*, p. 6, Headings 440, 441, 443, 444, 445 and 446 only; *Report on the Census of Production for 1954, v. 10, industry J* and *K*, Table 1, p. 3, but excluding non-printing publishers).

2 Williams, *Recruitment to Skilled Trades*, p. 116.

3 Howe and Waite, *London Society of Compositors*, p. 291.

4 *LTJ*, January 1956, p. 9.

5 *LTJ*, August 1956, p. 3.

6 *LTJ*, December 1958, p. 3.

7 *LTJ*, May 1959, p. 7.

8 *LTJ*, June 1959, p. 3.

9 A new agreement made in 1960 for a small section of the trade; see *LTJ*, May 1960, p. 7.

10 Carr-Saunders, Jones and Moser, *Survey of Social Conditions*, p. 144.

11 Zweig, *British Worker*, p. 41.

12 Laski, *The Village*, p. 17, 237.

13 'An Enquiry into some aspects of the working class life in London'. A survey of 203 working class households in the London area in 1957 by Lintas who kindly supplied the information. 20% of this sample were from less skilled workers, and therefore the proportion of non-manual fathers among the skilled only is probably under-estimated, though the difference would not account for the gap of 23% between this sample and the compositors.

14 Glass and Hall, 'Social Mobility in Great Britain: a study of Inter-generation Changes in Status', p. 183. Here the recruitment from non-manual backgrounds is probably over-estimated, for status category five, on which percentages are based, includes routine non-manual as well as skilled workers, and a higher proportion of the former are likely to come from non-manual homes.

15 Hall and Glass, 'Education and Social Mobility', p. 294–5.

16 Marsh, *Changing Social Structure*, p. 194; the proportion of non-manual workers is likely to have grown since 1951.

17 Ministry of Labour publication M.L.C.M./117/1955, which instructed ministry staff to collect educational data from young men in skilled trades; this survey found that, in 1955, about 75% of young men had a Secondary Modern school education.

VI

Way of Life and Ideology

In the last chapter we saw that the compositor, compared with either the working class as a whole, or even with the skilled working class alone, is obtaining fairly substantial average earnings and he enjoys a high status. By virtue of his material position and the social ranking he is ascribed, the compositor appears to be in just such an intermediary situation in which it might be expected that class and political affiliations are breaking down. This chapter is concerned with the extent to which the compositor is in fact adopting a middle class pattern of life, and whether this is affecting his class consciousness and political allegiance.

In discussing this way of life it is important to distinguish between two aspects: a) the material level of living, and b) the kind of values and aspirations that are held. It should not be assumed that the achievement of a middle class level of living necessarily leads to the adoption of middle class values. There might be a strong desire to acquire material goods, while other values of the middle class were still rejected – at least in the shorter term. In determining whether the compositor is adopting a middle class way of life it is necessary to deal with each aspect separately.

The information on compositors was collected by interviewing 100 compositors in the London area in the period December 1959 to February 1960. Appendix B shows that the sample was stratified by size of firm and a random selection was made of all compositors who were 30 years of age or over. Because of their special earnings position, newspaper compositors were excluded from the sample; it can be expected that the level of ownership of certain goods among them would be higher than it is for compositors in the other sections of the printing industry.

It is important to point out that though the compositors are analysed as a group, the pattern of life is by no means homogenous. This will be obvious from the figures given. In addition to a general lack of uniformity, differences in ways of life may well exist for the various sub groups, particularly composing machine operators, working overseers, and night workers. For example, of the 13 machine compositors not living with their parents 10 have their own home (77 per cent compared with 62 per cent for all compositors), 54 per cent have their own phone (compared with 32 per cent) and 54 per cent have their own car (compared with 25 per cent). The size of the sample does not permit a breakdown for such groups which would be statistically significant; therefore, comparison is made for compositors as a whole, irrespective of their actual work. It is emphasized that because of the small size of the sample, caution must be used in interpreting the data, and most of the conclusions must be tentative, but there is a consistency which is itself suggestive.[1]

A major problem has been to obtain comparative material which corresponded to the sample of compositors. What was specifically required was data for skilled workers, or for manual workers with comparable earnings to the compositor, 30 years of age or over, in the Greater London area. Material could be obtained for one or two of these characteristics but not for all three. For example, it was possible to obtain national figures for manual workers of similar income but not for Greater London only, and for certain items London was likely to show a higher degree of ownership. Where regional comparison was possible, the data included the less skilled sections of the working class with lower incomes. It was, fortunately, possible to obtain data that was gathered about the same time as that when the interviews with the compositors took place.

Level of living

With the decline in or eradication of differences in earnings between white collar and manual workers, distinctive ways of life are increasingly determined by how income is spent. Numerous items could be listed which show social class differences in ownership; here only a few items have been selected which are still regarded as reflecting distinctive ways of life.

An enumeration of items owned by compositors would not itself be very significant, so that only those items are given where some comparative data is available for manual workers in a roughly similar position in terms of skill or income. To avoid overstating the level of living of the compositor in relation to the better-off working class, data have been chosen which give the highest percentage ownership for the nearest comparable group; any important biases are referred to in the text. Ownership of a number of items that reveal the level of living is given in Table 11.

It will be seen that a very high proportion of compositors have and fulfil the desire to own their homes: 62 per cent have or are buying homes of their own. This is the outstanding feature of ownership amongst compositors. It might be expected that home ownership would be more widespread amongst workers in the London area than in the country as a

Table 11 **Ownership and Holidays**

	Compositors %	Manual workers %
Home ownership	62	35[a]
Car	25	32[a]
Television	90	82[a]
Telephone	32	9[b]
Holidays abroad	9	5[b]

a. These figures are for manual workers nationally whose annual income is above £625.[2]
b. These figures are for all manual workers in the London and South East region, irrespective of income.

whole, yet the difference of 27 per cent cannot be accounted for merely by regional differences. Indeed, data for the London and South East regions, though not giving separate figures for skilled workers, does give the extent of ownership amongst all white collar groups in that area, this is 57 per cent, with which the compositor compares favourably.[3]

In contrast, it would appear that car ownership among compositors is not as high as for other skilled workers, unless car ownership among them is more widespread outside the London area. Compared with manual workers in the London area, of whom 19 per cent own cars, the compositor is better off, but unlike the situation in home ownership, the compositor's likelihood of owning a car is only half that for all white collar workers. However, the differences between the compositor and other similar manual workers is not great, nor unexpected: it is not likely that the compositor on his earnings will possess, to a considerable extent, two items which involve substantial capital outlay and high regular out-goings.

Television sets are no longer really any guide to social differences; all social groups possess them to a similar extent, indeed skilled manual workers are likely to have sets more frequently than are white collar work-ers. Compositor's ownership of television at 90 per cent accords with the general pattern for manual workers.

About one-third of compositors (32 per cent) have a telephone. This is high compared with the nine per cent for other manual workers in the London area, though the comparative data cover manual workers of all income groups. The compositor is, however, very much below the level of telephone ownership among all white collar groups which is 61 per cent.

Holidays abroad are considered here as a substantial item of expenditure. Compositors do not go abroad regularly to any considerable extent: in one year nine per cent went to the Continent compared with five per cent for all manual workers; for white collar workers the number who went abroad in 1959 was 22 per cent. About one-third of compositors have taken a holiday abroad at some time in their lives; and several who said that they would like to go commented that they were dissuaded from doing so by their wives.

This analysis of a few major items of expenditure is limited, but revealing. Apart from car ownership, compositors spend more on these items than do other skilled workers. Particularly is this true of home ownership – the item that most especially expresses values that are associated with the middle class. The choice of the compositor as having an intermediary occupation in the social hierarchy is therefore justified: his material level of living is rather higher than that of skilled workers as a whole.

Aspirations of the compositor

We have next to consider whether a level of living which approaches that of the middle class is in fact accompanied by a wider diffusion of the values and aspirations characteristic of that class. It is difficult to find precise indicators of these values, but they find expression in various ways. They certainly include a high regard for education, and aspirations for one's children to achieve an occupational level preferably superior to one's own. The latter may involve deliberate limitation of family size.

Does the compositor have such aspirations? That one of the clearest expressions of middle class values is the emphasis placed on education has been shown in the clear differences that exist between manual and non-manual parents in their preferences for different kinds of secondary schools for their children.[4] If middle class aspirations were being adopted by the compositor, then it would be expected that this would be reflected in the education of his children.

Table 12 gives the secondary education experience of all the compositors' children over the age of 11.

Table 12 **Secondary Education of Compositors' Children**

	Boys	Girls	Boys & girls	
	No.	No.	No.	%
Secondary modern or elementary	33	19	52	54
Technical & comprehensive	6	1	7	7
Grammar	16	14	30	31
Unknown	2	6	8	8
	57	40	97	100

The proportion of 31 per cent of children attending grammar schools is fairly substantial. In a small study of the working class in the London area, of the 94 children in secondary education, 62 per cent were in secondary modern schools and 26 per cent were in grammar schools or in further academic institutions. Though it would appear that the difference between the compositors and other workers seems slight, it is important to stress that in the Lintas market research study comparator only the children who at that time were in full-time education were included, whereas the compositor study covers the educational experience of children of all ages. A substantial number of these received their education before the 1944 reform of secondary education, and it is likely that a higher proportion of the children of compositors are today receiving a grammar school education, or at least a non-secondary modern education.

The educational aspirations of compositors were ascertained by a question asking what kind of secondary education would be preferred for a son. The question was asked of all compositors, single or married, who did not already have a son attending a secondary school. The results are given in Table 13.

A considerable number of compositors were not very specific about their aspirations: nearly one-quarter just said 'as high as possible'. Further conversations with respondents revealed that in many cases this vagueness was due largely to ignorance of the educational system; 'as high as possible' could be variously interpreted and to suggest actual categories for these respondents to choose between might over-estimate the significance of these categories for the respondent. When such vagueness occurred, the choice was only included in the 'grammar school' category if

Table 13 **Educational Aspirations for Sons**

	Compositors		Skilled workers
	No.	%	%
Secondary modern	1	2	17
Technical	5	8	23
Grammar	51	82	48
Unknown	5	8	12
	62	100	100

other comments or occupational aspirations for their sons suggested that this kind of education was intended.

Compositors appear to place a very high valuation on education, with over 80 per cent desiring for their sons a grammar school education at secondary level. It should also be noted that about 20 per cent of the 62 compositors included in this part of the sample indicated a desire for their sons to have a university education.

In many cases this could be a hope rather than a firm aspiration, but even so it is revealing. It would certainly suggest a higher level of emphasis on education than is found among other skilled workers. Matched comparative material was difficult to obtain, but an approximate comparison can be made from the social mobility studies published in 1954. There are a number of sources of bias: the study of parental preferences in the social mobility studies is based on a different geographical area and, more important, was elicited from parents whose children were near the point of changing from their primary stage of education. The expressed preference is likely to be partly determined by the actual assessment of the child's probability of being accepted. Thus the large difference between the educational aspirations of compositors and skilled workers in general must be regarded with caution, yet it can be argued that it supports the view that compositors are likely to encourage education among their children to a somewhat greater extent than do skilled workers in general.

The kind of occupations that people desire for their children is also indicative of their values, and all married and unmarried compositors were asked the kind of occupations they would like a son of theirs to

Table 14 **Actual Occupation of Children**

	Boys	Girls	Boys & girls		Skilled workers	
	No.	No.	No.	%	No.	%
Professional & supervisory	4	2	6	13	2	2
Clerical	5	6	11	23	34	42
Skilled	20	3	23	49	20	25
Semi or unskilled	5	2	7	15	25	31
	34	13	47	100	81	100

enter. The compositors who had sons at work and had no aspirations for any others that they had were omitted. Fourteen compositors had no occupational preferences for their sons. Of the 70 who stated their hopes, 51 per cent desired professional occupations, ten per cent clerical, and 39 per cent wanted their sons to be in skilled trades. Understandably, many of these hopes were not very well formulated, but they showed a desire on behalf of a substantial proportion of compositors for their sons to be non-manual workers. Sixteen compositors thought that sons of theirs might go into printing; this covered all branches of the industry. Only a few wanted their sons to follow their own occupation; this confirms what we saw from current entrants to the trade that composing is much less a father-to-son occupation than it is often thought to be.

The extent to which these aspirations towards non-manual work fall short of reality can be seen in Table 14 showing the actual occupation of compositors' children. The total number of children is not very large, and therefore though the numbers for each sex are shown separately, only a combined percentage is given. Only those children in some kind of employment are included and those undergoing occupational training are classified in the occupational group they will be entering.

About half the children of compositors were recruited into skilled occupations, and about one-third entered non-manual employment. Under 20 per cent of the boys were in some kind of occupation in printing.

A comparison with other skilled workers is made with material from the Lintas study. Here there was a smaller degree of self-recruitment: only 25 per cent of the children of skilled workers entered skilled occupations, half of that for the compositors. An interesting distinction is in recruitment into non-manual work. More children of skilled workers entered all kinds of non-manual work than was true for the compositor, but a much higher proportion went into routine clerical jobs. Though the numbers are barely significant, a higher proportion of the sons of compositors enter higher non-manual work. It would appear that if the choice has to be made between routine non-manual work and a trade, the compositor would prefer his sons to go into a skilled occupation. Fewer children of compositors go into less skilled work: 15 per cent of them compared with 31 per cent of the children of all skilled workers entered semi and unskilled employment. Some of this difference may partly be contributed by the daughter: most of the 18 daughters of compositors who did not go out to work were housewives; this is 28 per cent of all the children of compositors. Only 11 per cent of the skilled workers in general had daughters in this category; daughters of skilled workers go out to work more frequently than compositors' daughters, and possibly enter less skilled employment. This might also suggest a social class differential in the marriages of the children of compositors: their daughters might marry men who prefer and are able to keep their wives at home.

In view of the high degree of self-recruitment into skilled occupations, it could be said that there is less social mobility among compositors. But the quality of the mobility is higher than for other skilled workers: fewer children go into less skilled work, and more are in non-manual work at a higher level than routine clerical employment.

Thus it would appear that educational and occupational aspirations of compositors for their children are high in relation to other skilled workers; their actual attainments are also somewhat higher than obtains among skilled workers generally. This would seem to indicate some acceptance of middle class values among compositors.

Fertility is affected by a number of social factors, including nature of work, health, and age at marriage. The aspirations we have so far been considering also have been shown to have some effect on the number of children people are willing to have. Is there any confirmation of the tendency to adopt middle class values to be found in the rate of fertility among compositors? Table 15 gives the fertility pattern for all compositors over 40 years of age who are or have been married. The assumption has been made that those of this age would, by and large, have completed their families, and some internal evidence shows that this is largely true: an analysis of the ages of children was made to see whether it was likely that compositors had completed their fertility at 40; in all but three cases there was strong evidence to suggest that this was so.

Table 15 **Fertility of Compositors**

Number of children	Married compositors over 40 years old		Total number of children
	No.	%	No.
0	9	13	0
1	27	40	27
2	21	31	42
3	7	10	21
4	2	3	8
5	2	3	10
	68	100	108

Average number of children = 1.6.

A higher age limit would have been more accurate but the slight advantage would have been reduced by a serious loss in the size of the sample.

At a completed family size of 1.6, compositors have a very low fertility rate.[5] This is very largely attributable to the fact that over one half, 53 per cent, of compositors have no more than one child. 13 per cent of the sample had no children at all. This fertility rate is in keeping with the other criteria which indicates the adoption of certain middle class values.

Two further areas throw some light on the way of life of the compositor: newspaper reading habits and religious activity.

Newspaper reading gives some indication of levels of interest and may possibly reveal aspirations to some extent, because of the relationship between reading and social class. In Table 16 the newspapers that are regularly read by compositors are given, and comparison is made with two of the social groups of male readers analysed in the National Readership Survey for 1959. C1 roughly corresponds to lower middle class including lower supervisory, minor professional and routine non-manual workers; C2 is the skilled manual group. The published results of the National Survey only give a social group breakdown nationally, not for Greater London. A total percentage for each newspaper is given for Greater London, and important differences exist for certain newspapers between this area and the National Survey. Therefore, in order to obtain an estimate of social class differences in newspaper reading for London, the figures by social groups have been given a regional weighting in the table; this has been done by taking the proportionate difference between the two areas for each newspaper, and applying the proportionate change to the percentage for each social class. This assumes, of course, that the regional difference will be the same for each social class, and this may not be true. The table also gives the national and Greater London figures from the National Readership Survey which will indicate the amount of change that has resulted from this weighting. The national survey includes males from 16 upwards; this is a source of bias only in the case of the *Daily Mirror*, the *Daily Sketch*, and the *Sunday Pictorial*, and even in these cases the main picture does not appear to be seriously distorted.

Compositors read newspapers to a considerable extent: 95 per cent of them read a morning paper and 89 per cent of them read a Sunday paper (several who did not read a Sunday paper said that this was because their religious denomination frowned upon it). The quality of newspaper reading is also much higher than for other skilled workers. The picture is distorted by the fact that one newspaper, the *News Chronicle* was read by a very large proportion, 52 per cent, of compositors who read newspapers. The reason for the large number of *News Chronicle* readers is partly explained by its quiet non-dramatic quality, likely to appeal to those whose familiarity with the printed word is likely to make them rather cynical; but another important reason is the fact that this paper was reputed to be the 'printers' paper'; it carried a larger section of printing advertisements than any other newspaper, and compositors would turn to this section when they thought about changing their jobs, or to see what rates of pay were being offered in other firms. The survey took place before the demise of the *News Chronicle*. Informal information suggests that ex-*Chronicle* readers are taking the *Herald* rather than the *Mail*.

It is the more popular papers that suffer from the large concentration on one newspaper. The frequency of reading the *Mirror* and the *Sketch* is much more similar to the higher white collar groups and the percentage who read the *Express* and the *Mail* is lower than any social group. The *Herald* is read to the same extent as the lower white collar group, and the *Guardian* and *Telegraph* are read at a rate somewhere between that for this group and the rate for skilled workers.

Sunday newspaper reading is not distorted by any concentration on one newspaper; therefore it is easier to make comparisons with other social groups. The most popular newspapers are read either at a rate lower than all social groups (true for the *Graphic*, *Herald* and *Empire News*), or at a rate similar to that of the higher social group (true for the

Table 16 **Newspaper Reading**

Newspaper	Compositors	National Survey of Social Groups (weighted for Greater London)		All social groups	
		C1	C2	National	Greater London
		%	%	%	%
	% of 95				
Mornings					
Daily Mirror	23	44	61	41	52
Daily Sketch	4	20	27	15	22
Daily Herald	11	11	20	17	18
News Chronicle	52	20	19	14	20
Guardian	5	5	1	3	3
Daily Express	26	34	33	37	33
Daily Mail	5	17	13	18	13
Daily Telegraph	7	21	4.5	8	14
Times	0	13	2	3	7
None	5				
	% of 89				
Sundays					
Sunday Express	22	36	25	27	29
Sunday Times	13	14	6	7	11
News of the World	36	46	63	50	57
Pictorial	26	43	60	41	49
People	36	36	46	42	40
Dispatch	8	17	14	14	15
Reynold's News	11	4	4	4	4
Graphic	7	10	10	8	11
Observer	8	19	5	6	11
Empire News	0	6	7	9	6
None	11				

News of the World and the *Pictorial*). The *Sunday Times* and the *People* are read at a similar rate to the lower white collar group, and the *Observer* at a rate between this group and the skilled workers. Reading of the *Sunday Express* conforms more to the skilled worker pattern; the only unusual preference among compositors is for *Reynolds News* which is generally read at a similar rate of three or four per cent for all of the social groups, whereas 11 per cent of compositors read this paper.

The pattern of Sunday newspaper reading confirms the view that compositors' newspaper reading habits are unlike other skilled workers and are more similar to those of white collar groups.

Another aspect of way of life in which social differences are displayed is in religious activity. Adequate comparative material is difficult to obtain, but it would appear that the compositor is not typical of the working class in this respect. Religious participation among compositors seems to be rather high: 19 per cent were practising Christians of various denominations, and 16 per cent of compositors attended church regularly or were active in their denomination. Studies of religious activity indicate that about nine per cent of the working class attend church at least once a week.[6] The amount of religious activity among compositors is especially high if sex differences are considered; for the rate of nine per cent for the working class includes both men and women, and it has been shown that women attend church about 50 per cent more frequently than men. The compositors' rate of religious activity is in fact similar to that of non-manual groups; for even without allowing for the sex difference it is nearer to the 22 per cent for the upper middle class in the *News Chronicle* survey, a similar percentage for the middle class as given in the Cauter and Downham study.

This level of religious activity among compositors may be claimed to be a further expression of their way of life; of their 'respectability' and also, possibly, of their aspirations.

Thus though there is a substantial group of compositors who still live what would be regarded as a working class way of life, the evidence suggests that middle class patterns of living are more frequent in this occupation than among other skilled workers.

Class affiliation

We have established that the compositor's way of life, as revealed by his level of living and his aspirations, shows some tendency towards a pattern of life that is generally associated with the non-manual worker. This process may lead to 'embourgeoisement' in the sense that not only is the middle class way of life adopted but that this brings with it a decline in working class identification. For it is argued that the adoption of middle class levels and aspirations is also a process of individualization: of concern with individual position and advancement rather than with the condition of the group. With the prosperity of the 1950s there had been a widespread view that economic progress depends more on individual effort than collective provision;[7] this would tend to weaken class feeling.

If such a weakening has been taking place, one would expect it to be most evident in those working class groups which have a strong tendency towards a middle class pattern. Is the adoption of a more middle class way of life leading to a weakening of working class consciousness among compositors?

Feelings about class are difficult to measure for class is not a discrete phenomenon, but an attempt may be made to indicate the extent of class feeling among compositors compared with other skilled workers at the present day. A distinction must be made between class affiliation and class consciousness. The former phrase is used in this survey to denote readiness to classify oneself in a certain class; the latter phrase denotes a certain cluster of attitudes towards class which reveals the strength of class feeling.

Class affiliation was ascertained by two questions. First the respondent was asked an open-ended question: 'To which social class do you feel you most belong?'; then he was asked to choose between middle class and working class as the class to which he felt he most belonged. The first question gave the opportunity to see how the compositor spontaneously felt about his position in the class structure; the second question would show the compositor's class affiliation when he was pressed into making a decision between the two classes.

It will be seen that a substantial proportion of compositors, 40 per cent, identified themselves as 'middle class' on the first question. What was meant by middle class varied considerably though this does not necessarily imply that they were confused about the class structure. To some, the majority of people today are 'middle class'. As one man put it: 'There are only two main classes now; the middle class, which contains 60 to 70 per cent, and the upper class; there is only a very small lower class, containing five per cent of the population'. The family played an important part in class affiliation: one referred to the fact that his father was a schoolteacher, so that he must class himself 'above the upper working class'; another also justified his self-assessment as middle class by the occupation of his father, a clerk, stating that he was 'brought up in a white

Spontaneous Class Assessment

	%
Middle class	34
Lower middle class	6
Upper working class	7
Working class	48
None	5
	100

collar atmosphere'. Those who were active in certain local organizations tended to rate themselves as middle class. There was, for example, a district Scoutmaster, who first tried to be classless: 'I meet them at the top and bottom: entertain van boys and solicitors and doctors' – the words he chose are rather significant and in the closed question he identified himself with the middle class.

Over half the compositors, 55 per cent, placed themselves, on the open ended question, somewhere in the working class. Rather surprisingly only a small number of those who placed themselves in the working class qualified this by specifying 'upper' working class. One wondered, therefore, what the compositor meant when he associated himself with the 'working class'. Did he have in mind the skilled worker, or does the identification imply a conscious preference to place himself with all manual workers rather than with non-manual workers? To suggest that there are definite reference groups of these kinds may imply an awareness of class that is too specific. Probably the knowledge of being a manual worker is important, but it is likely that particularly effective in this identification is the emotional appeal of being 'working class'. It is this kind of generalized identity that is meant when reference to working class is made, for example in the union journal. It is, therefore, hardly unexpected that different notions of what is meant by 'working class' are held.

The comments made by the respondents as they decided which class they chose to identify with, revealed the different motivation for so placing themselves; there was no one generally agreed reason. Economic motivations were frequent: 'Have to earn my living' was one comment; 'Can't be anything else can I?' was another. After stating that 'I like to be on the same level with everybody', one compositor chose working class because he felt that it was 'more honourable to say this'. This particular comment suggested that he was deferring to the class identification expected by the occupational group. Yet many who chose to be placed in the working class are obviously ambivalent. One man mentioned that he mixed in high circles when he was young because his uncle was a mayor: 'I got on well with everyone and wasn't looked down on', he said, 'whereas with the working class you get more "green eye" and they try to pull you down'. Another said 'I'm not a snob, but I don't like the crude, swearing working class.' From such observations one receives the impression that even among those compositors who identify with the working class, many feel themselves to be a shade superior; they bear out the popular view of the compositor as being among the higher ranks of the working class, socially as well as financially – a member of the labour aristocracy.

The available data to compare this free subjective class assessment of compositors with that of skilled workers in general is not really adequate. The 40 per cent of compositors who regarded themselves as somewhere in the middle class appears rather high if it is compared, for example, with the survey in Hertford and Greenwich,[8] which gives 30 per cent of skilled workers placing themselves in the middle classes. The Lintas market research survey gives 31 per cent. But it is important to note that the first study took place nearly ten years before the compositors were interviewed, a decade of important changes in material prosperity likely to increase the number who regarded themselves as middle class. The second survey, though nearer in time, includes unskilled as well as skilled workers. It is possible that the spontaneous self-assessment of compositors is not very much unlike that of other skilled workers today.

A rather different picture emerges when the compositors chose between two specific classes. One wondered what would happen when many who felt borderline in the class structure had to decide between two classes: would those who felt themselves to be around the lower middle class or upper working class sections choose upwards to the middle class or decide that they really felt nearer the working class?

When pressed to choose, a surprisingly large majority, 77 per cent, decided that their affiliation lay with the working class, and only 19 per cent reaffirmed that they were middle class. Considering the relatively high material position of the compositor, it is rather remarkable that such a small proportion should feel very strongly middle class. Certainly this degree of association with the middle class is lower than among skilled workers generally. A survey, carried out at about the same time as that of the compositors, asked skilled workers to choose their social status from a list. The results, modified to make them comparable with the closed

questions asked of the compositors,[9] give the extent of middle class affiliation among skilled workers as nearly three times that of compositors:
43 per cent as against 15 per cent; and 53 per cent placed themselves in
the working class. Thus it is clear that despite their material prosperity
and aspirations, there is still a considerable amount of feeling among
compositors of belonging to the working class; though the fact that 40
per cent initially located themselves within the middle classes indicates
that for a number of compositors class affiliation is not very specific at a
conscious level.

So far we have been discussing class affiliation. This does not tell
us very much about the strength of class feeling. Class affiliation could
be little more than a question of terminology: it may mean merely that
'manual worker' or 'skilled worker' is equated with 'working class'. In
order to ascertain the extent of class consciousness among compositors,
questions were asked which reveal class attitudes. Each respondent was
asked to say whether he agreed with, disagreed with, or had no opinion
on the following three statements:

1. The upper classes in Britain have always tried to keep
   the working classes from getting their fair share.
2. The men who own the big businesses have too much
   power in this country.
3. The trade unions have too much power in this country.

Similar questions had been asked in another survey[10] that had taken
place shortly before the compositors were interviewed, so that a comparison could be made with other skilled workers.

It will be seen from Table 17 that despite the crudeness of the questions there were strong negative or positive responses. Only one compositor felt that he couldn't express an opinion on all of the statements
presented, and there was a lower rate of no opinion than was true for
skilled workers in general.

About half the compositors interviewed felt that the upper classes
deprive the working classes of their due, a similar proportion as for other
skilled workers. But on this question the wording was not the same in the
two samples. It is likely that even more compositors would have agreed
with the statement in the form in which it was submitted to the working
class sample. Substantial differences in attitude are revealed for the next
two questions. 70 per cent of the compositors felt that big businessmen
have too much power, compared with 55 per cent for all skilled workers. An even wider difference was shown on the question of the power

Table 17 **Class Consciousness**

Question		Compositors	Skilled workers
		%	%
1	Agree	49	48
	Disagree	47	45
	No opinion	4	7
2	Agree	70	55
	Disagree	29	37
	No opinion	1	8
3	Agree	39	57
	Disagree	60	33
	No opinion	1	10

of trade unions. This sympathy towards trade unions no doubt partly reflects the degree of unionization among compositors and the high regard in which the compositors' union is held. Thus it would seem that class consciousness is stronger among compositors than it is for skilled workers in general.

The degree of class identification should not be exaggerated. Class attitudes among compositors are not highly structured: several who assess themselves as middle class have working class attitudes on class and vice versa. But there is some correlation between self-assessment and class consciousness as indicated by these attitudes. Among the 40 who assessed themselves as middle class, 35 per cent had working class attitudes compared with 54 per cent of those who assessed themselves as working class. Conversely, 40 per cent of those self-assessed as middle class had what may be regarded as 'reactionary' class attitudes, whereas these were held by only 19 per cent of those self-assessed as working class. One feature revealed in the analysis may be important if the feeling of belonging to the middle class increases within the working class. It is that those who place themselves in the middle class tend to be more hostile to the power of the trade unions. Such hostility was found to exist among 29 per cent of those who placed themselves in the working class, among 45 per cent of those who considered themselves middle class, and among 53 per cent of those who were strongly middle class, i.e. assessed themselves that way on both the open and closed questions on class affiliation.

The fact that nearly half the compositors in the sample (46 per cent) have a strong degree of class consciousness reinforces the previous findings: that despite their tendency towards a middle class way of life, compositors retain, to a considerable extent, a fairly strong working class identification.

Political affiliation

We now need to consider the voting behaviour of compositors, for the light it may throw upon the relationship between prosperity and political affiliation.

Before doing this it is pertinent to refer to the expected political behaviour among compositors. The references to politics in the *LTJ* give the impression that a majority of members support the Labour Party; indeed, that they are expected to support the Labour Party is confirmed by the suggestion that Conservative Party supporters were reticent about their allegiance. A quotation from a letter typifies the attitude: 'Yes, we have Conservatives in our midst, although they haven't the guts to identify themselves (except for one or two) at the quarterly meetings of the Society. Generally, they are to be found among the few who never knew what it was like to stand in the queues at Poppins Court, but always had a regular pay packet – and are afraid they might have to help their less fortunate workers in the world'.[11] Poppins Court was the lane behind the Society's offices, where unemployment pay was collected: the implication being that those who experienced unemployment were more likely to vote Labour. In fact, analysis of those who had been unemployed between the wars did not reveal any greater tendency to vote Labour, or to identify themselves with the working class more strongly than did compositors in general.

Though there were often leaders on political topics in the *LTJ*, comments by readers were rather infrequent. Occasionally there would be a spate of letters on whether or not the journal should include political comments, and discussion tended to centre on the extent to which trade unions should be politically active. Invariably at the time of a general election a leader would appear urging members to vote Labour, and rarely would opposition be expressed to this view.

However, views in a union journal, though revealing the kind of political behaviour expected, is not sufficient evidence of actual political affili-

Table 18 **Contributions to the Political Fund**

Year	Journeymen at trade plus out of trade members %	All trade unions[12] %
1946	66	–
1947	86	–
1948	97	90
1949	87	90
1951	84	88
1954	79	88

ation. The traditional association between trade union membership and political affiliation has never been coterminous; in the 1950s, with the Labour Party suffering a loss in popularity, it is likely that while the doctrine that trade unionists vote Labour is apparently accepted, there were union members who privately voted Conservative.

Before showing the actual voting behaviour of compositors as revealed by the sample, it is worth looking at the degree of support for the Labour Party which would be suggested from the number shown in Table 18 who contributed to the political fund of the union. Figures for compositors can only be given up to 1954; after that year amalgamation with the machine managers took place and only combined figures are given in the union's reports. For the post-war years, unlike the pre-war period, it is possible to make an estimate of the extent to which working members of the union contributed to the political fund. Enquiries from the union elicited the information that among superannuated members about one in three continue to pay the political levy, members who were working out of the trade tend to continue paying the levy if they do so before leaving the trade, and members working outside London tended not to pay the levy because they would pay it to the appropriate union in the provinces. Thus it was possible to give a fairly reliable estimate of the percentage of working members who contribute to the political fund.

In 1946 the Trade Union Act changed the procedure of agreement to pay the political levy from 'contracting in' to 'contracting out'. The particularly low percentage of that year compared with before the war was

Table 19 **Political Behaviour (1959 General Election)**

	Compositors	Skilled working class	Post election Gallup poll for skilled working class equivalent
	%	%	%
Conservative	14	29	34
Labour	68[a]	48	46
Liberal	14	–	5
Liberal and don't know	–	23	–
Did not vote	4	Not indicated	15
	100	100	100

a. Includes one communist.

probably due to the war which interrupted the continuity of payments. A rapid increase to 1948 brought the percentage of contributions to the remarkably high figure of 97 per cent. From then on selected years show the steady decline in support for the Labour Party, until in 1954 the figure had dropped to 79 per cent. It is likely that since that date there has been some further decline.

In comparing the pattern of contribution with that of other trade unions a prominent feature is the way in which the figures for the compositors' union has changed, whilst the overall percentage for all trade unions remains fairly stable. Considering the extent of support for the Conservative Party among the working class this stable high level of contributors is unlikely to reflect real support for the Labour Party. An important reason for the pattern being different in the case of compositors is that, despite the pressure to support the Labour Party, the procedure for contracting out is simple and in most cases straightforward; also the compositor is likely to be familiar with his rights. In some unions it is alleged that anybody wishing to contract out finds it extremely difficult to obtain the appropriate form: unless a man is sufficiently determined to make innumerable requests and possibly write several letters, he is likely to give up the attempt.

By looking at the actual support for the Labour Party as shown by the sample enquiry, we can see how far the index of political support indicated by contributions to the political fund is a reliable guide. This can be gauged by reference to Table 19.

The voting pattern of compositors reveals a very high degree of support for the Labour Party; the figure of 67 per cent is not very far below that suggested by the evidence of contributions to the political fund (allowing for some decline in contributions since 1954).

What is very surprising is the very small proportion of compositors, 14 per cent, who vote Conservative. One observer analysing the self-image of voters, has suggested that people who see themselves as intelligent and educated are more likely to vote for the Conservative Party. If this were true then one would expect that an occupation which has high status through its associations with literacy, and one whose members are conscious of being educated, would be likely to have a large number of Conservative voters; yet this occupation votes Conservative to a far less extent than do other skilled workers.

Compositors vote Labour at a much higher rate than do skilled workers in general; and this political identification with the Labour Party is not confined to voting: a fairly high proportion of the sample were individual members of the Labour Party; 12 were members, one was going to join and three had been members in the past.

Conversely, the Liberal vote is relatively high and it may be that those who cannot support Labour find it easier to withdraw from the expected voting pattern by voting for the Liberal Party, rather than for the party that would be directly counter to the ethos. There is some evidence to suggest that a number of compositors vote Liberal as a stage on the way to voting Conservative. A classic example was the compositor who as a young man was a member of the Left Book Club and voted Labour up to and including the 1945 General Election. By 1950 he was becoming disillusioned with the Labour Party and voted Liberal because of his concern with the dangers of State monopoly; he continued to vote Liberal until 1959 when (had he not been away on holiday) he would have voted Conservative as 'the only alternative to something I don't want'. There were a number of others who changed to voting Conservative after a period of voting Liberal.

This factor of change in political allegiance would suggest some conscious reappraisal. Yet a more permanent identification is also apparent. This is particularly seen in the considerable association that exists between voting behaviour and class of origin. It must be noted that in the following tables, though separate numbers are given for Conservative

Table 20 **Political Behaviour and Social Origin**

	Labour		Conservative	Liberal	Conservative & Liberal	Non-voters
	No.	%	No.	No.	%	No.
Non manual	18	32	9	5	52	2
Skilled	24	42	5	6	41	1
Unskilled or semi-skilled	25	26	0	2	7	1
	57	100	14	13	100	4
Father not alive	11		0	1		0

Table 21 **Political Behaviour and Ownership**

	Labour		Conservative	Liberal	Conservative & Liberal
	No.	% of 68	No.	No.	% of 28
Own house	41	60	10	8	64
Telephone	20	29	6	5	39
Car	15	22	4	4	29
Television	61	90	13	13	93
No. of voters	68		14	14	

and Liberal voters, a combined percentage only is given because of the small numbers involved. Justification for this is given above where it is suggested that Liberal supporters among compositors tend to be right-wing and would be nearer the Conservative than the Labour Party.

Table 20 shows that over half (52 per cent) of those who voted Liberal or Conservative had non-manual social origins, whereas only 32 per cent of Labour voters originated in these groups.

We now need to consider whether material prosperity has any influence on voting behaviour. In Table 21 the percentage comparison is still made between Labour voters with the Conservative and Liberal votes combined; the actual numbers in the latter two groups of voters show that there is very little difference between them.

In each case Conservatives and Liberals together have a higher rate of ownership than do Labour supporters. But this difference is small: the largest gap between the two groups is only ten per cent for telephone possession. For the other items the difference is not significant. Especially revealing is that the possession of one's own house does not appear to be related to voting behaviour: 60 per cent of Labour voters had their own house compared with 64 per cent of Conservative and Liberal voters. It would seem that for compositors at any rate relative prosperity has not, as yet, had a profound effect on voting.

Conclusion

Looking at the relatively high earnings, high social status, and origins of the compositor, one would expect that this kind of upper working class occupation is one where the members would be less willing to identify with the working class and support the Labour Party. Yet from the evidence submitted this is clearly not the case. From the comparative data that is available it would appear that compositors more readily associate themselves with the working class than do skilled workers in general; also, in their political allegiance, compositors are by no means typical of skilled workers, nor indeed of the working class as a whole, for the Labour Party continues to attract a very high proportion of votes among them, and of the non-Labour voters, Conservative and Liberal supporters are equally distributed. The existence of such affiliations in a group which has a relatively high level of living and considerable aspirations requires explanation.

This thesis suggests that the forces that maintain the compositors' allegiance to the working class and to the Labour Party are to be found in the pressures of the occupation itself. The occupational community helps to maintain a cluster of attitudes that can be called an occupational ethos: the good compositor is a good trade unionist, a member of the working class, and a supporter of the Labour Party. The ethos is not peculiar to compositors, yet, though by no means all compositors are receptive to it, its acceptance appears to be more widespread among compositors than it is among skilled workers as a whole. This relationship, between the occupational community on the one hand, and class and voting affiliations on the other, is discussed in the next chapter.

Notes

1 Readers with a statistical bent might challenge the absence of tests of significance. But the size and nature of the cells generated by a sample of this size make the use of such tests of dubious value. Further, this is an exploratory study making such tests less relevant. A further valuable discussion of these issues can be found in Lipset, Trow and Coleman, *Union Democracy*, p. 427–32, an interesting study of the International Typographical Union in the USA.

2 Abrams, 'Who owns household goods?', *Financial Times*, 9 December 1959, p. 10, cols 3–6.

3 Comparison may also be made with type of residence lived in for compositors and skilled workers:

	Compositors	Skilled workers
Own house	62	26
Privately rented	16	21
Council rented	20	51
Other	2	2

Source: Lintas.

4 Martin, 'Inquiry into Parents' Preferences in Secondary Education', p. 163; see also Floud, *Social Class and Educational Opportunity*.

5 This average family size is similar to that of non-manual workers. Assuming that most compositors above 40 years of age would have had at least 15 years of marriage, comparison can be made with the Family Census data for years of marriage 1915 and 1930. The non-manual group had an average family size of 1.61 children for 1930 (Table E22), rising to 2.12 for 1915 (Table E7); while the family size for the manual group was 2.19 children for 1930 (Table F22), rising to 2.90 for 1915 (Table F7) (Royal Commission on Population, *Trend and Pattern of Fertility in Great Britain*, pt 2, p. 103, 98, 115, 110 respectively).

6 Cauter and Downham, *Communication of Ideas*, p. 52; a survey in the *News Chronicle* of 16 April 1957, ('Are we still Christians?', p. 4, cols 3–7 at col. 5) gives a similar figure.

7 Crosland, *Can Labour Win?*, p. 12.

8 Martin, 'Some Subjective Aspects of Social Stratification'. This is based on a survey made in the two areas in September–October 1950.

9 The figures are derived from the article 'Why Labour has Lost Elections' by Mark Abrams in *Socialist Commentary*, May 1960, p. 6 and 8; see also his *Must Labour Lose?*, p. 14–18.

10 Kindly supplied by Allan Silver whose research work was published as *Angels in Marble: working-class conservatives in urban England*, by Robert T. McKenzie and Allan Silver.

11 *LTJ*, May 1950, p. 7.

12 Gregory, '"Contract out" Percentage Lower: Political Levy', *Daily Telegraph*, 10 November 1959, p. 20, col. 5.

VII

The Occupational Community

An occupation is more than just the work involved: occupations have various social aspects which give rise to numerous perceptions and social relationships. A number of features lend social importance to an occupation: the abilities and educational requirements that are necessary for the job are obvious aspects and help to determine the prestige accorded to the occupation; the nature of the work will determine the kind of communication that is possible and whether the communication takes place through a hierarchy of levels or with one's peers; the quality of communication that is possible, whether it is restricted to the needs of a job or whether more general conversation can take place, also has its effect. Such factors may influence the kind of relationships possible and even the way of life of the members.

Of particular concern to this thesis is the kind of community that has developed amongst compositors and what makes such a community possible. Three particular aspects of the occupation need to be considered: the nature of the work that encourages the occupational community; the kind of occupational community that exists; and the kind of influence that this has on the compositor.

Basis for the occupational community

The work situation is important in facilitating an occupational community. Usually each compositor has his own frame at which he does most of the operations necessary for the job: setting the type where necessary, correcting galleys, and making up the pages or advertisements (see Appendix A). The 'frame' can be regarded as the compositor's home: here he keeps his tools, any reference books and other private possessions; here he usually drinks his tea at morning and afternoon breaks; this is where he arrives in the mornings and leaves at night (one of his last actions being to switch off the individual light that often hangs over his frame). A compositor feels possessive about his frame and protests against others entering it without his acquiescence ('What are you doing in *my* frame?' is often asked in mock hostility of a trespasser). The frame is likely to have other frames adjoining it at the side and at the rear, occu-pied by other compositors who are thus in familiar contact. A man work-ing at the frame alongside a compositor is known as his 'side page', and the phrase 'my side page', or 'side 'un', often carries with it a note of affec-tion (though it is not unknown for it to contain the bite of sarcasm similar to that in the term 'my mate' applied to a person with whom one has a long-standing feud!).

The nature of the work itself allows for fairly easy contact between the men. This is true even where a job is being done entirely by one man; it is even more true when the job is large enough to have a number of men engaged on it. A large job which is done regularly (for example, a periodi-cal) will usually have several men permanently engaged on it, known as a 'companionship', or more generally as 'a 'ship'; this tends to give rise to a special sense of group feeling, and contact between the men on that 'ship' will often be more than is functionally necessary for the job.

Some men prefer working quietly, but the more garrulous have ample opportunities to express themselves. Although most of the work demands concentration, there are periods or kinds of operations that do not require complete absorption, and thus a man can communicate and express him-self not infrequently. During a day in the composing room expression can range widely from a general chat, discussion about the football game of the previous Saturday, domestic complaints or problems, political controversy, whistling and even singing. Though there are exceptions to this, many composing room overseers would not inhibit such forms of expression so long as the work was not hindered. The work itself rarely flows evenly and in many shops there are slack moments, for example when a job on which several men have been engaged has been sent to the machine room for printing. Opportunities occur to lighten the day by playing jokes and particular enjoyment is derived by encouraging people to lose their equanimity: 'getting him out' or 'having him on' as it is called. This kind of activity serves a valuable function of 'levelling' by prevent-ing men from showing arrogance, conceit, or straying too far from the accepted code of behaviour or even way of life – to do so will invite com-ment and sarcasm sufficiently friendly to be heeded.

There is no intention of presenting a picture of the work life of the compositor which exaggerates the time and attention given to relaxation. It is true that the work norm must not be raised too high by individuals and comment is likely to be invited by the person who works intensively the whole time, with 'his skates on'. Yet the man who continually chat-ters and avoids 'pulling out' is also likely to be scorned. This possibility is less likely, because of the docket system that operates in most firms: in order to cost a job more precisely, a daily docket is made of the previous day's work so that the time spent on a particular job can be ascertained. The compositor is usually anxious to present a fairly full docket, though whether this is possible is partly determined by the character of the job: some kinds of work will give a fair amount of 'fat', which means that more time can be put down to the job than was actually worked, whilst other kinds will produce a 'tight docket'. What is important here is that the length of time that a job takes is difficult to measure precisely: the considerable number of non-mechanized processes in composing makes it difficult to construct precise output norms; therefore the compositor can decide, within limits, whether he needs to 'pull out' or if he is able to slacken his pace of work.

A sense of community is also fostered by the fact that the help of other compositors is often required. Though there is not the kind of intense solidarity that is developed by a working group faced with a common danger, compositors are often dependent on friendly relations in order to prevent frustration or wasted time. There are many occasions when this help may be sought: in deciphering badly written manuscripts; in locating a rarely used fount of type; in identifying a piece of type that requires changing, or where the customer has attached an example of the typeface he desires but cannot name. In firms where spacing materials are in short supply a fellow craftsman may have a little hoard that he has hidden somewhere (a 'slum') from which he may be willing to supply a friend; the loan of a composing stick of a certain size might be useful; or help may be required in lifting a forme of type on or off the stone, or to the lift for transportation to the machine room. Much of this reliance on the help of others may be declining: typewritten copy is replacing manuscript; super-casting machines are eliminating the shortage of materials; layout artists are deciding the typeface to be used and thereby reducing the need for advice from colleagues; the use of trolleys reduces the need for aid in transporting formes. Yet contingencies where the aid of others is necessary still occur. Such need for help and the possibility for considerable communication gives the kind of conditions in which a sense of community is encouraged. Another factor is also relevant: the compositor enjoys considerable prestige within the firm; this helps to isolate him from other departments and thereby tends to reinforce the existence of a separate occupational community.

The Chapel organization

'Every Printing-house is by custom of Time out of mind, called a Chappel', so wrote Moxon in the seventeenth century. The Chapel has long attracted the attention of writers, and it is necessary here only to state briefly the historical development and some of the main contemporary functions of the body. The Chapel is the formalized expression of the occupational community: its traditional function was the laying down of rules for the customary practices of working within the firm, and it inevitably developed procedures for regulating the relations between the men, especially in respect of disputes. We have seen that the Chapel later became a basis for union organization: firstly, as the means of organizing the union (Chapels would establish contact with each other and send delegates to meetings); then, later, the Chapel became the means of delivering union policy and this aspect, rather than the role of the Chapel in formulating union policy, became emphasized.

Chapel organization tends to be similar in most firms except those that are very small. A Chapel committee is elected through which Chapel policy is carried out. This is composed of the FoC (the Chapel's representative and intermediary with the union; he often also acts as chairman); chairman, where the FoC does not also occupy this role; Chapel clerk, who acts as treasurer and writer of minutes; and one or more committee men, according to the size of the Chapel. There is also an auditor, but usually he is not a member of the committee. Chapels usually have their own set of rules, regular meetings and regular procedures for their activities. But the extent to which the Chapel is well organized is strongly related to size: the organization is much more structured in larger firms. All the compositors in a Chapel have to pay Chapel subscriptions in addition to those for the union. Chapels vary in the amount they impose, usually between 2d and 6d a week: this covers Chapel expenses and the small 'salaries' paid to Chapel officers.

The Chapel as a community

Writers on the Chapel have tended to consider the Chapel as an organization;[1] stressing its function as an intermediary with the union or with the management of the firm. But the Chapel can be defined in another way: as the men working at a particular place. Considered in the second way the Chapel has a community aspect that is not included in the Chapel as an organized association.[2] Indeed, occasionally a firm is to be found that does not have an organized Chapel, for example in some non-union firms, but still has, to some extent, an occupational community.

To avoid confusion it is desirable to reserve the use of the word 'Chapel' for the formal organization, and use the phrase 'occupational community' for the activities of the Chapel members which are outside the activities of the Chapel as a part of the union organization.

One important aspect of the Chapel as a community is the emphasis on equality. Within the Chapel any status differentials which result from differences of type of work or responsibility are reduced and all members are equal; thus all are subject to equal criticism, at least theoretically, in practice this is probably more true of the larger Chapels. There may be difficulty in expressing criticism: individuals may prefer not to arouse the possible hostility of another Chapel member who because of special responsibility may be able to exploit his resentment. In larger Chapels greater vigilance can be kept on this kind of situation and the Chapel is strong enough to make its pressure effective. A myth of equality of skill is, in consequence, also encouraged: all members of each group, hand compositors, Lino operators, Mono operators and proof-readers, are regarded as being equally capable of similar work. This idea of equality is given expression by the enforcement in many Chapels of equal opportunity for overtime.

This aspect of equality in the Chapel can be highly beneficial. Personal animosity and possibly misunderstandings tend to be uncovered at these meetings, and members are not averse to making charges, which then may be clarified, justified, or denied by the accused. The Chapel then decides what action should be taken. The procedure, where used, acts as a valuable safety valve in getting rid of aggressions. Of course, the crystallizing of hostility in the form of actual complaints to a Chapel meeting might act as a means of making the hostility even more rigid, but experience suggests that the Chapel usually acts reasonably in these cases and tends to cool passions rather than inflame them.

To see the contemporary importance of the Chapel as an occupational community, it is necessary to look at the range of activities that it has, which reveal the richness of the community, and help to determine the extent to which this community is participated in.

Friendly societies

Most firms have compositors who collect for various friendly society organizations. Some of these organizations are restricted to the printing industry. Amongst these is the Printers' Pension Corporation (PPC), to which members have to be elected in order to receive a pension when

they retire, so that on retirement members advertise that they are applying for a pension and hope to obtain sufficient votes. There are also the
Sick Fund Union and various local auxiliaries of the PPC in different
parts of London; by belonging to these a member subscribes additional
funds into the Corporation, but also hopes to become more widely known
and thereby secure more votes when he retires. There are also printers'
organizations that provide convalescent homes: Caxton Home, Lloyds
Memorial Fund, and the Printers' Medical Aid which also gives various
forms of assistance to cover the cost of certain surgical appliances, specialist fees and has other benefits. The union itself, the LTS, has a separate
section, to which members may belong, which provides additional sickness benefit.

Friendly societies which are not peculiar to printing also have collectors in printing firms. These include the Hospital Savings Association,
and the Saturday Hospital Fund. Many firms also have collectors for various charities, e.g. the Manor House Hospital, spastics, the blind, tuberculosis victims, etc.

Collections for such organizations usually take place after the men
receive their pay packets on Fridays. These collections are nothing to do
with the Chapel as such: the collectors are ordinary Chapel members who
volunteer to be responsible for the task of collecting. The extent to which
firms have these activities varies. Few firms will have collectors for all
these organizations, but most firms will have some represented.

The extent to which compositors contribute to these organizations is
suggested by the sample. 58 per cent were members of at least one printing organization. This is likely to be an underestimate as some compositors pay into these funds so automatically that they may well have forgot-
ten to mention that they belonged.

The decision to join an organization is not simply a personal matter; it
reflects to some extent the pressure of the occupational community; and
it is suggested that the existence of these organizations in firms tends to
reflect or reinforce the existence of the occupational community. This
community is likely to be stronger in large firms where organization generally is more formalized. If this is so, one would expect membership of
organizations to be heavier in larger firms. This was in fact the case: 45
per cent of those in small firms (with fewer than 20 compositors) were
members of some printing organization, whereas 76 per cent of those in
very large firms (those with over 100 compositors) were members.

In addition to these outside organizations, a number of Chapels run
their own sick clubs to which members may belong. Seven of the 28
Chapels had their sick clubs. In addition four firms had sickness benefit

schemes to supplement the National Insurance benefits. Only two firms had pension schemes for their employees.

Pass rounds and outings

On certain occasions, it is necessary to pass round a list for voluntary contributions for a Chapel member. This happened in all but four firms, and these were the smallest with only five or fewer compositors working there; thus 94 per cent of compositors in the sample worked in Chapels which had 'pass rounds' on some occasion. Usually this was done either when a member married, if he were sick, or when he retired; in small firms, the list would often not be confined to the Chapel but would go round the whole firm. In 19 Chapels a list would be sent round when a member married; the sum collected was used to purchase a present or was given in cash. In one Chapel it was customary for the member getting married to 'push the boat out', that is buy drinks for the whole Chapel (which had over 30 members). 18 Chapels had a list that was passed round if a member was ill; the reason for the custom being less frequent in this case, when the need may be more immediate, is because many Chapels have a sick club. However, frequently a list is customary even where a sick club exists, and often there is a qualification that the list goes round only after the member has been away for a certain specified period. The sick list gives the members of the Chapel the opportunity to make a contribution during a possibly difficult period for a fellow member, a contribution more personal than the sick club provides: it would be very rare for a compositor to pass on such a list to his neighbour's frame without signing up to a contribution. Pass rounds for sickness were probably more frequent in the past when sickness meant absence of income and when there was less possibility of saving.

The most frequent occasion for a 'pass round' is when a member retires: this was customary in 22 firms. One firm had no pass round but the Chapel held a dinner, and invited Directors. Presentations are usually fairly formal (unless the member is especially easily embarrassed); a special 'Chapel' (Chapel meeting) is held, generally during the lunch break, and speeches are often made referring to the idiosyncrasies of the member or particular experiences during the period in which he has been a member of the Chapel. These occasions give a particular emphasis to the existence and continuity of the occupational community, and reinforce the feeling by the members of belonging to a group. After retirement, the member's link with the Chapel is frequently continued and retired members visit firms and go round chatting to the men; in one firm the Chapel sends a gift of £5 every Christmas to superannuated former members of the Chapel. Over 90 per cent of compositors worked in firms experiencing some form of recognition of retirement. If a Chapel member dies it is customary to send a wreath and a Chapel representative to the funeral.

Another activity of the occupational community is the periodic outing. This is a long-standing tradition in printing: Moxon in the seventeenth century described the printers' annual 'way-goose' and Charles Manby Smith in the nineteenth century describes a 'weigh-goose' held in the second week in September. The tradition is still fairly widespread,[3] though a number of firms indicated that they had held outings in the recent past but no longer did so; in one firm the decline in the number of men working there was blamed for the tradition fading out. Of the 28 firms in the sample, 18, embracing nearly 80 per cent of compositors, had some form of regular outing (in three of these the term 'wayzgoose' was still used). Very few of the outings were run exclusively by the composing room Chapel: they were organized by the firm, or by the firm's social club, with all the printing departments going on the outing; only five composing Chapels had an outing entirely on their own.

The form these outings takes varies: often they are large outings to the coast where the day is spent consuming large intakes of beer, and a formal meal is arranged where speeches are made; such outings may be 'stag affairs' or include wives and girlfriends (presents of flowers were given in one firm to the wives who attended). One firm had an institutionalized pattern each year of a trip to Brighton stopping at the same hotel for lunch on the way down and tea on the way back. It was a 'stag do' and in the afternoon a comic cricket match was played; it was not known whether the comic aspect of the game was originally intentional or whether the intake of liquid refreshments made it inevitable. Other outings take the form of a Chapel evening (a 'Chapel supper' it is often called) with dinner followed by a visit to the theatre, or a dinner and dance, or cabaret. On many of these occasions the craft element would be introduced by the printed menu being designed and set up by a member of the Chapel. In one firm the dinner was explicitly seen as having an integrating function, for the overseer was invited and in addition to the inevitable 'back slapping' there were serious criticisms about events that had taken place in the firm.

Bang outs

The 'bang out' is given when a compositor leaves the composing room in unusual circumstances. It consists of the creation of as loud a noise as possible by every member of the room and is maintained for several minutes. Any tools that come to hand are used to heighten the noise – a cacophony produced by the ring of metal knocking against stone or wood, banging of wooden mallets, and the shaking of large drawers filled with little wooden blocks called 'quoins' and used for locking the type into a metal 'chase'; these are shaken about. One large Chapel was visited when a bang out took place. It started as a fairly quiet rhythmic beat as the man about to leave prepared to go; gradually as the man passed through the room it mounted to a crescendo in which the rhythm disappeared; the banging lasted for seven to eight minutes. Some firms had bang outs when men retired – sometimes this was not a regular feature but only happened if the member was particularly well liked. In some Chapels bang outs are fairly frequent and take place whenever a member of the Chapel leaves off early from work. The practice was rarer in the very small firms: eight out of 17 firms with fewer than 20 compositors (seven of them employing less than ten compositors) and only one of the larger firms had no bang outs. In the last case the practice had been specifically banned by the overseer.

Other customs

In any community customs develop that reinforce the identity of that community. Amongst compositors, customs are frequently to be found in addition to those to which reference has already been made. The origin of these customs can partly be explained by the need to relieve the long hours of work, and the ability to do so when the processes of the work were so unmechanized. When leisure time was restricted, until the twentieth century, a certain degree of leisure was introduced at the place of work. But customs may also become institutionalized and widely known because of the existence of a community which possesses and wants to retain a sense of identity.

One important factor in the development of customs has been the existence of apprentices. The apprentice has greater opportunity to seek relief from continuous work, and his youth gives some explanation for any irresponsibility. It is not unexpected, therefore, that the most widespread customs centre around the apprentice.

Medium to large size firms tend to have various methods of initiation for new apprentices: sending them on false errands; blacking parts of their body, especially the genitals, with printing ink; making the youngest apprentice sing, standing or dancing, on the stone.

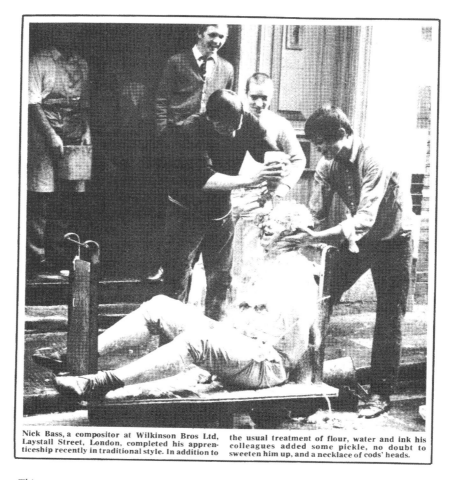

Nick Bass, a compositor at Wilkinson Bros Ltd, Laystall Street, London, completed his apprenticeship recently in traditional style. In addition to the usual treatment of flour, water and ink his colleagues added some pickle, no doubt to sweeten him up, and a necklace of cods' heads.

This apprentice pictured in 'Print', the NGA journal in 1969 was coming out of his time. Not all rituals were as gruesome as this.

    A most critical point in the compositor's life is when he passes from being an apprentice to being a journeyman; then he is free to move to other firms, receives more wages, is expected to have more responsibility, and becomes a full member of the Chapel. It is an event that is likely to produce a ritual; and the ritual reinforces community feeling. In 19 of the 28 firms regular bang outs take place whenever an apprentice 'comes out of his time' – that is, when he has completed his term of apprenticeship and receives his indentures, which are signed stating that his term has been satisfactorily completed. The bang out usually occurs when he is leaving the firm on the day when the apprenticeship is completed, and the apprentice is frequently given the afternoon off.

Several firms have additional ceremonies when the apprentice comes out of his time. Frequently the frame where the apprentice works is decorated the previous evening by fellow-apprentices. Often 'ordeals' have to be undergone; whilst these are rather less elaborate than we saw in Chapter I described by Gent in the eighteenth century, they tend to be joyful occasions. At one firm the apprentice is put into a truck and taken around the composing department, and attached to the truck is a slogan pertinent to the boy's personality. At another firm the apprentice is dressed up according to his past behaviour or interests, for example, in the attire of a particular sport, and is paraded throughout the firm. One firm had a more formal custom involving the Chapel itself: a gathering takes place around one of the stones at 12 noon when the works manager hands the apprentice his indentures, and he receives a money grant from the Chapel. After this he is dressed up, put into a trolley and taken around the firm and outside the building; on his travels various, non-harmful, objects are thrown at him. In 17 firms representing 73 per cent of the sample the apprentice, after receiving his indentures, buys drinks, often for the whole department. The management of one firm went so far to encourage the custom that they gave the apprentice £5 to help with this expenditure.

There are also customs which are participated in by the journeymen only. As we have already seen, overtime has always been a prominent feature in the life of the compositor, and whether overtime is available at any time is frequently a topic for discussion. Though overtime is generally desired, only a few men eagerly anticipate regular long periods: the man who is notorious for the frequency with which he is willing to work overtime is referred to as 'a gobbler'. As might be expected customs tend to develop around the practice. One Chapel has a crown that is presented to the 'King gobbler of the month', i.e. the journeyman who has done the largest amount of overtime during the previous month; and for the next month the man concerned is known as 'The King'. In another Chapel, until a strict rota system was introduced and organized by the Chapel, a large medal, known as the 'Gobbler's Medal' was presented at regular periods to the man with the highest total (in the same Chapel the overtime rota list is pinned up in the FoC's frame with a photograph of a large elephant's trunk hanging over the list and on it the printed words 'trunk out'!).

One Chapel that tended to maintain customs has a yearly tradition at Christmas Eve. This is known as the 'Pottiest Awards', when journeymen who have gained some notoriety for some peculiarity of personality or activity is voted in these terms by the whole Chapel; for example as the biggest tall storyteller, biggest gobbler, etc.

In some Chapels the sense of community is heightened by the obligation to share one's pleasures with other members. For example, anybody winning over a certain amount on gambling always buys tea and cakes for the Chapel. In another firm anyone returning from his summer's holiday always brought sticks of rock to work; these are broken up and placed on the stone, 'rock up' is cried and a scramble for the rock takes place.

A 'swear box' is sometimes organized either by the whole Chapel or by a group within it; whenever a person swears he puts in a predetermined amount of money (often 1d a word, but the value may vary according to the quality of the word used). The money collected may be put into Chapel funds or be periodically distributed amongst the participants; it used to be frequently a source of buying drinks.

Customs such as those described have an important function. They help to maintain a feeling of community and a sense of belonging to a group. It may well be that such feelings tend to give to the members some degree of identity. In this regard there is a tendency developing; as the work process becomes more rationalized, especially with the development of production control, many of these customs are seen as delaying production either directly or in producing a light-hearted atmosphere which is seen as possibly deleterious. It was mentioned in a number of firms that the overseer had stopped various customs; this could be an unfortunate trend, not only because traditional practices add colour to the working life, but also because such practices may help to produce a more satisfactory working atmosphere. It may be argued that in fostering the occupational community the management would be encouraging a basis for solidarity. This may be true, but such feelings of community may also encourage a sense of satisfaction with and responsibility towards the occupation itself.

Language of the community

Communities have a strong tendency to develop words and phrases peculiar to themselves. Such a language is likely to include various aspects of the work that is performed (a colloquial expression may be used instead of a technical one), and the social situations and relationships of the group.

A common language has existed for centuries amongst the compositors. Some of the terms used are not peculiar to compositors, nor are they confined to printers. For several of the words have a long history and have been absorbed from or transmitted to other occupations. Yet it would appear from discussions with apprentices from different printing departments that the compositors have the widest vocabulary, and when the terms are used they foster the awareness of belonging to a group where the meaning will be understood. The existence of a common language reflects the separateness of the occupational community.

How widely known is this language and is the usage declining? One indication of the extent to which the language is known and used today was ascertained during the survey of compositors. A list of words and phrases was compiled from personal experience of usage, reading, and as a result of discussions with apprentices. At each of the firms the FoC was asked whether he knew the meaning of the term and also whether it was used regularly or rarely in that Chapel. The list was not exhaustive and other phrases that had been overlooked or used occasionally were revealed during the enquiry. These additional phrases are included in Appendix C separately from those submitted to the FoCs.

On average, 62 per cent of the 42 words and phrases submitted are still used, the majority of them (over 80 per cent) regularly. The frequency with which each term is used in the firms sampled is shown in the Appendix. Infrequent use of words is the result of a number of factors: changing conditions, technical changes (though despite supercasting machines the word 'slum' was used surprisingly widely), and the fact that certain phrases may not have caught on. For example, Ralph and Miles' Boy were in use in the eighteenth century and the words reflected the attempt to impose the authority of the Chapel on its members; as the authority became more firmly accepted – especially when it was reinforced by the authority of the union – the terms probably fell into disuse. The use of clocking-in machines and the decline of piece work, where it was possible to make up for lost time by greater effort, have resulted in the loss of 'bridging' in the vocabulary. With the advent of composing machines, men no longer stand at the case for days or weeks setting type and consequently 'pica thumper', though still widely known, is not in regular use. Terms such as Hope Springs Eternal (HSE) and All Hope Abandoned (AHA) do not appear to have extended their use beyond a few firms – a possible factor here may be that overtime is now more regular and a man usually (though not always) knows in advance if he is to stay late on a given night.

We have already mentioned that there is a tendency for the occupational community to be stronger in the larger Chapels and this is confirmed by the distribution of language usage. Though the average usage

Table 22 **Language and Size of Chapel**

Chapel size	No. of firms	Total words used	Average words used			Both as a % of the 42 words submitted
			Regularly	Rarely	Both	
Small (under 10 compositors)	10	176	13	5	18	43
Medium (10–19)	7	196	22	6	28	66
Medium/large (20–60)	9	273	26	4	30	71
Large (over 100)	2	71	30	6	36	86

is 62 per cent of the 42 phrases submitted, firms of different size use the language to a varying extent. This is shown in Table 22.

A clear correlation exists between size of Chapel and the extent to which the terminology is used. In the largest Chapels 36 of the 42 words submitted were used, that is 86 per cent – twice as many as those used in the smallest Chapels. In the larger firms there are more opportunities for using the words because of the more varied circumstances. Also a larger number makes it more possible for the language to be kept alive by those who particularly enjoy using the vocabulary, and the greater likelihood of new men entering the firm makes possible a further injection of terms.

There are signs that the vocabulary may be used less frequently than hitherto. In addition to the reasons already given why specific words may be falling into disuse, it would appear that more words are known by older compositors than are actually in use. Whereas 62 per cent of the terms submitted were used, on average 80 per cent of the terms were known by the compositor answering the question. It may be argued that knowledge of the terms is likely to exceed usage; also the information was usually given by older men with experience of other firms and it may be that the younger men will in due course likewise accumulate a larger vocabulary than that used where they work. This may be so, but it was observed at several Chapels that the terminology was used less frequently than it used to be. Apart from technical changes which make terms obsolete, the fact that the men are being more subjected to a common mass culture outside the workplace also has its effect: there is a tendency, for example, for 'cap I' to replaced by 'big head', 'wrong fount' by 'beatnik' or 'a square', and 'n.f.' by 'cat'.

It is clear from all this evidence of specific organizations, customs and language that a strong occupational community exists. The basis for this community is to be found in the work situation of the compositor, and his status and isolation within the firm.

Notes

1 For example Sykes, 'Trade-union Workshop Organisation in the Printing Industry: the Chapel'.
2 Max Weber's concepts of community and association are useful, see Aron, *Main Currents of Sociological Thought*, v. 2, p. 278–9.
3 Just after World War II, Ellic Howe stated that the custom of the Wayzegoose (normally spelled wayzgoose) 'seems almost to have died out'. Howe, *London Compositor*, p. 26n.

VIII

The Influence of the Occupational Community

The question that now needs to be considered is whether this community has any influence over the behaviour of its members, and if so of what kind.

We have seen that certain kinds of behaviour are certainly influenced by the existence of the occupational community; those that are directly associated with the community itself: membership of friendly societies, participation in customs and outings, and the use of a certain vocabulary. But it is likely that the community exerts an influence that is wider than these activities. A strong community is able to impose on its members a code and moral values, and to influence their way of life. The community may not be able to change the personality of its members, but it will exert pressure on behaviour that is considered undesirable and will inhibit manifestations of such behaviour; actions that are regarded as extreme will come under criticism. Such criticism may not be formal, as in the case where the behaviour is regarded as undesirable for the working community; but if the criticism is widespread in the community it is likely to be heeded: dress, manner of speaking, even leisure activities and reading matter may be topics for comment. Unless the member does not mind too much the feeling that he is outside the group, he is likely to take cognizance of any disapproval that is shown. The working group also has a more positive function in promoting participation in topics of general interest: sport, music, television, home ownership (even gardening and 'do it yourself' jobs) become areas that are subjected to group pressure, albeit unconsciously, which thus encourage conformity.

There may be no uniform acceptance of these areas, and therefore the pressures to conform may not always be strong, or that they may be stronger in certain firms than in the occupation at large. But where the values are widely accepted by the occupation, where they are continually reaffirmed (for example, by the union itself), then there are strong pressures towards conformity. We have already suggested that a certain group of values does exist among compositors: it is that the good compositor is a strong trade unionist, belongs to the working class, and supports the Labour Party. This ethos, as it may be called, though not peculiar

Table 23 **Attitude to Trade Unions and Class Affiliation**

Opinion of statement that trade unions are too powerful	Working class			Middle class		No class
	No.	No.	% of 58	No.	% of 40	No.
Agree	36	17	29	19	48	0
Disagree	63	41	71	20	50	2
No opinion	1			1		0
	100	58		40		2

to this occupation, is strongly maintained among its members. The ethos certainly fits with the attitudes of the compositor which are displayed in their degree of working class identification, sympathy towards trade unions, and support for the Labour Party.

Considering their level of material prosperity, this ethos among compositors is unexpectedly high. This cannot be explained in terms of social origins, for the social origins of the compositor are relatively high and yet, despite an association between high origin and rejection of the ethos, the compositor exhibits a high degree of acceptance of the ethos.

In this chapter it is suggested that a further variable needs to be considered: the occupation itself. The hypothesis is proffered that a major factor in the persistence of these attitudes is the existence of the occupational community, which is a strong pressure for inducing conformity to the ethos among compositors.

The occupational community and ideology

Direct evidence of the influence of the occupational community in supporting the ethos is not easily available. Yet something of this influence can be inferred by trying to relate the different aspects of the ethos to what can be ascertained about the occupational community. Only two aspects of the ethos will be considered in detail: class identification and voting behaviour. But before doing so some evidence will be presented to indicate that the third part of the ethos, support for trade unionism, correlates with the other two.

Table 24 **Attitude to Trade Unions and Political Affiliation**

	Labour		Conservative	Liberal	Conservative & Liberal	Didn't vote
	No.	% of 68	No.	No.	% of 28	No.
Agree	16	24	9	9	64	2
Disagree	52	76	4	5	32	2
No opinion	0		1	0		0
	68		14	14		4

We have already seen that trade union sympathy, as revealed by the compositors' level of negative attitude to the statement that 'the trade unions have too much power in this county', is higher among compositors than it is among other skilled workers. It is, however, worth providing some additional evidence that trade union sympathy is part of the ethos, by showing that working class affiliation, Labour Party support and trade union sympathy tend to hang together.

In the following tables the attitude of compositors to the statement on the power of trade unions is related to their class and political affiliations.

Strong associations are shown between class and political attitudes and a sympathetic attitude towards trade unions which may be deduced from the replies to the statement. 71 per cent of those who considered themselves to be working class disagreed with the statement that the trade unions are too powerful, whereas 50 per cent of those who placed themselves in the middle classes disagreed. A stronger association was shown in relation to political support. Three-quarters of Labour voters (76 per cent) disagreed with the statement, compared with only one-third of the Conservative and Liberal voters (32 per cent). It is doubtless true that a distinction should be drawn between having a general sympathy towards trade unions and being a 'good trade unionist' – the latter being the operative part of the ethos. A man may be a strong supporter of his own union, yet be more critical of the trade union movement as a whole. He could thus conform to the trade union aspect of the ethos, while at the same time agreeing with the statement that trade unions have too much power. It can, however, be expected that the compositor who is a strong supporter of his union is more likely to have a more generalized sympathy towards the trade union movement.

The evidence submitted indicates that the three aspects of the ethos tend to hang together, and that the findings from the analysis to be presented in respect of class and political affiliations are, in general, likely to obtain for trade union sympathy also.

As already pointed out, it is not easy to obtain direct evidence of the occupational community in supporting the ethos. Some estimate of this influence, however, can be made by taking two approaches. One is to relate the class and political affiliations of individual compositors to their degree of participation in the community. The other is to relate the affiliations of individuals to the strength of the occupational community in the firms in which they work. Both these approaches will now be attempted.

Individual participation in the community

To make a more satisfactory assessment it would be necessary to know much more about the relationship between the individual compositor and the rest of the men: how far he feels a part of the community, his attitude to Chapel meetings, to what extent he takes part in its customs. This would have required a rather different study. Certain clues, however, can be used that may be some guide to the extent of participation. In the first place there is membership of friendly societies in the printing trade. It is true that membership of such societies is often dependent on whether easy facilities for making contributions exist in the firms; yet it may be expected that the compositor who identifies himself with the community is more likely to belong to one or more such societies than the compositor whose sense of belonging is less strong.

Another guide may be found in the choice of one's friends. The fact that a man chooses his friends either from his own occupation or from associated trades may also be indicative of his sense of belonging. Such a choice certainly shows the kind of influence that one's occupation can have, and it is likely that leisure time conversation will not ignore topics centring on work and therefore reinforce the impingement of the community on the individual member. Of course whether a friendship develops in one's occupation is affected by other factors: for example, the size of the firm worked at, opportunity for contacts, experience in a number of firms, and the age at which the friendship was made. But there is no clear reason why these in themselves should be related to differences in class and political affiliations. For similar reasons, it might be suggested that having members of one's family in the industry may also have some influence. Here the element of choice is absent, so that the effect may not be so strong, but it can be argued that interest in the occupation may be fostered or maintained by contact with members of one's family with similar work experience and interests.

Official activities in the Chapel are likely to reflect or promote a strong sense of belonging to the community. Men who accept office as FoC, clerk, or committee member are likely to be self-recruited to some extent from among those who are especially interested in the community; they are politically inclined in the sense that they enjoy, in varying degrees, this kind of organizational responsibility. If it is argued that such men are likely to be recruited from those who are already more interested in the Labour and working class movement, then this is further evidence of the existence of the ethos.

Participation and class affiliation

Earlier we saw the extent of this participation in general. Now the indices of participation will be related to the participant's own subjective assessment of his social class. As in Chapter VI, because of the numbers involved, assessment of social class is based on the open-ended question asking respondents to which social class they felt they most belonged.

The first point that is obvious from Table 25 is that there are no strong differences in participation between those who assess themselves in the different social classes. Yet the hypothesis that participation in the community is likely to be related to affiliation to the working class, is not entirely invalid. Though the size of the groups makes all the figures statistically suspect, it may be relevant that for most of the cases there is a consistently higher degree of participation for those who assess themselves as working class.

It may be noted that a very high proportion of the sample, namely one-third, have had some experience of Chapel office. Not all of these are eager for office: a number would have experience in small shops, where it may be difficult to persuade sufficient members to take office, and the more responsible compositor may feel it as his reluctant duty to agree to occupy a vacant position. Also in such small offices, the absence of a real community may make the official positions that do exist rather nominal and therefore lack those factors which are likely to produce a strong identification with the community. Some Chapels have a rota for certain positions.

Table 25 **Participation in Occupational Community and Class Affiliation**

	Middle class		Working class		No class
	No.	%	No.	%	No.
Membership of printing friendly societies					
None	19	48	22	38	1
One	11	27	16	28	1
Two or more	10	25	20	34	
Total	40		58		
Friends in printing	15	38	24	41	1
Held office in Chapel					
FoC	5	12.5	10	17	1
Other	7	17.5	8	14	
Family in printing	20	50	35	60	

Compositors who had one or more members of their family in printing (including both the immediate family and the wider kinship group), were to be found among 60 per cent of those who considered themselves to be working class and 50 per cent who placed themselves in the middle classes. The difference should, however, be regarded with caution: the fact of having a member of the family in the same industry may not involve contact with him. Also 29 per cent of the sample had fathers in the printing industry, of these a high proportion were from semi-skilled manual occupations, and it has been found that those from manual origins have a higher tendency to regard themselves as working class than middle class. Thus the difference in class feeling for those who have family in printing may be said to be partly a function of social origin. The choice of one's friends from the printing trade appears to bear no relation to class assessment.

Table 26 **Participation and Voting**

	Labour		Conservative	Liberal	Conservative & Liberal	Didn't vote
	No.	% of 68	No.	No.	% of 28	No.
Membership of printing friendly societies						
None	23	34	9	7	57	3
One	21	31	2	4	21.5	1
Two or more	24	35	3	3	21.5	
Total	68		14	14		4
Friends in printing	33	49	3	2	18	2
Held office in Chapel						
FoC	15	22	0	1	3.5	
Other	10	15	2	3	18	
Family in printing	38	56	9	8	61	2

Participation and political behaviour

We now need to see whether any relationship exists between participation in the community, as indicated by the clues already outlined, and voting for the Labour Party. Because of the small numbers involved, Conservative and Liberal voters are combined for the percentage figure, though the actual numbers in each case are shown in the table. Support for the different parties is based on actual voting in the 1959 General Election when the Conservatives were re-elected; one compositor voted Communist, he is included under Labour as being on the left.

The relationship between participation in the community and support for the Labour Party would appear to be much stronger than the relationship between participation and class affiliation. Only 34 per cent of Labour voters do not belong to any printing friendly society compared with 57 per cent of Conservative and Liberal voters. Conversely, 66 per cent of Labour voters belong to one or more societies compared with 43 per cent for the supporters of the other parties. Multiple membership is to be found among 35 per cent of Labour voters, but only 21.5 per cent of Liberals and Conservatives.

Choice of friends from the printing trade is also related to voting behaviour, though there was little difference in class affiliation. Among Labour voters 49 per cent had friends in printing, whereas this was true for only 18 per cent of Conservative and Liberal voters. If it is true that the fact that one has a friend in the trade is likely to reinforce one's identification with one's occupation and therefore with the ethos, it may be suggested that the high correlation with voting behaviour and absence of a relationship with class affiliation may be evidence that the ethos is breaking down in relation to working class affiliation, but is still maintained in its appeal to support the Labour Party. As was suggested earlier in relation to class affiliation the fact that one has a member of one's family in the industry does not appear to strengthen the ethos: 56 per cent of Labour voters had family in printing compared with 61 per cent of Conservative and Liberal voters.

Experience of holding Chapel office also appears to have a strong relationship with voting: 37 per cent of Labour voters having held office, compared with 21.5 per cent of Liberal and Conservative voters. Of particular significance is the experience of having been a FoC. Of the 16 men who at the time of the sample were or had been holders of this office, 15 voted Labour and the other one had voted Liberal – no Conservative voter had been a FoC. It is not suggested that the experience of this position makes compositors support Labour – though this is not entirely unlikely. Probably there is a strong self-recruitment factor. Labour supporters being more willing to take this office, and possibly also, that Chapel members are more likely to elect as Fathers of Chapels men who are known to be Labour supporters as more likely to represent their interests more vigorously. In either case, however, the fact that Labour supporters are more likely to want office or are more likely to get elected may be suggested as a reflection of that part of the ethos that exhorts compositors to vote Labour.

This evidence on the relationship between participation in the occupational community and voting behaviour is clear. There is a consistent tendency for Labour voters to participate in the community. In particular the association is strong for membership of printing friendly societies, friends in printing, and the experience of having held office in the Chapel. Thus there is much stronger evidence from these clues that participation in the community is related to voting behaviour rather than to class affiliation; this reinforces the contention that class affiliation is breaking down more quickly than voting patterns. The political ethos, that part of the ethos that has reference to voting, is being maintained, whereas the class ethos is less strong.

Influence of the occupational community in the firm

Another way of assessing the influence of the community on these affiliations is by trying to assess the strength of the occupational community within the firm and to try to relate this to the incidence of class and political affiliations among the men working in the firm. Justification for this procedure is twofold. In the first place it is difficult to assess the degree of an individual's participation in the community, and the items that have been analysed are only clues to the amount of participation or sense of belonging that an individual has; looking at the strength of the community in the firms can therefore be regarded as a supplementary way of ascertaining the influence of the community. In the second place the willingness of an individual to participate in the community may not be sufficient: the facilities for participation may be absent. Further, the communities within different firms vary considerably in strength, and this strength itself may be a powerful influence in the maintenance of the ethos. Where the community is strong in organization and in the maintenance of customs, where an occupational group, with a peculiar culture is therefore clearly discernible, it is likely that the values and ethos of the group will be more vigorously maintained.

A number of items can be enumerated which could be said to give some indication of the strength of the occupational community among compositors in the firms sampled. These items comprise the following: the extent to which the compositor's vocabulary is used; the organization of periodic outings; the institution of pass rounds; the use of bang outs; and the practice of any other customs. By relating the existence of these features to the class and political affiliations of the compositors who work in the firms it is hoped to show something of the influence of the community. These features of the community have already been discussed, but a few special points need to be noted here. In the first place the existence of these features within a firm does not necessarily mean that the compositor who was interviewed is personally involved in them. All that is being suggested is that the existence of these features is some indication of the strength of the community, and that it is likely that compositors working in such firms are likely to be affected. A factor that could not be taken into account was the length of service that a man had

Table 27 **Class Affiliation and the Occupational Community**

	Working class		Middle class		No class
	No.	% of 58	No.	% of 40	No.
Use of the vocabulary					
More than 30 terms	36	62	18	45	1
30 terms or fewer	22	38	22	55	1
Outings					
For the Chapel only	25	43	15	38	1
For the whole firm	14	24	11	27	
None	19	33	14	35	1
Bang outs					
Practised	40	82[a]	28	76[b]	
Not practised	9	18[a]	9	24[b]	

a. This is a percentage of 49 (excluding the banned firm).
b. This is a percentage of 37 (excluding the banned firm).

with the firm: for the longer the service, the longer the period in which he was subjected to the influence.

Secondly, it must be emphasized that this is not a random sample of firms based upon the degree of occupational community that exists in their composing department. Thus the information does not show the extent to which compositors in general are subjected to this influence: the sample may over or under represent the proportion of men in firms which have a strong community. We are concerned here with evidence of whether there appears to be any influence, not the size of the influence.

Thirdly, it was not possible to construct an index of strength of the occupational community. Only four firms containing a total of six men had none of the features of a strong community; conversely only three firms, containing 21 men, had all the features. It was impossible to give a weight to the respective importance that each of the features has for the occupational community; therefore, it is only possible to relate the class and political affiliations of individual compositors to the existence in their firm of each feature separately.

One feature of the occupational community had to be abandoned. Pass rounds were so frequent an institution that only six men come from

Table 28 **Political Behaviour and the Occupational Community**

	Labour		Conservative	Liberal	Conservative & Liberal	Didn't vote
	No.	% of 68	No.	No.	% of 28	No.
Use of the vocabulary						
More than 30 terms	41	60	6	6	43	2
30 terms or fewer	27	40	8	8	57	2
Outings						
For the Chapel only	30	44	4	5	32	2
For the firm only	16	24	4	3	25	2
None	22	32	6	6	43	0
Bang outs						
Practised	46	82[a]	9	10	70[b]	2
Not practised	10	18[a]	4	4	30[b]	1

a. This is a percentage of 56.
b. This is a percentage of 27.

Chapels where the institution was unknown, therefore the analysis was not worth making, for the proportions expressing class and political affiliations were bound to be similar to the whole sample. In addition a modification had to be introduced in respect of 'bang outs'. In one large firm, with a strong community in other respects, a ban on bang outs had been imposed by the management. To have included this firm among those which had no bang outs would have been an artificial estimate of the strength of its community. In order to avoid this source of bias, the figures, in the case of bang outs only, exclude this Chapel entirely.

It had to be decided at what point the use of the language of the community reflected the strength of the community. All the Chapels in the sample used a varying number of words in the vocabulary, regularly or rarely. A number was taken that would be high enough to reflect a wide usage, and also would include a sufficient number of men in those Chapels to permit some analysis in relation to class and political affiliation. An arbitrary division was made between those Chapels using 30 words or fewer, both regularly or rarely, and those using over 30 words; 45 men came from the former Chapels and 55 from the latter.

Table 27 shows that for each of these indices there is a consistent relationship between the strength of the occupational community and the existence of working class affiliations among its members.

Use of language shows the most important difference: 62 per cent of those who consider themselves working class were in Chapels where more than 30 words or expressions of the compositor's language were in use, compared with only 45 per cent of those 40 compositors who first placed themselves in the middle class. For outings and bang outs the differences in class affiliation are not significant, but they are in the expected direction; this is the case especially where the compositors have their own outing for then the separateness of the occupational community is likely to be stronger. Bang outs are very widely practised, even so a small difference can be seen in class affiliation.

Thus though the differences are very slight, except in the case of the use of the language of the community, the consistency of the relationship between these indices of the community strength and class affiliation may suggest some relationship between them.

On most of the items a stronger association was found between the strength of the community and voting behaviour than existed for class affiliation.

It will be seen that on language usage the percentage difference (17 per cent) was the same as in the case of class affiliation: 60 per cent of those who voted Labour were in firms where the language was more widely used, compared with 43 per cent who voted Conservative or Liberal. Firms where the compositors' Chapel had separate outings contained a higher proportion of Labour Party supporters, and notwithstanding the high degree to which bang outs are practised, a clear difference in political affiliation was still shown.

The evidence so far presented on the association between the strength of the occupational community and class and political affiliation is not conclusive. In the first place the indices that have been taken to show the occupational community are hypothetical, and they may be disputed. Secondly, the figures are not, in the main, statistically significant. Yet the consistency of the findings is suggestive and for certain items, especially the use made of the community's own vocabulary, the association is strong. The results also confirm the evidence already shown of the relationship between the individual's participation in the occupational community and his class and political affiliations.

The factor of size may be mentioned. Size brings the need to organize more formally in the larger Chapels: the organization tends to be stronger, meetings more regular, and procedure more rigid; in larger firms there is a greater consciousness of being separate from other departments. We have noted that the occupational community is stronger in the larger firms and would expect to find there a greater degree of working class affiliation and willingness to support the Labour Party. Though the number in the very large firms was very small (there were only 25 in the sample in Chapels of more than 100 compositors), the differences were fairly clear: 76 per cent identified themselves with the working class compared with 58 per cent in the sample as a whole; in these firms 88 per cent voted Labour compared with 68 per cent in the whole sample.

One final point needs to be made about the influence of the occupational community. So far we have been considering the direct relationship between the occupational community and class and political affiliation. In indicating the relationship between these affiliations and individual participation, the strength of the occupational community, and the size of the Chapel, we have been stressing the direct influence of the local occupational community within the firms. As the occupational community described so far is centred on the place of work, it should be asked whether this community is any more than a working community. Is there any sense of communal feeling outside the actual place of work? To answer this it is useful to distinguish the foregoing activities into those which are part of the working community and those which are part of the occupational community. The working community includes activities such as the Chapel sick club, pass rounds for members, periodical outings, and certain customs peculiar to the firm. The occupational community has activities that extend beyond the workplace: the various friendly societies, the customs that are widespread amongst compositors, the Chapel organization, and the common language. Such activities give a sense of belonging to an occupational group.

This community is reinforced by other factors. In London, the printing industry is still heavily localized in the central districts, it is thus fairly easy to meet fellow craftsmen in pubs and eating places, and to maintain contact with previous friends after changing jobs. From personal observation, there appears to be some not inconsiderable contact with previous workmates and men visit firms where they have worked. Contact is facilitated by the union's delegate meetings where old workmates may be seen, sometimes after a period of several years; these meetings themselves, and of course the union, tend to heighten the awareness of being part of an occupational group. There is also the *LTJ*, the organ of the LTS. In addition to technical articles and union affairs, a good deal of space is devoted to 'gossip' about members and Chapels; one compositor remarked that the first thing he turned to in the journal was the monthly list of union members who had died during the previous month 'to see whether any old acquaintance had passed on'; another compositor said that reading this list was the only reason for taking the journal. Thus the *Journal* helps to maintain the sense of awareness of belonging to a group wider than the immediate working group. The existence of the local advisories might be expected to add further to the sense of community.

Thus the occupational community should not be interpreted too narrowly. The occupational community extends beyond the workplace and influences can be exerted wider than the confines of the Chapel itself. It is possible for the occupational community in the Chapel to be weak, but the influence of the wider community may still be felt. Therefore it is possible to suggest a relationship between the occupational community and class and political affiliations without establishing that relationship directly within the Chapel in which the compositor works. However, that the immediate occupational community is able to exert an influence to some extent has now been established, and in particular this is true for the very large Chapels.

Is the influence breaking down?

The evidence presented in this chapter shows that there is some relationship between the community and the acceptance of the ethos. The association was not always strong, but in general the pattern was consistent: the stronger the participation in the community and the stronger the community itself, the higher the likelihood that compositors involved would identify themselves with the working class and vote for the Labour Party. The relationship was particularly true in respect of voting behaviour and would suggest that this part of the ethos is stronger than the appeal to class.

Whilst correlations do not necessarily show a causal relationship, the consistency of the evidence strongly suggests that the occupational community is a powerful influence in producing the high degree of working class affiliation and Labour Party support that is found among compositors. These affiliations are much higher among compositors than they are among other skilled workers and they fit into the ethos that is strongly current among compositors and which is maintained by the strength of the community feeling.

Is this pattern likely to continue in the future? Two aspects are important here. Firstly, the possibility that the occupational community may become less strong and less important to the compositor. Secondly, that the ethos itself may be subjected to change, or at least will weaken in its appeal. Nothing certain can be said about either of these factors, but attention can be drawn to a number of signs, some of which point in opposing directions.

There are signs that the occupational community is being subjected to strain. The two parts of the community within the firm need to be distinguished in order to discuss this: the community and the association that is manifested in the Chapel organization. In the Chapel organization, the assertion of union supremacy over the local unit may help to weaken the occupational community. In respect of the community itself it has been noted that as the work becomes more rationalized there is less opportunity for relaxation at work; customs that appear to be time-consuming are frowned on by the management, and indeed the men themselves may prefer not to be disturbed in their work if the process becomes more highly geared. Already in one large Chapel bang-outs no longer take place, and in a number of others it has been reported that customs, especially those centring on the apprentice, are discouraged.

The community may also be affected by external social changes. The development of the community was partly a response to the long hours, bad conditions and limited leisure time of an earlier period. Support for the community was found in the easy contact between compositors not only at the workplace but also outside it: men lived at no great distance from each other and often travelled to work together; frequent recourse was made to public houses where compositors would meet in groups and maintain contact even when they no longer worked together; such possibilities for contact were facilitated by the geographical concentration of the printing industry. Today, hours are much fewer, and there is less need for diversion at work in order to relieve the conditions of labour (though it may still be an important factor in maintaining or increasing satisfaction with one's work). With movement of place of residence to the suburbs and some loosening of the geographical concentration of the industry, contact between compositors is less easily maintained, and may be confined more to working hours. The stimulation of other needs and the rise of other activities, especially in the house and garden, have made the public house less attractive; the opportunity for other activities may weaken interest in the occupational community; even the compositor's language is having to struggle against the more popular phrases in an age of mass entertainment. Also, with the development of the National

Table 29 **Class Affiliation of Journeymen by Age**

	Number	Working class		Middle class		No class
		No.	%	No.	%	No.
Born before 1918	68	42	62	25	37	1
Born 1918 +	32	16	50	15	47	1

Health Service several compositors stated that they no longer contributed to certain friendly societies.

Some of these are signs for the very long-term future, and countervailing trends may be noted. First, union amalgamations may have the effect of reinforcing the local unit of the Chapel; this would be especially true if amalgamation produces a lack of contact between union officials and the rank and file, or at least the feeling by the men that the union is 'out of touch'. Such amalgamations might help to reduce the isolation of the compositors in the firm. Already, for example, since the amalgamation with the printing machine minders some joint social activities are taking place. Also, we have seen the importance of the size of the Chapel in both maintaining a strong community and in imposing the ethos. If the tendency towards larger units in the printing industry continues, then the increased Chapel size could well help to maintain the community.

Much of this is hypothetical, and because most of these factors are long-term trends, it must be noted that in the future, technological changes might alter the occupation very radically. In the long term, photo composition, for example, could change the basis of the occupation; its possible effects cannot be discussed here.

More pertinent is the possibility that the ethos itself will change or will be less attractive in its appeal. It is likely, of course, that the appeal to trade union sympathy will continue. But given the continuance of the present political and economic conditions, it is not unlikely that the class and political aspects of the ethos may prove less attractive. If this assumption were true then it would be expected that young people in the trade would be less receptive to the ethos; for these have only experienced the relative prosperity of the post-war years, and have been led to associate much of this prosperity with a Conservative government; it may also be expected that they have been less subjected to the ethos, which is more likely to have been apparent in the 1930s when Conservatism was more easily associated with depression. One would expect that the younger

Table 30 **Political Affiliation of Journeymen by Age**

	Labour		Conservative	Liberal	Conservative & Liberal	Didn't vote
	No.	%	No.	No.	%	No.
Born before 1918	43	63	13	9	32	3
Born 1918 +	25	78	1	5	19	1

journeymen would be identifying themselves with the middle class more frequently and supporting Labour less.

The sample was confined to journeymen over 30 years of age, and it might well be that greater changes have been taking place among those who are younger than this. Yet if the age group of approximately 30 to 40 is taken some of the signs of change should be revealed. The upper age limit might appear too high, but it is necessary to obtain a group large enough to permit some analysis. These men have experienced being journeymen in the post-war years only (the majority of those who finished or were due to complete their apprenticeship before the end of the war would have been called up into the Services). They would have known only the full employment of the post-war period, and have no doubt benefited from the prosperity of the 1950s. Do they show any difference in their class and political affiliations from their older fellow workers?

This rather limited evidence in Tables 29 and 30 is suggestive. Considering the numbers on which the sample is based there would seem to be some difference in class affiliation between the post-war journeymen and those who had some experience of being journeymen before the war. The difference is in keeping with the earlier findings that the appeal to working class affiliations has lost something of its strength and it would appear to have done so especially among the younger age group. 2 per cent of the older men felt themselves to be in the working class whereas 50 per cent of the younger men did so. But the appeal of the Labour Party does not seem to have diminished at all. Indeed, on the basis of these figures an increase in Labour support is shown: 78 per cent of the younger journeymen voted for the Labour Party in 1959, compared with 63 per cent of the older journeymen. Of the 19 per cent, compared with 32 per cent, who voted for the non-Labour political parties, only one voted for the Conservative Party.

There are a number of elements in this result which may not apply in the future. In the first place the origins of the two groups may have some effect. Many of the older group came into the trade in the period between the end of the First World War and the depression of the early 1930s. The trade was difficult to enter and the boys entering may have been of superior status; certainly as has already been shown the position of the compositors during that period led to some aloofness from the working class, and this may have encouraged a different voting pattern; in addition, the Labour Party in that period had yet to win major working class backing; the support of these older men for the Conservative and Liberal parties may reflect their already established voting pattern. Secondly, the post Second World War struggles for improvement in wages may have helped to identify the compositors with the Labour Party through associating the employers with the Conservative Party; though if this were a factor one might expect that it would have also encouraged more working class identification in this group; it may be, however, that the appeals to wage differentials may also have assisted ambivalence about such identification. A third element is that a very high proportion of these younger journeymen were employed in the very large firms. It has already been shown that these firms have a high degree of working class affiliation and Labour Party support. It cannot be ascertained whether all large firms tend to have a higher proportion of younger workers. However, this element reinforces the suggested potential influence of the occupational community.

It must be stressed that there are signs of change; that the ethos appears to be losing something of its appeal. We have already observed on several occasions that it appears that class affiliation is breaking down more rapidly than voting patterns. Possibly because class feeling is more vague it breaks down more rapidly with economic and social changes, whereas voting is more specific and habitual and is therefore more resistant to change: though there are some signs of weakening support for Labour, a number having shifted towards the Right since about 1950.

But the emphasis of this chapter has been that up to the present, at any rate, the occupational community has not broken down, its ethos still has appeal. It is suggested that this community influence has been one important factor in the high degree to which compositors display identification with the working class and support for the Labour Party.

IX

Conclusion

The problem stated in the introduction to this thesis centred on the current controversy over the effects of prosperity on manual workers. We have found that among one section of the working class a way of life nearer that of non-manual than manual workers has not prevented a relatively high level of working class and Labour Party affiliations; and evidence has been presented of how one occupation has been affected by social change. We now need to consider more fully our main area of interest: the relationship between the social condition of the members of an occupation and their class and political affiliations. In order to do so adequately, it is necessary first to re-state the major historical trends.

The conditions of identification with the working class

A number of stages can be discerned in the development of class consciousness among compositors.

The first stage belongs to the early history of the compositor up to the middle of the eighteenth century. By the end of the period there is evidence of the development of 'group consciousness' – awareness of belonging to an occupational group. This can be seen in the kind of community that was developing in the period and in the widespread practice of common customs. Temporary combinations were formed, and towards the end of the period, attempts were made to establish various forms of permanent unions among compositors.

Several conditions helped to foster such consciousness. In the first place there was a sense of separateness, both economically and socially. Although work was not always regular, wages were higher than in most skilled trades; in addition, the compositor enjoyed a high status, which was derived largely from the need for a level of education sufficient to read and interpret written manuscript into type, in a period when literacy was restricted. The prestige with which the general public invested the occupation is indicated by the substantial number of boys who were attracted into the trade, not only from artisans but also from higher social groups; premium payments were common, though by no means universal. Another factor was the existence of the Chapel. This institution helped to maintain common traditions, customs and language; though not itself a union, the Chapel aided the attempts to form a union. A third factor in the development of a group consciousness was the close proximity of the working places of the journeymen compositors. Though the trade was on a small scale, the industry being regulated by the State through the Stationers' Company, almost from the introduction of printing there was a distinction between the masters and a body of permanent journeymen. These journeymen were employed in rather small establishments which were densely concentrated in a particular area of London: such geographical concentration was important for the formation and maintenance of group awareness and facilitated intermittent mutual action in complaints over working conditions; such action was itself a reinforcing agent in the development of group consciousness during the period.

A second stage of widening consciousness is observable in the period approximately between the mid-eighteenth and mid-nineteenth centuries. During this period there was a major expansion of printing; the regulation of the industry broke down, and large-scale firms developed. Yet despite the increase in the volume of work this was a period of relative decline for compositors. And there emerged among them an awareness of the similarity between their condition and that of other artisans; expressions of identification with the 'working classes' in this period implied, in general, the older skilled occupations, 'the trades'.

The relative decline in the position of the compositor which encouraged the emergence of this artisan consciousness was due to several factors. In the first place employment became much less stable: persistent unemployment became a feature of the occupation from the end of the Napoleonic Wars to, more or less, the end of the period. Paradoxically, a period of increasing demand for reading matter and thereby for printing did not improve the situation of the compositor. This demand was greater than the journeyman labour force could supply; and with the use of faster printing machines, typesetting became a bottleneck. In the subsequent expansion of the industry boy labour increased, and was facilitated by the nature of the demand for reading matter which involved the relatively simple process of straightforward typesetting. Boy labour was cheaper, and was thus often preferred to journeymen, who found it increasingly difficult to advance their wages. Though wage rates continued fairly high there was a decline in the relative position of the occupation in terms of income as the newer and more highly paid manual occupations, which resulted from mechanization, emerged. The consequent loss in status was reflected by the recruitment into the trade of boys from lower social strata than hitherto. These factors combined to encourage an awareness of sharing a common experience with other sections of the working class, especially in certain bad years of trade. Resistance against the masters was a further factor: the attempts to alter traditional modes of working with the advance of industrialization,[1] or to modify the system of payment in order to reduce labour costs, and the largely ineffectual attempts by the men to limit the practice of boy labour, all produced opposition to the masters which helped to identify the compositors with other workers, especially those in occupations similarly threatened. The struggles of the period and the need for mutual aid to modify the effects of unemployment encouraged attempts at organization which eventually resulted at the end of the period in the formation of the LSC. The unions were important means of making contact with organizations of other workers, and promoted sympathy and mutual aid in distress; thus they contributed to the widening of consciousness.

Yet expressions of sympathy and militancy were largely of a temporary nature or only affected a small part of the occupation. The occupation was still regarded as being among the higher paid and members were conscious of their status. Enthusiastic participation in the revolutionary or reform movements in the period was thus inhibited, and whilst individual compositors were associated with such movements (e.g. Chartism), these were, in the main, educated idealists. The union organization always acted with caution and restraint, reflecting in part the endeavours of the members to preserve their respectability and to maintain their status of belonging to the aristocracy of the working classes. Supported, no doubt, by the majority of the members, the union kept aloof from mass working class activities: the widening consciousness tended to be confined to an identification with 'the trades'.

From the middle of the nineteenth century until the First World War, a third stage of widening consciousness can be discerned. Printing continued to expand, but employment remained unstable. In this period the area of consciousness was no longer confined to the skilled trades: there was a definite emergence of identification with the working class. The major cause was the serious deterioration in the position of the compositor. Though the reduction in the cost of living until the turn of the century prevented real hardship, the position of the compositor declined not only relatively but absolutely as other occupations, particularly in the new metal industries, replaced the compositor in the best paid group of manual occupations.[2] Unemployment persisted and to some extent was temporarily aggravated by the introduction of composing machinery. Composing machinery, it must be stressed, aggravated but did not cause the decline of the compositor; this was well advanced before machinery was introduced. Unemployment as a result of this factor was not as severe as it might have been: there was a large expansion of printing and the union had become sufficiently strong to bring, gradually, the problem of boy labour under control and to restrict the supply of labour through the apprenticeship system. Composing machinery made boy labour less attractive and the threat of mechanization possibly discouraged recruitment into the trade; the union was also strong enough to minimise any harmful effect on wages from the introduction of composing machinery.

Another factor that might be suggested as affecting the declining position of the compositor was the extension of education. Wider educational provisions did affect the position of certain occupations, which hitherto benefited from the fact that education was restricted. The compositor certainly lost something of his relatively superior position educationally; but it would be untrue to regard the wider opportunities for education among the working classes in the second half of the century as important in the decline of the position of the compositor. Other factors can be adduced for this decline, which was taking place before the period of large-scale educational provision towards the end of the century. It is unlikely that the educational backgrounds of compositors were very different from those of other skilled artisans, especially in this period, and education often came as a result of the work rather than preceding it.

It was in this period that that part of the ethos was formulated which appeals to identification with the working class. As the conditions of life became similar for a wider part of the working class, so there was a greater readiness to identify with the labour movement. Unionization among the unskilled and the revelation of the living standards of the less skilled generated a sympathy for and readiness to help this section of the working class. Sympathy was paralleled by the wave of socialist thought and the growth of a social conscience, both of which helped to promote feelings of solidarity; these feelings were probably aided by the increased number of compositors who were recruited from the more specifically working classes. In the decade and a half prior to the First World War wage advances were at a standstill, despite increases in the cost of living, and relations with the employers became embittered by disputes. From such conditions emerged the working class ethos. Expressions of this are to be found in both political and industrial activity, as compositors became actively involved in the labour movement both through the union organization and as individuals. Gradually there was a willingness to participate in national politics through the Labour Party. Also a trend towards industrial solidarity is evinced in the joint activity of several printing unions and the attempts at amalgamation. Further indices of working class identification can be found in the support given to other occupations and the affiliation of the union to the GTFU; the compositors' union, the LSC, became a focus for working class identification which was fostered by other institutional contacts through such links as the LTC and the TUC.

It must be stressed that any idea of a fairly homogenous working class in this period is false: there were considerable differences in the material condition and outlook of different sections of the working class. Even within an occupation, differences existed, and it is emphasized that the emergence of class consciousness does not at all imply that it was universal among compositors. Probably a not insignificant proportion of the occupation did not associate themselves with these expressions of working class identification. There were still highly paid sections of the occupation, and expressions by individuals indicate that strong status feelings persisted, doubtless aided by some association of the compositor with literacy by the general public. Substantial evidence suggests a not inconsiderable unwillingness to support the new Labour Party, and in order to win support appeals had to be made to the need for trade union representation in Parliament for the printing industry. Perceived narrow sectional interest rather than political idealism was a substantial part of the basis for the Labour Party. There was also a lack of enthusiasm about amalgamating or concerted action with other unions: some of this came from sceptical 'realists'; but there were also those who wanted to maintain their 'respectability' and preserve what status they had, who looked back with nostalgia to the days of the 'gentleman compositor', and who were concerned with the threat of being engulfed in the working class. However, though the numerical strength of this group should not be underestimated, appeal to a more widely based working class consciousness appears to have emerged in this period.

The establishment of this ethos makes the inter-war period an ambiguous one in terms of class consciousness. For in this period the position of the compositor improved considerably, and the compositor re-emerged among the labour aristocracy. Three important factors were responsible for this. Foremost was the union. The First World War had encouraged the development of a powerful organization which had to be consulted on a large number of problems that the war had produced; the growth in the union's influence and scope was paralleled by a high degree of unionization among compositors. Fairly firm control was secured by the union over recruitment, the introduction of machinery and working conditions. Secondly, wages steeply increased to the early 1920s, and then at a time when wages were being generally depressed, the union was sufficiently powerful to restrict the extent of wage reductions; thus important benefits were gained from the fall in living costs, and the position of the compositor in relation to other working class occupations improved. Thirdly, though unemployment was considerable, especially during the depression of the early 1930s, it was not as high as in those industries which were less sheltered from foreign competition. The occupation became a desirable one to enter, and was highly regarded. This was reflected in a reversal of the trend in the previous period and there was an increase in the intake of boys from higher social origins and from printing occupations.

The improvement in the position of compositors brought some decline in the earlier trend towards militancy. Evidence of this can be found in the response to the General Strike, when the majority of compositors, though perhaps sympathetic, were unenthusiastic. The earlier trend towards industrial solidarity was also restrained and amalgamation was hardly mooted – the union was able to gain more by standing on its own. With the relative absence of large-scale trade disputes there were fewer expressions of hostility towards the masters. So far as the Labour Party was supported it continued to be mainly on the basis of trade union interest. Yet the forces operating in the previous period had committed the compositors to a sense of class affiliation and obligation, and in particular stress was laid on the importance of support to the trade union. The ethos had been established, and a basic sympathy was heightened by the experience of the depression of the 1930s.

From this historical evidence it is clear that class consciousness is neither a unitary nor a static phenomenon. Through the periods that have been outlined, class consciousness and political ideology have undergone development and modification with changing social circumstances. Though the occupation has always contained members of very diverse backgrounds who, therefore, never displayed uniformity in attitudes and identification, a clear relationship has been observed between the position of the compositor and his inclination to participate in the wider labour movement.

This relationship would lead one to expect that the material position of the present day compositor would result in a weakening in his class and political affiliations. The survey reveals that the compositor is enjoying a material prosperity that is higher than that of skilled workers as a whole, and enjoys a relatively high status; yet it would appear that he identifies himself with the working class to a greater extent than do other skilled workers, and certainly supports the Labour Party more strongly. It may well be that these affiliations are weakening, yet it is worth enquiring why they have remained so strong up to the present.

This thesis suggests that an important reason for this is that the occupation itself has an important role in influencing certain social attitudes of its members. Through the mechanism of a strong occupational community, an ideology developed over a long period is imparted to the members: that the good compositor is a strong trade unionist, belongs to the working class and supports the Labour Party. This 'ethos' still obtains, despite the relative economic prosperity of the compositor.

The historical development of the occupation is thus shown to have an important influence on certain aspects of the contemporary position of the compositor. There is a continual reference back to the condition of the occupation and its economic rewards in the past; past position has often been the justification for present demands. Also the public image of the occupation (which affects, for example, recruitment) is partly a result of its past status and associations with literacy. The members of the occupation are thus still influenced by the past social development of the occupation. There is also the occupational community which has its roots very early in the history of the craft; it has developed and undergone modification, yet it has essentially been maintained to the present day. This community acts as an important mechanism in sustaining the ethos which, as we have seen, gradually emerged with changes in the social position of the compositor.

The relevance of Marx

The findings of this thesis raise the problem of the relationship between ideology and the conditions under which it emerges. We have seen that there has been a broad relationship between certain 'structural' factors in the occupation and the development of an ethos. These structural factors include wages, employment prospects, hours, conditions of work, physical concentration and the social status of the occupation (this status being reflected in the social origins and educational background of the entrants, which can also be considered to be structural factors). As these elements in the 'market situation' of the compositor worsened, and the compositor was drawn more definitely into the working class and its movements, so the ideology or ethos developed. It was these elements, structured in the occupation, that largely influenced this growth of class consciousness and political affiliation, and not the external appeals of sympathy, justice and socialism.

This conclusion is relevant to Marx's thesis that ideology is a superstructure based on the structure of economic conditions. But we have seen that the economic basis for that superstructure is breaking down with the contemporary growth in material prosperity. We are not concerned here with the extent of this prosperity which, it is true, is still limited. What is important is that there is evidence to suggest that the ideological appeal to identification with the working class and support for the Labour Party is weakening in the working class generally. Yet this ideology is still well maintained in an occupation, which in terms of the economic and status elements in its structure, would be expected to be considerably modifying its superstructure.

An explanation of this in terms of Marxian theory is possible by a modification of the narrow economic interpretation that is usually given to 'structure'. Certainly, as we have seen in this thesis, economic elements have engendered the ideological super-structure. But the independent existence that the ethos appears to be able to maintain is not merely due to time lag: it has structural support. Though the economic elements have been changing, other elements (which have emerged as a response to the social conditions) can help to support the ideology. It is here suggested that in the case of the compositors the occupational community is an important structural element in supporting the ethos.

Reference may also be made to other aspects of Marxian theory regarding the development of class consciousness. First, there is the view that class consciousness increases with the development of industrial capitalism. As industry develops, workers combine and class consciousness grows. This combination has the double effect of preventing competition between the workers and dealing more effectively with employers. As the employers unite, so these combinations unite and form into associations. In the struggle, the mass becomes more unified and in doing so becomes 'a class for itself', that is, conscious of more positive aims than merely defence against the oppression of the employer. The struggle becomes one of class and takes on a political aspect. The essential conditions for the development of social class can be summarized: the conflict over economic rewards; physical concentration and ease of communication; and the development of solidarity and political organization, in place of organization for economic ends. The second theory is that as industrial capitalism develops so the conditions of life of the working classes become more uniform, especially as a result of the introduction of machinery. 'The various interests and conditions of life within the ranks of the proletariat are more and more equalized, in proportion as machinery obliterates all distinctions of labour, and nearly everywhere reduces wages to the same low level.'[3] Both these theories are, of course, interrelated: increasing uniformity is also a condition for the development of class consciousness. But they each contain certain observations that are worth evaluating in relation to the development of the occupation of composing.

It may be argued that this occupation is not typical, especially in view of the elite position it held. But the changing position of the occupation had features likely to be paralleled by other occupations; also it might be suggested that the superior education that compositors in general gained, was likely rationally, to make them better able to assess their true position as members of the working classes and to take action accordingly. Even if the occupation were exceptional this does not detract from its value as one means of assessing Marx. The importance of variables, other than the ones he observed, may be noted; and the studies of exceptional cases may help to explain unexpected behaviour within less exceptional occupations.

Marx and the growth of class consciousness

It is clear that there has been a general movement towards class consciousness among compositors, paralleling structural changes in the economic and social position of the occupation. As we have seen this has emerged in three stages: from occupational consciousness, via artisan consciousness to working class consciousness. But for a number of reasons, this consciousness has not taken on the quality envisaged by Marx. By 'quality' is meant the extent and depth of this feeling: working class identification is by no means true for all members of the occupation; also absent among the majority are revolutionary aims to change the capitalist system.

Economic changes and improvements in social conditions have obviously weakened revolutionary appeals. Can other factors be adduced for indicating where Marx failed in his prognosis? One important key to the explanation of the limitations of Marx's theory regarding the development of class consciousness is to be found in the study of occupations. Occasionally there is a half-conscious suggestion in Marx[4] about the importance of occupations, but by and large an estimate of their significance is lacking in his writings; yet they are the basic mechanism through which class consciousness can be developed, and their study reveals the limitations of the theory. For Marx, class had a special role in effecting change, which may have led him to neglect occupational analysis. That Marx neglected their significance may explain a particular ambiguity. His references to combinations of workers are not clear; they may refer, for example, to workers in one occupation or to all the workers in one factory; nor can this be deduced from the fact that most of the unions at the time were occupationally based – Marx, in talking about the increasing equalization of workers as a unifying factor, for example, is obviously thinking about something wider than occupation. Nor is it clear what is included in the larger associations of workers: are they associations of crafts, factories or industries? Because of his wider concern with the broad development of class leading to eventual political action, Marx ignored what would be the essential mechanisms for organization. These mechanisms may themselves inhibit the development of a common situation and common interests.

Trade unions are the means of establishing contacts with other working class organizations, in doing so they are a focus for class feeling and encourage this among their members. But the basis of trade union organization is occupation; this is true in the last analysis for all trade unions, but it is especially true for craft organizations confined to specific occupations. They could, therefore, only encourage a limited working class identification. By their very existence the trade unions helped to prevent the creation of a uniform working class: for their function was to at least maintain differentials between occupations. In so far as they are successful for their own members trade unions can only encourage a limited class identification. Only when it is felt that one's occupation is being repressed or is undergoing deterioration in common with the rest of the working class, can strong identification with the working class be aroused. If the occupation is able to withstand deterioration, as happened in the case of the compositor between the wars, identification with the working class is less enthusiastic. In a period of relative prosperity, as in post-war Britain, attempts are made either to maintain differentials or to increase them.

Once established, a union has every incentive to continue as a separate entity. Growth in bureaucracy and the provision of services for its members combine to make it unlikely that the union would easily relinquish its position. Even links with other working class organizations – trades councils, the TUC and political activity – tend towards preserving the unit rather than assimilating it into a wider working class movement. In the movement for amalgamation in printing varying friendly society benefits have often been the justification for preserving the union identity, but this obstacle, though difficult, is by no means insurmountable. Other recurring problems have been the autonomy and control by the occupational group and the preservation of the position or privileges of the union bureaucracy. Throughout the last century and a quarter there has been a continual refusal by the craft unions to be merged into a wider association. Thus combination into unions, based as it is on occupation, tends to preserve both occupational differences and their own separate entities. Occupations and the associations that they develop may act as a focus for working class action but they are also a conservative influence in limiting class solidarity.[5]

Participation by trade unions in political activity at the beginning of the establishment of the Labour Party is often regarded as a sign of working class militancy, a sign of the political expression and aspirations of class interests. We have seen that, for the compositor at least, such participation was motivated (or at least had to be justified to the members) not by working class militancy but by a narrower group interest: trade union representation for the printing trade. It was to keep vigilance for the printing industry and to watch especially any decision that may affect the conditions of the workers or trade unions within it; to try to encourage more printing and to ensure that the customs of the trade were recognized by the Government in placing printing contracts. Appeals to compositors to support trade union representation in Parliament were thus justified in terms of self interest.

By the beginning of the twentieth century political activity was also seen as providing the worker with the means of expressing his class view, but this aspect was always subordinate to the narrower kind of justification. One explanation of this restricted view may be that a well-formulated working class ideology was absent. There had been many theoretical constructions of socialism, but socialism was regarded as something external to the working class. Perhaps the nearest approach to a working class ideology that was beginning to emerge was the idea of a basic standard of living and the freedom to negotiate above the minimum.

Other comments may also be made on Marx's theory. First, that the initial factor of concentration of workers in factories is essential for combination.[6] The history of the compositors shows that attempts at combination developed before the rise of large-scale industries; the facilitating factor here being not factory concentration but geographical concentration which made for easy contact. It should also be stressed that the combination was motivated not simply by the need to resist oppression by the masters and the awareness of a similar interest in the productive process, but also as a means of organizing more permanent friendly society benefits (at first for sickness and later for unemployment). It may also be observed that formal organization of the men preceded those of the employers' associations, though, of course, it was easier for masters to meet informally to make decisions; formal organizations of the masters arose partly from the need to negotiate with the men's organizations.

A further factor inhibiting the development of class consciousness is the existence of status differentials between occupations. We have seen that despite his economic deterioration by the end of the nineteenth century, the compositor still retained semblances of his old status. A time lag occurs between a changed economic position of an occupation and the reconstruction of the image held of the occupation to conform to the new position; an image developed in one period persists into the changed conditions of another period. The image of composing was a fusion of different elements: the high wages of certain sections; the regularity of work for certain groups of compositors; and the combination of a high degree of literacy and skill with which the occupation was associated. From this image the compositor derived a certain degree of status to which he tended to cling, and which clung to him, as his economic condition deteriorated. There was a continual reference back to an earlier position, and the desire to preserve this traditional status helped to inhibit the enthusiastic identification with the working class.

Related to this factor of status was the existence of differentials within the occupation. Wide differences in earnings obtained among compositors, according to the section of the trade in which they were engaged; newspaper work had different rates and different sections of the trade had varying possibilities for piecework. Such differences if they do not prevent identification by the different sections with compositors as a whole, tend to inhibit them from sharing any fervour which may be displayed for a wider working class solidarity.

Marx and increasing uniformity

The second theory of Marx, that there is a growing uniformity of the working class, demands further comment in the light of the evidence of the compositors, in addition to the above remarks on the endeavours to preserve differentials.

Marx believed that it was the introduction of machinery that would help to obliterate differences between workers. Machinery would reduce the need for skills and thus reduce the need for wage differentials, the unemployment it causes would also tend to make wages more uniform. This tendency could be interpreted as applying both between and within occupations: there would be an increasing trend toward similarity of economic reward. The evidence of the compositor does not bear out this view. The deterioration in the compositor's condition preceded the introduction of composing machines. Indirectly it is true that machinery and technical developments in other departments encouraged the social deterioration of the compositor: printing machines and stereotyping, for example, affected in different ways the amount of work available for the compositor and also encouraged the use of boy labour; but this labour was being used before these innovations were widely adopted. Nor were the effects of the introduction of composing machines as severe as those that Marx observed in other trades undergoing mechanization. Indeed, machinery made possible even greater differentials within the occupation. In part this was due to the ability of the union to regulate the conditions under which machinery was operated; this is particularly possible where machinery is introduced in circumstances where it is most desirable to avoid conflict. But a major factor was the greater output of the machine which made it possible for the employer to pay rates higher than those paid to hand compositors. The very introduction of machinery also facilitated a greater control over boy labour and thereby eventually diminished the problem of unemployment. Union control and the increased demand for printing avoided the long term unemployment and consequent depression of wages which might have resulted from the introduction of machinery; though the number of hand compositors gradually contracted, many workers were able to benefit from the profitability of the composing machine. Thus machinery was neither the cause of depression nor did it make for greater uniformity of wages among compositors.

It should be stressed that Marx's more general thesis regarding the conditions necessary for the growth of class consciousness generally is not being challenged. Class consciousness among compositors was certainly given expression when their position became depressed and their condition became more similar to that of other sections of the working class. Thus, the Marxian type of analysis, emphasizing the structural factors influencing ideology, is valuable; but Marx's omissions, founded perhaps on hope, led him to a false prediction. From the evidence of the compositor (the study of other occupations may prove Marx less limiting) it must be concluded that in his concern over the widening of class consciousness and the development of a unified working class movement, Marx neglected an analysis of the forces that tend towards separateness and the conservation of existing differentials and institutions. These tend to inhibit the growth of and participation in a unified working class movement.

Structure and ideology

We have suggested that there is a direct relationship between the structural elements in the condition of an occupation and the ideology that emerges. It might be argued, however, that the development of class consciousness among compositors was due to external rather than to structural causes. In support of this it would be adduced that such consciousness developed among compositors at a time when it was becoming extensive among workers generally, and the atmosphere generated a greater influence on class feeling than did the more specific structural elements within the occupation itself. Whether there was a similar development of class consciousness among occupations that did not suffer a decline in their socio-economic condition would require another study. But certain historical comparisons, using the compositors, could be made briefly which would suggest that this criticism is not sufficient. An example may be taken from the mass movements of the 1830s and 1840s. These did not appear to have a great attraction for the large body of compositors, whose position though relatively reduced was still high among manual occupations. Those individual compositors who were drawn into the movements tended to be educated idealists protesting rather against general injustice than only against their own conditions. The value of using this period is limited for it may be said that a working class movement was only beginning, it had not established a full body of organizations such as unions, trade councils and congresses in frequent contact. A better example would be found in the period between the two world wars. Here was a period of strong working class activity, yet the compositors in general were not strongly militant, and this can be attributed largely to their improved position. Though not denying that the external 'mood of the period' may have strong influence, the structural factors appear to be more important. From this it may be concluded that extensive solidarity can only be expected among those sections whose economic position is affected or immediately threatened; it is the structural specifics of the occupation that are the means of engendering militancy, not class membership merely.

In the present situation it would appear that the economic elements in the structure are breaking down and that the working class ethos, still widely adhered to, finds its support in the less directly economic elements in the structure, namely the occupational community. But is it likely that the ethos can continue resting on non economic supports? We have seen that working class affiliation appears more likely to break down than political affiliation. If the material condition of the compositor continues to improve it is possible that class consciousness will further decrease, and the tendencies toward changing political allegiance will become more explicit. It seems unlikely that the occupational community would be able to continue alone to maintain the ethos. Over a long period of time its influence on these ideological aspects is likely to diminish, especially as there are indications that the occupational community itself is showing signs of strain.

Yet a number of factors may combine to add to the structural factors affecting class consciousness. Firstly, the continuation of regular industrial disputes may encourage the retention of the ethos. Secondly, the recent attempts at amalgamation with other unions may be more successful than they have been to date. A possible attempt to lay down a similar basic wage for all skilled workers, and the certain appeal to solidarity with other workers as a result of amalgamation are likely to reinforce the appeal to the ethos. Thirdly, recent wage agreements have included clauses about using less skilled workers for certain operations in the composing room; the unions have been extremely wary about such clauses, but have preferred to try to alleviate the labour shortage in this way rather than by increasing the number of apprentices. If the division of labour increases by such dilution, any consequent labour surplus could well affect wage rates or at least restrict the level of higher rates. Because of the strength of the union, however, this factor is unlikely to be important in the near future. Fourthly, there is the possibility of drastic technological changes in the printing industry; this is likely to affect the composing room in particular if the use of metal for typesetting is replaced by other processes now being developed. It is impossible to assess the effect this will have on the compositor, his rewards, his work situation, and, if he continues to exist in his present form, on his ideology. These factors have to be balanced against the influence of the incidence of prosperity on class and political affiliation.

Changing ethos and occupational influence

Mention has already been made about the ethos itself undergoing possible modification. In the absence of the above factors proving able to maintain the ethos, it is probable that for skilled occupations, at least, the continuation of the material prosperity of the 1950s might affect the ethos. The experience of the USA would suggest that in conditions of prosperity, whilst industrial harmony may be absent working class militancy declines. Reduced appeals to class solidarity may be paralleled by a weakening readiness to support the Labour Party, especially if the image remains of the Party being associated with the underdog. In these conditions it may well be that the ideology that becomes more explicit would be what can be called a trade union ideology rather than a class ideology: that is the idea of a basic standard of living for all workers and the freedom of occupational associations to negotiate above the minimum. This idea is by no means new. We have already suggested that it was emerging among compositors at the beginning of the century. But the socialist influences on the trade unions, their association with the Labour Party, the appeal to working class solidarity, and the links with the TUC may have inhibited this idea becoming more explicitly an ideology. The weakening of the influence of these forces may encourage a more conscious adoption of this view.

In discussing the influence of structural factors in the adoption and maintenance of the ideology, we have been considering one of the roles of an occupation: its ability to impose certain social attitudes on its members. Are such occupational influences likely to continue? An occupation is more than a job: the relationships that emerge from the work situation affect the way of life of members of the occupation in numerous ways. We have already noticed its effect on attitudes and friendships, and its probable effect on leisure activities and interests, dress, behaviour, and other aspects of a material level of living that the occupation economically permits and socially encourages. The extent to which it has this influence depends largely on the nature of the occupation and its social setting. Where the work situation demands that a number of men of the same occupation work in close proximity, the influence is heightened. Especially is this true where the work encourages close living together also, such as in mining. The study of such occupations is likely to reveal more homogeneous patterns than exists in those occupations where the work situation is less integrating and does not involve the socially reinforcing factor of proximity of residence.

It may be expected that occupations will continue their roles in influencing areas of behaviour outside that demanded by the nature of the work itself. What is likely to change is any peculiar influence that the occupation may exert; such an influence is likely to arise in certain circumstances and in special areas, where the occupation becomes a focus for other activities. Under these special conditions the occupation may develop a culture of its own through which it moulds its members in various ways. We have seen, for example, that the occupational community of the compositor influences certain attitudes. This kind of influence is likely to decrease if the culture of the occupation weakens. Social separateness stimulates the development of the culture, and this is likely to break down as other influences of the wider society become pervasive: shorter hours, mass entertainment and communication, wider opportunities for leisure, the geographic dispersal of members of the occupation, all tend to weaken the occupational culture.

This thesis argues, however, that the compositors' occupational community has remained sufficiently strong to be an important factor in the maintenance of an ethos that developed under different conditions in an earlier period.

Notes

1 Composing was not affected by machinery in this period and thus the outcries against industrialization (e.g. Williams, *Culture and Society*, p. 87–109) are absent in this occupation, printing was, however, affected by other technical changes in the printing machine department and in stereotyping.
2 Hobsbawm, 'The Labour Aristocracy in Nineteenth-century Britain', p. 284.
3 Marx and Engels, *Communist Manifesto*, p. 11–12.
4 Marx, *Selected Writings*, ed. Bottomore and Rubel, p. 179, extract from 'Capital', v. 3.
5 Strachey, *Contemporary Capitalism*, discusses the neglect by Marx of the power of trade unions to raise living standards.
6 Marx, *Selected Writings*, ed. Bottomore and Rubel, p. 186–8, extract from 'Poverty of Philosophy'.

Epilogue

'This old comp can lament, with Othello, that his occupation's gone.' [1]

Occupational transformation

At the time the thesis was written, the scent of technological change blowing across the Atlantic and the North Sea was very mild. Few sensed how powerful it would become, how much change would be wrought. Only one observer, Ellic Howe, mentioned to me in the late Fifties the likelihood of major change, saying he thought that within twenty years hot metal composition would be dead. He was not far out. Yet none of the senior management of the 28 firms visited, nor the well over a hundred compositors I spoke to during the period December 1959 to February 1960, said anything about the new technology; not a single concern was expressed about photo-composition and its radical implications. Had there been widespread concern at the time it would surely have been mentioned by someone.

Despite some experiments, the only major innovations in composition that had taken place in the five hundred years of printing's existence had been the introduction of Linotype and Monotype machines in the late Nineteenth Century. But whilst these had considerably changed typesetting speeds and consequently output, they both used hot metal, the casting of type characters from matrices into which molten metal was injected. The hand compositor's work had hardly changed, just less day-long hand setting, 'pica thumping' as it was called, and he (it was almost always a 'he') still retained the essentials of his skills: his knowledge of fonts, layout ability, and know-how in making up the type in readiness for the printing stage. The industry had experienced sporadic attempts at major innovation as early as the 1890s when a form of direct inputting was prophesied;[2] a photographic process for typesetting was patented, and further experiments had been made sporadically into the 1940s. But it wasn't until the mid-Fifties that processes other than using metal type began to seem commercially viable.[3]

This outline cannot do justice to all the technological experimentation that then took place; its intention is to provide a brief account of some of the major developments and their impact, including some of the responses made by the industry, employers and unions, and especially to provide examples of how individual compositors met the challenges they faced. The purpose of this Epilogue, then, is to relate something of the devastating change that has taken place for the compositor since the submission of the thesis; a change from a flourishing occupation to its demise.

For background, I had also intended to include some basic data, such as the number of working compositors and their wage rates since 1960. This proved much more difficult than anticipated. With amalgamations over the years, the unions ceased to record much detail by occupation, as if the newly amalgamated organizations wished to play down differences; it also had the effect of avoiding the difficulty of designating new occupations in what was a highly fluid situation. In the decennial censuses the categories used changed as the technology and operations evolved. From initially using 'compositor' alone, to adding or replacing it with 'originators' and 'print preparers' or 'prepress', and separately using the generic term 'printers' when the specific occupation was an amalgam or unclear. All this, while itself a marker of the rapidity of change and the declining importance of the craft, made detailed comparisons over time impossible. It was as if the compositor was being air-brushed from the record.

Overall numbers engaged in the industry have fallen drastically, from around 202,000 males and 100,000 females in paper and printing in the 1961 Census for England and Wales to, according to the British Printing Industries Federation (BPIF), 190,000 overall in the early 1990s, and falling to about 140,000 in 2009. Of this last figure about 12 per cent, i.e. 16,000, work in the general area of prepress which overlaps with some of the functions of the hot metal compositor. Prepress is a much broader concept, it can include graphics, keyboarding, the production of images and illustrations, litho processes, platemaking, and proofing, all prior to the actual printing. It has been described as 'a complex composite of slowly evolved traditional techniques and "new" technology'.[4] Despite the extended coverage of the term, the total numbers engaged in these various processes are much reduced from the heyday of hot metal when there were over 39,000 male and 330 female compositors in the 1961 Census.

Regarding wage rates, the old, elaborately complex London Scale of Prices, fully understood only by a few experts, appears to have been replaced by a simple national structure. A Partnership at Work Agreement between the BPIF and the union Unite lays down minimum weekly rates for different categories of skill for the industry. There are three classes: Fully Skilled, Semi-Skilled, and Unskilled, with prepress work generally falling in the first, the Class 1 category. The minimum rate in April, 2008 was £281. Most firms, union and non-union, would take this as a baseline figure. There is no maximum and additional earnings are possible depending on the type of work, kind of machine used, overtime, call-out charges, and payments for shift work; many individuals negotiate their own rate independently from fellow workers. Weekly earnings frequently total around £500.

Technological change

It is difficult to unpick the complicated story of technological change in a few paragraphs. Change was to come in two major phases; these can be broadly described as analogue-based photographic composition and digital-based electronic composition. These developments also depended on changes in the way the product was actually printed; this required moving away from the raised surface of letterpress to printing from the flat surface of offset lithography, which was more compatible with photographic or film composition; and lithography underwent its own process of technical development.

From around the mid-Fifties to the end of the Seventies many different photo-composing machines using film were being produced with different advantages, and manufacturers of traditional typesetting machines, such as Linotype and Monotype, had to develop their own photo-composing versions to stay in the business of typesetting.[5] Manufacturers competed with each other offering different advantages. But the early versions tended to share a similar problem: that of making corrections. These could only be done by physically stripping a small piece of new film into the existing one, a tedious, fiddly procedure. The economic downturn of the Seventies reduced the level of experimentation that manufacturing firms and individual printing offices were making. But by the end of the decade the era of hot metal was almost over (apart from in the national newspapers which will be referred to later). The occupation of the traditional compositor was coming to an end.

The next radical shift was from photographic to electronic digital composition. Though there were earlier examples, this was heralded in particular by the introduction of the Apple Macintosh computer in January 1984, with its mouse and graphics interface. This included a screen able to show fonts, sizes and style, for example italics and bold type, and the

Kentish Times *in the 1980s. The new technology had radically altered working conditions.*

ability to lay out the product to be printed. Eventually this innovation was adapted by personal computer providers such as IBM. Other providers entered the arena around the same time and soon the film medium was replaced.

The 'Mac', and other personal computers, have become so much a part of the technological landscape of publishing that it is already difficult to appreciate how radical a development it was. The whole panoply of skills formerly largely covered in the design and composition departments could now potentially be performed by one person with a small computer; some familiarity with layout and fonts could be of value, though more typically the design aspect is pre-specified by a typographer/graphic designer.

The take-up of these developments by industry appears initially to have been very patchy. The new machinery was not cheap nor always reliable: early Macs were notorious for frequently crashing. A firm which had recently purchased new traditional machinery and equipment wanted to see a return on that investment rather than incur capital loss. A small employer might have preferred a reduction in profit rather than make a new, and to him untried, capital investment with all the associated headaches and implications for staffing; this would be especially so if he were

approaching retirement. In addition, choice was wide, sometimes confus-
ingly so, with different new machinery offering various functions, some
of which were modifiable by the purchaser. Early reactions to change in
the industry were thus very varied: some felt that hot metal would exist
alongside these innovations, others believed that it would be displaced.
There were also employers and journeymen, according to one informant,
who thought that the new technology would prove 'a flash in the pan'.

So innovation didn't proceed with the wholesale replacement of one
set of developments by another; instead different technologies were to be
found in use in different parts of the industry. The three major branches
of the trade, bookwork, general jobbing including periodicals, and the
national newspapers, were affected at different times. Indeed, one
informant relates that the firm he worked for had into the 1970s three
composing departments existing at the same time, differentiated according to function: the general jobbing section contained traditional hand
compositors and Lino and Monotype operators, feeding into letterpress
printing machines; the provincial newspaper section had Lino machines
similarly printing letterpress; it was the book production department
with its more straightforward demands that initially used the new technology of photo-composition.[6]

Technological change, with the objective of trying to improve performance in the industry, brought one kind of attack on the occupation of
compositor. But there was also a more direct assault on another front,
from political and social forces. This came about especially as the period
of major technological development coincided with the coming to power
of a government committed to breaking the power of the unions, and
supporting employers prepared for confrontation. Dramatically significant examples were Eddie Shah in 1982 and Rupert Murdoch around
1985. As the owner of six local newspapers, Shah used the recent anti-
closed shop legislation to bring in non-union labour and defeated the
print unions after national strikes that went on for seven months. He
introduced advanced technology which required less skill, paving the
way for non-union labour. Three years later, News International, controlled by Murdoch, clandestinely built and equipped a new printing
plant for all its titles in the London district of Wapping.[7] When the print
unions announced a strike mainly over direct inputting by the journalists,
Murdoch activated this new plant with the assistance of the Electrical,
Electronic, Telecommunications and Plumbing Union (EETPU).[8] With
such changes in the national newspapers, the last bastion of union power
collapsed, along with their ability to achieve high earnings. These developments also saw the end of the geographical association of newspaper

production with Fleet Street.[9] The decline in union power now covered all sections of the industry.

A few years earlier the Greater London Council produced its report on the decline of the industry in London, concluding that there was less need for publishing and printing to be geographically close, nor was there a need for either to be so centrally and expensively located, in terms of real estate and wage levels.[10] This was another incentive for change in London.

Neal Archerson penned a nostalgic piece on the move of the *Observer* to Battersea in January 1988, concluding with this observation: 'We the journalists, are going to a handsome white building between Battersea Park and the old power station, a place of space, light and computer screens. Others, who we used to know so well, will not be coming ... After more than 400 years, the printers of the City of London are finished ... the unions finally lost at the battle of Wapping. There was protection, overmanning, some extortionate wages – "Spanish practices" that were less than honest. Less than honourable all the same, was the part played in the printers' defeat by the journalists, who took their jobs.

'Even if the printers had been saints, the new technology meant that their trade was doomed. But I will miss them: often eccentric, kindly, sometimes inflammable, they helped to keep our feet on the ground ... Looking at the long rows of basins where they used to clean up, it occurred uneasily to me that their kind of dirt was easier to wash off than ours.'

Some institutional responses

As the scale of technological innovation increased, clearly the industry needed to adapt to the new technology. Some idea of the forms this took can be seen by looking at a few examples of the ways in which the organizations representing master printers and print workers engaged with different aspects of change.

Responses by employers

The BFMP had a long-standing *Members Circular* which dealt with issues facing the industry. The first reference found to photocomposing was a brief note in February 1958 that the unions were working on a demarcation formula;[11] and the issue of demarcation featured in a number of circulars at this time. Not until 1963 did the BFMP find it important to help organize a course on computer typesetting, aimed at providing members with some appreciation of what this new technology could do. This was a 10–15 day course at Newcastle University under the auspices of Nato, to bring the latest experiences in the US and Europe into contact with those in Britain.[12] In the same year the *Circular* welcomed the union amalgamations taking place between the London Typographical Society and the provincial Typographical Association, with further unions considering joining, as helping to reduce demarcation disputes.[13] This was considered increasingly urgent with the wider use of film and new plate-making processes for printing surfaces, and the introduction of web offset into letterpress firms. In 1966 there were references to more frequent one- and two-day courses being set up for members, especially for the Young Master Printers group.

Another indicator of change was in the content of the BFMP's publication *Estimating for Printers*. This publication had its first edition in 1916, and went through several editions as changes occurred in the industry. No reference was made to photosetting systems until the ninth edition in 1970; this was just a half-page reference to some of the systems in use. Not until the end of the decade had the level of change become apparent: in 1979 the new tenth edition contained material on both hot and cold composition, giving more detail on the latter. In the following year, 1980, the eleventh edition had just a few pages on hot metal composition; and in 1989 the publication was completely revised in a thirteenth edition when the focus changed with only a tiny section on 'hot metal setting [which] has now been overtaken almost completely'. These publications are no more; the BPIF which replaced the BFMP, has published a new handbook in the area of estimating[14] and also offers courses.

In 1968, another problem was being stressed: the production of new printing work 'outside our industry'. This was difficult for employers and unions to control, and the situation was exacerbated for the London print trade by the flight from London as land values became more expensive and communications and transportation improved. Though there was some compensation for this loss as the volume of demand for print in general increased, the problem remained. A *Members Circular* in that year wondered if the NGA, the new union, could help in retaining type origination within the traditional printing industry, for this was 'one of the biggest [problems] which we have ever faced together'.[15]

In the post-war period the demand for compositors had intensified and had remained difficult to satisfy. Employers attempted to increase the supply by introducing women and streamlining apprenticeships. The two problems were mentioned in the September 1968 *Circular*: in referring to the lack of skilled labour it was stated 'that any attempt to maintain this area of work as an exclusively male preserve is doomed to failure'.[16]

Union responses to change

The union's response to the gender issue was indicated at a delegate meeting of the NGA where it was recognized that the period from 1969 had been noteworthy for the introduction of new techniques, and that radical changes were overtaking the industry. The question of women as keyboard operators was stated to be a 'difficult and emotive issue, but all too often the Association is presented with a *fait accompli* and learns that equipment and typist have been installed simultaneously'.[17] The report of the meeting recognized that many compositors were reluctant to undertake keyboard duties; this reluctance was associated with a view that keyboard operation was unmanly, which added weight to the argument that women were more temperamentally suited to such work. The writer goes on to assert that the National Council of the Association did not agree with this view despite the acceptance of the use of females as keyboard operators by the Scottish Typographical Association: 'we as masters of our own destiny do not intend to depart from the firm stand we have taken to resist the introduction of such labour'. But on both issues, keeping printing within the industry as then known and female labour, change had to be accepted.

The union was more constructive with regard to apprenticeships, agreeing over the years to reductions in length from the customary seven years prevailing until after the Second World War to half that length; this was partly related to the raising of the school-leaving age; the reduction was accompanied by tighter regulation of the training. A review of training as a whole presented its conclusions in 1973, which tightened up the system of training.[18] Yet despite these efforts, firms, especially those that had been set up outside the traditional printing industry, felt they didn't require the same level of training, and could largely undertake this on their own. The apprenticeship system, which had been for centuries the primary form of training in the industry, was being abandoned.

Nationally, printing apprenticeship numbers are today minuscule: the total number of apprentices in the industry has been reported variously as anything from under 200 (168 in 2007/8) to around 400, few of them it would seem in prepress, of whom there are no more than 40. The period of apprenticeship varies with the firm, generally between two and three years for prepress. There is still a City and Guilds in Origination and Prepress, and NVQs in three areas: Machine Printing, Mechanized Print

Finishing, and Prepress. These are taken by a total of 200–300 students a year, with only about 25 taking the Prepress qualification.[19]

The decline in apprenticeships in printing, although accelerated by the technological changes, coincided with a wider disenchantment with the apprenticeship as a form of training for modern industry in general. This was reflected in government policy in the 1980s in favour of work-based learning when the number of Industrial Training Boards reduced generally. How far recent government attempts to resuscitate apprentice-ship schemes for skilled workers generally will be successful in printing, remains to be seen.

Both employer and worker organizations took steps to ensure that their members understood and could adapt to the new challenges. We have noted some such responses by the employers. Union responses are also worth noting. The NGA Delegate meeting in 1972 stressed that the introduction of computers was the area of greatest technological develop-ment. New techniques were bypassing composing rooms, and 'since we cannot expect to prevent progress we must seek to harness it so far as we are able'.[20] Already in 1965 several large printing firms were launch-ing into computer typesetting, and approached the NGA regarding the training of existing staff as computer keyboard operators. The *Graphical Journal* proclaimed: 'This is, indeed, great progress and will demonstrate how adaptable our members can be if given, and willing to accept, the opportunity'.[21] A two-week full-time course sponsored by the union was held in November that year at the LCP; there were over 200 applicants for the 16 places.[22] By the late 1960s, the LCP was organizing numerous photocomposing courses.

On pay, from 1973 the BPIF and NGA had worked out a series of agree-ments on photocomposition which took into account virtually all equip-ment, with different pay rates according to the work done. There were also agreements on hours and it was expected that a thirty-seven-and-a-half-hour week that had been agreed would be general by 1981. By this time the widespread use of metal type had practically ceased. This was reflected in the decline in production of hot metal composition machin-ery envisaged in the ten-year forecast made in 1979 by PIRA.

Whilst there was cooperation between employers and the unions, there were also disputes, some arising from inter-union concerns over demar-cation. One solution was to be found in further union amalgamations, and as already noted a series took place over the years (see Prologue).[23] As already noted, union amalgamations were welcomed by the Master Printers which saw them as a way of reducing disputes.

Individual experiences of change

The compositor together with a few smaller occupations, such as stereo-typers and Monocasters, bore the brunt of these changes. Over a period of about two decades from the 1970s, at first slowly and then with increasing momentum the traditional compositor's occupation became virtually extinct. The nearest equivalent replacement has the unromantic and ambiguous title of 'originator' or 'prepress worker'. The copy is now usually word processed by the author, and is either designed by the author or, more probably, a typographer/graphic designer.

Clearly major challenges had to be faced by compositors both personal and professional, how were they affected by the decline in hot metal composition? In order to get some notion of what it meant to individuals it seemed important to meet up with some former traditional compositors to hear their stories. By a number of routes, several were found who agreed to be interviewed; these were often followed up by email. They are not a representative sample, but provide some examples of how compositors were affected; this section briefly outlines their experiences.[24]

i) DF was a little older than most entrants at the time he entered the print at 17 years old in 1955, and served a five-year apprenticeship at Hackers, a general jobbing printers at Clapham Junction. After a year at the Central School of Arts he transferred to the LSP where he first heard about photo-composition. When he came out of his time in 1960 he was beginning to wonder how long hot metal would last. He joined another jobbing printers and became the FoC within five weeks of completing his apprenticeship. He joined the Baynard Press in 1962 working on periodicals, and again became the FoC. Though threatened, photo-composition never came to the Baynard, and he stayed there until 1973 becoming redundant when the firm, then part of Southwark Offset, was sold. At the time many hot metal firms were under-cutting each other. In 1973 he joined Reveille as a hand compositor and became the Imperial FoC (the term used for the chairman of all the FoCs of the different sections of a large printing house). New technology was introduced there in the late 1970s, and he did inputting including advertisements, cut and pasting, and corrections; he was trained in-house. Robert Maxwell took over in 1984 and imposed a reduction in wage rates by one-third, despite agreements with the NGA. The work was changing by the month and he was becoming very apprehensive about the future. Young girls were brought in, and rather bizarrely he was expected to teach them to cut and paste at dramatically lower wages. He was pleased to get out when he was made redundant in 1993, and took early retirement, aged 56.

ii) Barrie F was born in 1946, and started his six-year apprenticeship with the Eden Press in January 1963, when he was 16. He took his C&G Intermediate Certificate in compositor's work in 1967 while on day-release, and came out of his time six months early, the certificate of indentureship completion noting that 'his application to his task made it possible to allow a reduction in the full period'. The firm was outside the main union structure, being a part of the non-militant PTA, which represented both employer and employee. He recalls that, atypical for the industry at large at the time, the firm engaged a woman Linotype operator. She was Russian, and had been trained in her country of origin; she was very good – it helped to adjust him to the idea of women in the trade. Around 1968-9, after a few months in a small printers and having joined the NGA, he moved to HMSO, working as a Monotype keyboard operator. It was not until the mid-1970s that he began to be aware of photo-composition. He then worked as a keyboard operator at a typesetting establishment until a take-over by Maxwell threatened when he returned to HMSO in the 1970s. Barrie had wanted to work in Fleet Street but was strongly put off by his father who seemed to be aware even then of the likelihood of major change ('he went ballistic at the idea'). It was around this time in the late 1970s that he began to be fully aware of the extent of the threats facing his occupation, and was 'frightened out of my life'. Until then, it seems that many in the industry felt that photocomposition was just another process in addition to hot metal composition, not an entire replacement. He recalls that hot metal didn't finish at HMSO until 1986.

The firm expected him to multitask in the various processes involved in photo-composition and provided training in computer typesetting, proof-reading, platemaking, and pagination, the process on film of what had been known in hot metal as imposition. There was no additional remuneration for this, but a high volume of overtime became the expectation. Apprentices were phased out by the mid 1970s. When women were introduced into the firm in 1987, the Chapel was sufficiently strong to insist that they should be trained in the same four areas of work performed by men; the women did so despite some reluctance by them, though they tended to do more keyboarding and proof-reading. This enabled the Chapel to insist on the women getting the same rate as the men. In 1995, Barrie, along with over 100 men in the composing Chapel, was offered redundancy, which he took along with 80 others, several of whom decided to retire. The firm secured many replacements from former Fleet

Street print workers. He then joined the British Medical Association, key-boarding on an electronic computer until retirement in 2005.

iii) JF, born in 1944, entered the trade in 1961 aged 16 and undertook a six-year apprenticeship at Odhams. [25] He took a C&G Intermediate Certificate in Compositor's Work. Whilst on day-release classes he was introduced to the idea of photocomposition as something for the future, not as a threat to the whole occupation. He felt that by the mid 1960s there was an increasing awareness of impending changes with developments in photocomposition, 'though compositors may not have realized how swift and complete they would be'. He recalls working at a small printers over the summer of 1970: 'I remember the comps., middle-aged men always working in small shops like this one, being depressed about the future and telling me that I should get out of the trade. ... Soon the industry would receive a number of shocks, especially with Eddie Shah's confrontation with the unions at his Warrington print works and Manchester news offices in the early 1980s, invoking Margaret Thatcher's Industrial Laws and undermining the closed shop.'

When JF came out of his time he was well aware of impending change, but didn't expect that he would need to adjust in major ways every couple of years. He was aware that different compositors had different experiences depending on how much a firm decided to invest in new technology. 'From the day I started work, the technology began to move under my feet. And so I was constantly adapting to new techniques through my working life – film setting, paper paste-up, computer typesetting, digital desktop publishing, etc. ... So, shortly after my apprenticeship finished I steered myself towards typography ... later becoming creative director of an agency'.

By the late 1970s he had become a freelance designer, a position he still occupies. He is also a trained London guide, taking groups around central London, often with a focus on printing and its history.

iv) VH came from a family of printers extending back 150 years. He passed the entrance examination for Keliher, Hudson and Kearns and that of the JIC, and started work aged 15 in January 1952. He undertook a five-year apprenticeship in composing, and attended the LSP where he took his C&G examinations in Composing, at both Intermediate and Final levels. In 1957, realising that the industry was likely to change, though unsure how, he thought he should widen his experience and joined a small general jobbing firm, where he became Clerk to the Chapel and attended union meetings. In 1961 he moved to Tompkins, a well-equipped colour printers, where he did a good deal of advertisement design, and then in 1963 to another jobbing firm where he decided to become a Monotype keyboard operator. He took a 13-week course attending the Monotype school in Chancery Lane for five nights a week. In 1964 he moved to the Adelphi Press combining keyboard operating with hand composing. There he became FoC. He also 'went on the road', getting work for the firm, which he didn't enjoy, so in 1965 he went to Daniel Greenaways, doing company printing which he thoroughly enjoyed, working on nights. After a short stint with another company printer he moved to a typesetting firm.

By now, new methods of typesetting were emerging: 'it fell to me to retrain the staff; I soon realised the older men didn't have the ability to pen rule, a steady hand is required, also a good eye for cut and paste was necessary'. This was the time of the three-day week and the company closed when clients went into liquidation. He was now out of work, at a time when there was very little work for hand compositors. However, keyboard operators were required.

It was 1975 and film setting was making inroads in the industry, so he decided he had to learn about the new systems and had several jobs over the following ten years. By 1985 'film setting was in big time. ... One of the directors was pushing to introduce the Apple Mac, but it was falling on deaf ears with the others'. When the Director set up his own company in 1992, VH joined them with the prospect of training on Apple Macs, which could do the whole job on screen. In 1996 the firm set up a studio in a major advertising agency, an environment completely different: 'we worked directly with art directors and copywriters as the job took shape'; he experienced many further changes to the technology, before retiring in 2006.

The industry had changed radically from the one he entered in 1952, 'and I enjoyed every moment of the way'. The only informant denying any feeling of threat from the new technology, VH said he was aware that the industry was changing but was not worried, by working in different offices every few years he felt able to keep abreast of technological developments and 'stay ahead of the game'.

v) PL also came from a printing family. His father had been a compositor at the Pergamon Press until he was 74, yet given full redundancy pay by Maxwell in 1966. PL in turn entered the print at 14 in 1946; he had signed a seven-year indentureship at C and E Layton, which was reduced to six. PL's next firm sent him to Germany to look at their new technology in the mid-1960s; he was very impressed. He didn't feel threatened at first for he felt confident that his firm would provide a good training, but he began to feel concerned when the firm brought in youngsters and paid them half the compositor's rate; they then got rid of the compositors. He was made redundant in 1993, aged 61. In his 47 years at the trade he worked for 11 firms none of which still exist. He knew many compositors who 'packed it in', several moved into quite other work, for example, as security guards and in sports centres.

vi) JV, born in 1946, entered a six-year apprenticeship at the Cornwall Press, taking a C&G Intermediate Certificate in Compositor's Work. After becoming a journeyman he moved through a couple of jobs in 1968-69, following which he worked for two years as a hot metal compositor at a typesetting firm. With various further changes of employment between 1969 and 1983, there followed a series of adaptations to different aspects of photocomposition: proof-correcting, film make-up, camera work, paper paste-up, and plate-making, experiencing short periods of a few months unemployment. He recalls the period as being somewhat messy in terms of earnings, as whilst national wage agreements were made by the union, they tended to be implemented by firms in different ways, and local bargaining became widespread. With skill shortages, men would change jobs if sufficient overtime was not available or after learning new techniques that were in demand. In one of the firms women were intro-duced as keyboard operators, the employer warning that the company would lose work otherwise; the Chapel had to accept this but insisted they joined the union.

Any new piece of equipment that came into any department of his last but one firm, the Tabloid Press, had to be reviewed by a team representing management, the Chapel and human resources. A new keyboard machine would have to be demonstrated to such a team by a Chapel member, where he would put the equipment through its paces and answer detailed questions. The machine would be graded for pay at a later date according to how much it was an improvement on a previous machine. The flex-ible working practiced within the Chapel meant that when a machine went into a higher grade all members of the Chapel would benefit as they would all use it. The system was at the mercy of rival Chapels trying to stop another department from getting too far ahead in the grading stakes. In 1983 he moved to the Wellcome Foundation, where he remained until taking early retirement in 2002. There, too, he experienced a very wide range of changes in work, including keyboard operating, with the firm having a policy of moving the men to different sections every couple of weeks, so that staff were familiarised with the different and changing aspects of photo-composition. 'One was expected to be flexible and accept continuous relearning, undertaking numerous in-house or print-ing school training schemes.' Many major adjustments were made with little, if any, financial remuneration. Income levels were maintained by a higher grading because of the range of skills required and a high volume of overtime. In retirement JV also became a London guide, with special printing-trade orientated trips.

vii) PS was born in 1955. At 15 he started a six-year apprenticeship at a small jobbing printers in New Cross, London. He did his day release courses at Camberwell College of Art where he took his C&G Basic Craft, Composing certificate, and then to the LCP (previously LSP), where he took his C&G Advanced Craft, Composing, and another course in Graphic Reproduction. During his apprenticeship the period reduced periodically to a minimum of three, maximum of four years, with a requirement to pass a C&G in composing and an employer's recommendation.

He became a compositor technician, first at Camberwell College in around 1978, then at the LCP (now part of the London College of Communication, itself a college of the University of the Arts, London) in 1980. He then assisted the delivery of graphic reproduction to design students, prepress students and, until the mid-eighties, those hot metal composing apprentices still existing in the trade. During his time at the college he witnessed the demise of the apprenticeship system. Employers generally relinquished apprenticeships, and the college experienced a considerable fall-off in demand for day-release courses, as employers pre-ferred to provide their own in-house training for prepress and origina-tion. The City and Guilds withdrew their Composing qualifications in 1981, and these were replaced by a C&G qualification in Origination and Prepress. This was dropped by the College as it moved into higher-level education.

Today, the London College of Communication appears to be the only educational institution in the country specializing in the printing indus-try. Amongst the courses they offer is a two-day-a-week one-year Diploma in Digital Origination, covering design, text inputting, page make-up, and litho printing, as well as a general introduction to the printing industry. This course is taken both by those already working and by students wish-ing to enter the industry. Interestingly, the College offers letterpress to certain graphics students studying Foundation or B.A. courses in Graphics and Media and in the Foundation or B.A. in Book Art Design (see Green Shoots, below). PS is now on the lecturing staff of the College and teaches on the letterpress courses; he never felt threatened by the possibility of losing his job, nor did he resent learning new skills: 'On the contrary, I appreciated being in an establishment where I was required...to learn new skills (which appeared to be in sharp contrast to the experience of many working in the industry at the time, who came to us as students to learn new skills at their...own behest and cost)'.

From the examples above it would appear that the majority of compositors felt threatened, with the occupation facing crisis. One has a sense of men who were no longer able to determine how they did their job, no longer in control of their work situation, and having to adapt to survive. The compositors interviewed in this section were men who were able to respond to the different and frequently challenging demands. They remained in the print, sometimes changing their area of work or setting up on their own, though several felt so vulnerable that they seriously considered other alternatives. Two other conversations with skilled workers from related letterpress occupations which had similarly collapsed suggests that they, too, found other opportunities. One was a Monocaster who grasped unexpected possibilities to become a successful entrepreneur as an employer in a typesetting office, an ambition he hadn't previously considered; the other was a stereotyper who took early retirement and loved it.

But not all were able to adapt; some were so overcome by their experience that they never recovered, and sought less demanding work. One informant related that one compositor ended up working in a refuse yard (almost literally 'on the dustheap'). Another tells of a man who became a solicitor's messenger. Other accounts of printers' lives refer to similar examples: one former compositor wrote of his colleagues 'some could retire early, others retrain, but a minority would slip into decline and suicide'.[26]

One researcher reveals some of the ambivalence that was felt: of the 50 compositors she interviewed many expressed 'nostalgia for the old and gripes about the new'; but the factors of cleanliness and ease of work 'swung most of them finally in favour of the new. They tend to feel that the office style of work is a step up the social ladder'. However, change was not easy, there were accounts of stress, heart attacks, and breakdowns.[27] This confirms the view that some adapted well, others less so, or not at all.

Change: negatives and positives

Whilst the changes were clearly seen as a threat by many compositors, there were also advantages. It is worth drawing together some aspects of both from other sources.

The negatives

Compositors were affected at different stages in the process of techno-logical change, depending on the level of change at the firm they worked for and its employment and payment policies. Generally, levels of remu-neration had less potential for higher earnings, and at some point peri-ods of unemployment or redundancy were experienced. Such negatives were in addition to having to get to grips with completely unfamiliar processes, the psychological impact of uncertainty, a sense of loss of con-trol, no longer being buttressed by a powerful union. Consider what the changes must have meant to a man who had served a six- or seven-year apprenticeship in a seemingly safe and fairly well-paid, prestigious occu-pation; an occupation which had also imparted a strong sense of self and was an important source of identity and satisfaction.[28] Life seemed secure and comfortable, but soon he was to witness changes over which he had little control with many of his skills no longer of use. His expecta-tions and assumptions about the future were seriously undermined.

One compositor working for a firm which made a complete transfer to photofilm as early as 1963 remembers a meeting called by the Managing Director. The MD focused on the favourable aspects of change: in film-setting, the comp. would sit at a light table, working with scissors, scalpel and ruler. There would be no more standing at frames and lifting heavy formes, no dissing or picking for sorts [that is, finding rarely used metal type characters] to replace damaged or missing letters, or running out of spacing materials. But, the compositor observes, these had always been accepted as part of the work. 'We were soon to experience a new and com-pletely different set of frustrating problems' which he goes on to describe in detail, such as making fiddly corrections and coping with problems of film imposition. 'We compositors had gone along with the transition to film. We had endured the frustration that came with it and suffered the loss of our letterpress craft status, only to find ourselves more or less aban-doned by management.' Later, the firm sold out to a large printing con-glomerate which closed the firm, 'a real shock to the local community'.[29]

As the traditional compositor's work situation changed, his skills diluted by performing less skilled tasks, together with the introduction of new forms of labour, some of the conditions for the compositor's own community also began to be undermined. Today there appear to be only remnants left of this colourful aspect of his working life; already its customs and language are gradually dying.

In relation to printing output, several informants referred to a decline in printing standards with the move from hot metal composition. One example has been the decline in the use of specialist proof-correctors and the increased reliance on computerized instructions resulting in more grammatical errors, spelling mistakes, inappropriate word breaks for hyphenation, and poor spacing justification. The use of the author to proof-read his own work has been a particularly dangerous trend, over-familiarity with the text leading to errors remaining unnoticed. It may be that further sophistication of software will help overcome some of these problems.

Some benefits of change

Nostalgia can be dangerous, leading to over-romanticizing the past. For the changes taking place also had positive results. New skills, some transferable such as computing, were being learnt – though many compositors would probably have preferred not being forced to learn them.

As already mentioned, an important benefit for those working in the print, has been a cleaner and seemingly healthier environment. Over the years there had been repeated reference to the health problems of compositors, a source of concern in the days of hot metal; indeed, several research projects on the matter had been undertaken in the 1920s. One of these selected the compositor's work to look at the relationship between illumination, efficiency, and fatigue.[30]

Another important study found that though printers had a lower mortality rate than other males, they experienced a higher rate of tuberculosis, and this was especially marked among the compositors.[31] Explanations for this couldn't be determined, either boys of lower physique were attracted into the trade, or there were environmental factors, such as working with lead (which could lower resistance to disease and infection), inadequate ventilation, cramped conditions, gas lighting, and dust. Of the last, one printer commented, 'the dust had to be seen to be believed: I doubt if the place had ever had more than the floor swept since the day they opened, and certainly the cases were never cleaned out'.[32] To attempt to overcome this problem, St. Clements Press devised a dust extractor which it sold to the trade.[33] In addition, there was the hazard of bad backs due to lifting heavy cases and formes without care or training. Today there would have been litigation on such matters as the working environment and the non-provision of adequate instruction on health hazards.

It should be said that modern technology, though cleaner, introduces other health issues, such as the possible deleterious effects of a high usage of visual display screens for keyboarding; increased laser use; and the need for appropriate seating and posture.[34]

Other benefits have also been effected: printing costs have been reduced; and fewer inter-union demarcation disputes are experienced. But the major gains have been those impacting on society: the widespread availability of the technological changes has made self-expression and publication easier. Further, whilst overall numbers in printing have substantially declined, the new technology has extended the range of occupational opportunities for women.[35]

Green shoots?

Hot metal composition isn't completely extinct. First, there are the hobby printers, men and women who enjoy working with metal type; some are former printers, others did a little at school, art school, or were even introduced to the idea when young by the present of a small John Bull printing set. More seriously perhaps, there are a number of small printing shops producing generally small scale or fine art work, sometimes using hot metal. An umbrella organization, the British Printing Society, which covers a variety of such interests, has about 400 members; they publish *Small Printer*. One member firm visited, which undertakes a wide range of work, is housed in a tiny workshop[36] run by two ladies in Archway, London. They were both trained as graphics students but wanted to engage in print production from start to finish. They appreciated the appearance that letterpress gave, particularly in smaller kinds of work. They managed to accomplish good quality work, using hot metal and electronic type-setting with letterpress and litho, in a very confined space (indicated by the name of their accommodation).

In recent years, some graphics educators have begun to feel that knowledge of letterpress can be valuable for students, even though they are unlikely to use it much directly in their careers. There has been a concern that with technological sophistication almost anything visual is achievable. Without the limitations of letterpress, two problems in particular have been highlighted: first, design possibilities are so open-ended that students are baffled by the range of choices available to them; secondly, graphic designers have tended to focus on the design aspect rather than

The Corridor at Harrington and Squires. Copyright Hege Saebjornsen

the purpose of the printed matter to be produced, designing to capture attention rather than for readability. A desire for creativity can result in, for example, the choice of unsuitable font and type size, over-varied fonts, or using combinations of colour for print and paper, all of which can reduce legibility or readability, with the reader being visually distracted. Aesthetics overrides function. There is a view which may be growing that by reintroducing and working with letterpress some discipline can be provided to budding designers. It might be said to support a view expressed in an earlier phase of technological change, that 'almost all the really good photocomposition that is to be seen comes from those printing houses where the letterpress memory lingers on.'[37] Whether this still holds true it would be difficult to judge. But it can be argued that without a good understanding of the rules of typography, the visual norms on readability which evolved over centuries of typesetting, it is very hard to produce well-laid out text; and there is no better way of learning these rules than to work with letterpress. Further interesting arguments on the value for graphics students of experiencing letterpress, emphasizing, for example, the physicality or tactile aspect of letterpress composition, can be found in a conference on the subject, as well as other writings.[38] Though whether sufficient attention can be given to this in the curriculum to be really effective has to be questioned, at least students would be provided with some knowledge of the sources of much printing terminology used today.

These are hardly green shoots for hot metal, rather ignited embers kept alive by enthusiasts; but they help keep a light on a technology now largely in the past.

Closing comments

It has always been difficult to hold back technological advance when it brings with it major economic benefit. The field of digital printing will continue to change, in ways difficult to predict; already there is talk of the death of the printed book, and of newspapers being replaced by web-sites and hand-held readers. The experience of the compositor epitomises much of what will continue to be experienced with the sweep of techno-logical development. The rapidity and scale of the internet revolution suggests we are only at the beginning of this process.

This book has indicated the importance of the occupation and the role of the occupational community, as a source of wider influence on the compositor's life-style, and of satisfaction in his work, providing not only skill, but status and identity. Could those who have replaced the com-positor develop anything akin to this occupational community, which developed over centuries? Whilst this is impossible to predict, it seems unlikely that with the speed of technological change and the wider social changes that have taken place, a fertile environment can arise for any-thing parallel to this kind of community to develop. The colourful world of the compositor is a world that is lost.

Thus this has been an epilogue in two senses: it is an afterword, a finale to the book; it also bids farewell to a well-regarded occupation established for half a millennium and overtaken by technology; as indeed was the scribe by the compositor and his moveable soldiers of lead.

Notes

1 Clapham,'Typographer and Comp', *Matrix*, no. 18, 1998, p. 5.

2 Duffy, *Skilled Compositor*, p. 69, cites the *Star* and *Press News* foretelling this in 1897.

3 The first fairly durable installation of a photo-typesetting machine in the British printing industry was in 1956 (Wallis, *Electronic Typesetting*, p. 3).

4 Birkenshaw, *Ten Year Technology Forecast*, p. 73.

5 Excellent, clear accounts of developments are to be found in two books by Wallis: *Electronic Typesetting* and *A Concise Chronology of Typesetting Developments 1886–1986*. Seybold's *Fundamentals of Modern Photo-composition* (1979) gives a useful history of some early developments with charts that survey the different typesetting machines, while the periodical *Seybold Report* covers the field in great detail from 1971 onwards. A brief account can be found in Cockburn, *Brothers: male dominance and techno-logical change*, p. 61–4. A very useful recent overview is Mosley,'Technologies of Print', in *Oxford Companion to the Book*, p. 89–104.

6 *Private Angelo*, by Eric Linklater, privately printed at Christmas 1957 for Allen Lane and Richard Lane 'is believed to be the first book produced in England entirely without the use of metal type' (the quotation is from the accompanying greetings card tipped into the St Bride Library copy, 30179).

7 Another factor possibly affecting the date was the age of current machinery; PIRA's ten year forecast for the industry made in 1979 had noted that in the newspaper industry hot metal machines were likely to finish their lives within five to seven years, (Section 5.2).

8 Rupert Murdoch wanted to break what were called 'Spanish Practices', which were especially strong in newspaper production, where the significance of deadlines gave the union extra power. He said that he got pretty tired of restrictive practices 'So we brought in computers from New Hampshire, printers from Australia and truckers from outside London, and secretly began building a system to print and distribute all of our papers from that one site [in Wapping, London] – that is to say, more than 35 million newspa-pers a week [*The Times*, the *Sunday Times*, the *Sun* and *News of the World*]' (Murdoch, 'Publishing Revolution' (Online resource)). By 1988 most national papers had abandoned Fleet Street having relocated to the Docklands and other areas. For a readable, journalist's account of the Murdoch/union bat-tles over introducing technological innovation, which changed the balance of power between owners and the unions, see Melvern, *End of the Street*, and more particularly Littleton, *Wapping Dispute*.

9 Barson and Saint, *Farewell to Fleet Street*.

10 Maitland, *London's Printing and Publishing Industry*, p. 10 sect. 2.4, p. 13 sect. 2.4, p. 14 sect. 3.4, and p. 19 sect. 5.16.

11 'Photo-composing', *Members Circular* (BFMP), February 1958, p. 38.

12 'Course on Computer Typesetting', *Members Circular* (BFMP), December 1963, p. 448.

13 'To Merge or Not to Merge', *Members Circular* (BFMP), September 1963, p. 329. Inter-union demarcation disputes were reduced but not eliminated: for example, a major dispute in 1974 between SLADE and the NGA, had to be resolved through the ACAS process; see Great Britain, Department of Employment, *Report of a Committee of Inquiry into the Dispute at Odhams (Watford) Ltd.*

14 *Estimating for Printers*, 9th ed., London: BFMP, 1970, p. 32–6; 10th ed., London: BPIF, 1979, p. 21–31; 11th ed., London: BPIF, 1980, p. 24–8; 13th ed., London: BPIF, 1989, p. 217; Spiers, *Print Estimators*, London: BPIF, 1996.

15 'Staffing of Typewriters and Tape-producing Keyboards', *Members Circular* (BFMP), September 1968, p. 226–7; quotation from p. 227, col. 3.

16 'Staffing of Typewriters'; quotation from p. 227, col. 3.

17 NGA, *Report of the Third Triennial Delegate Meeting*, 1972, p. 29.

18 'Joint Apprenticeship Study', *Members Circular* (BFMP), November 1973, p. 254–5; for further detail see 'Structure of Printing Education in State of Flux', *Members Circular* (BFMP), December 1973, p. 276–7.

19 Information from Proskills, the national body for skills training, and the BPIF. Numbers taking City and Guilds courses in print were not available.

20 NGA, *Report of the Third Triennial Delegate Meeting*, 1972, p. 30.

21 'Computer Training', *Graphical Journal*, March 1965, p. 70.

22 The syllabus covered tape controlled composing systems for hot metal and film, general and special purpose computers, programming, and trends and developments ('Computer Course', *Graphical Journal*, August 1965, p. 266, and December 1965, p. 397).

23 It is interesting to note that the last address of one retiring president in 1974, Fred Simmons – who was urging further amalgamations – referred to a delegate meeting of the Typographical Association, the provincial union, held as early as 1908. A motion on amalgamation was carried, with acclamation, to the effect that there should be one union for the printing industry, an idea which may have been influenced by notions of syndicalism which were around at the time. Tommy Naylor, a famous and long-remembered General Secretary of the LSC supported the motion in his fraternal address to the meeting ('Fred's Farewell', *Print*, July 1974, p. 2–3 at p. 2, col. 1). It was to take about 55 years for the provincial TA and the LTS to amalgamate into the NGA, and more years for other print unions to join together.

24 Further examples can be found in the Donald Milham Archive, which records the experiences of individual compositors and other printers in the later twentieth century. (Typescript copies can be consulted at the St Bride Library and the University of Reading.) The Sound Archive at Reading

University has additional cds, videos, and dvds compiled by researchers recording memories of printers who experienced the transition from letter-press to lithography. (A word of warning: dates recalled after many years are notoriously unreliable and should be treated with caution.)

25 The Odhams Chapel had a small library and he recalls that the FoC, Charlie Bowdler, a name well-known in the trade at the time, loaned him a copy of *The Ragged Trousered Philanthropists*, a popular portrayal of working class life.

26 Donald Milham Archive, 052.

27 Cockburn, 'The Printers and their Skills: a craft destroyed', *Matrix*, no. 3 (1983), p. 94–7; quotations from p. 95.

28 Identity could sometimes take on an almost literal form. I recall one compos-itor, who used Gill Sans for all advertisements, being known as 'Gill' Bryant; another, with a different penchant, was called 'Garamond' Goodgame.

29 Donald Milham Archive, 071.

30 Weston and Taylor, *Relation between Illumination and Efficiency in Fine Work (Typesetting by Hand)* (Medical Research Council and Department of Scientific and Industrial Research). Also J. H. Sutcliffe, Superintendant of the Army Spectacle Depot, had delivered a lecture on 5 December 1919, 'Care of the Printer's Eyesight'. Speaking of the problems of eyestrain, he suggested that potential printing apprentices be examined for eye defects which could be made worse by their trade.

31 Hill, *Investigation into the Sickness Experience of Printers* (Industrial Fatigue Research Board of the Medical Research Council).

32 Dodson, 'Shadows in the Composing Room', *Matrix*, no. 21 (2001), p. 167–8; quotation from p. 168.

33 Clement Dust Extractor Co., *The Printers' Enemy* [brochure advertising the Clements Patent Case Dust Extractor, ca. 1913].

34 *Printers Guide to Health and Safety* (Health and Safety Executive), particu-larly p. 26, 69–70 and 91–2.

35 Hayton, 'Women, Work and New Technology'.

36 Harrington and Squires, The Corridor, 136a Fortess Road, London NW5 2HP.

37 Randle, 'Hot-metal Typesetting in 2000', *Matrix*, no. 3 (1983), p. 142.

38 Edwards, Lockheart and Raein, *The Codex Project* (online resource). A plea to introduce letterpress composing to typography and design students is made in David Jury's lively and insightful *Letterpress*.

Appendices

The three appendices to the original thesis have different purposes.

Appendix A gives a description of the hand compositor's work and the kinds of abilities required by the craft.

Appendix B sets out the methodology used to obtain the sample of the hundred compositors who were interviewed, in order to arrive at a reasonably representative group. The sample was based on different sized firms reflecting the non-newspaper industry in the London region; another consideration was the need for a total number of firms manageable enough to handle. The account is given of how the different relevant bodies, the master printers, the union, and the chapels were approached to gain their agreement. The Appendix also discusses the sample of apprentices.

Appendix C is the vocabulary of special words that compositors have developed over the years. The vocabulary is used in the thesis as one measure of the occupational community. The list is not exhaustive, nor are the words necessarily used solely by compositors. An assessment of how much the words are known and used is made.

Appendix A

The compositor's work and work situation

The compositor sets up or arranges type from which the printing is to be made. Originally the printer both composed the type and printed from the press – and this still happens in one- or two-man firms; but these two operations soon became two distinct occupations and then, particularly with the introduction of printing machines, separate departments. Today most type is set by machine, either single letters (Monotype) or in complete lines (Linotype or Intertype), and hand setting is generally done only when the amount of copy to be set is small, or when the type is for display purposes (as for example, in advertisements and headlines). Hand compositors are, however, still numerically the largest section of compositors, outnumbering the operators by nearly four to one.

Work procedures will vary in different firms but an approximate outline for the hand compositor can be given. The copy for a job is sent to the composing room and given to the compositor who is to be responsible for the job. He will ensure that the copy is marked up correctly, and that the type face and size, and the measure (line-length) in which the type is to be set is indicated. The copy is then taken to the composing machine section to be set up. After the type has been set it is placed on long, narrow trays called 'galleys' and an impression is taken; this is sent to the reading department to be read with the original copy for checking. After the galley proof has been read, the compositor corrects the type; then the type is 'made up' in the way it is to appear when printed. This is the stage when most skill may be required: arranging the type to get the desired effect, and choosing and setting typefaces as necessary for lines that are to appear differently from the main text such as side headings. Proofs of the made up job are checked by the reader, and then the completed type pages are placed into steel frames (called 'chases') and positioned so that the pages will appear consecutively when they have been printed and folded; this operation is called 'imposing'. The combined type and chase (a 'forme') is then ready to be transported to the printing machine department. Unless there are further corrections to be made when the job is on the machine, that is the last the compositor sees of his work before it is printed. If the job is not required again the formes are returned to the composing department for dismantling.

All compositors have to complete an apprenticeship (now six years). Mode of entry has been largely informal, that is by some personal contact with, or application to, a firm. Attempts to formalize entry by selective procedures via the JIC have been made and applicants are examined in English, Arithmetic, General Knowledge and have an IQ test. Though many firms do not use the scheme the proportion of composing apprentices selected in this way is increasing, and it would appear that about 60 per cent of composing apprentices in London are now being selected through the examination. Training varies from firm to firm, a problem of concern for the unions and the master printers; one means of securing a wider training is the release from work to printing schools for one day or half day each week; this practice is widespread in London.

Certain qualifications are desirable for the work: the ability to manipulate small objects, which involves both dexterity and patience; some appreciation of design and layout; some acquaintance with English punctuation and simple grammar; and sufficient intelligence to interpret the needs of the customer, and to enable the job to be read easily (a large number of decisions may have to be made here, from how to group the type, to deciding where it is most desirable to hyphenate a word that has to be divided because of lack of space).

Qualifications such as these are not always demanded. The extent to which the compositor needs to be creative in designing a job has declined. The growth of the industry has encouraged specialization, and this aspect of the compositor's work has been increasingly taken over by typographic artists employed in advertising agencies, publishing and printing firms, who design the job before it is seen by the compositor. This decline in creativeness does not mean that compositors do not need to appreciate design. Design standards have increased in printing, and schools try to imbue craft students with some appreciation of good layout. Further, the designs of the typographer may not be precise, and the compositor may still have to interpret the intention of the artist and select typefaces accordingly. (It may be noted that in this country the word 'typographer' is reserved for the layout artist, whereas in the United States compositors are also known as typographers).

With the reduction in the number of compositors engaged on hand setting, the need for knowledge of the English language has also declined; today this is more essential for composing machine operators. However, the hand compositor spends a considerable portion of his time in the course of a week setting type and he can reduce corrections to this work if he is familiar with the language; the inability to spell could slow down his speed of setting.

Different sections of the industry tend to emphasize different qualifications. Very roughly it may be said that the general printing firms require the widest range of ability and knowledge; it is here that the compositor may still have to design the job and decide which typefaces are most suitable; however, many of the very small printing shops, which generally only do general printing, tend to lack high standards of design. Firms combining general printing with the printing of periodicals require fairly high standards of versatility, and a knowledge of a wide range of typefaces is desirable and can be learnt in such offices; the amount of initiative required in these offices varies considerably, but some of the craft has been taken out of the work in offices where mechanization has been introduced and materials have been standardized. In newspaper offices the emphasis is on speed in putting into effect a layout that is largely predetermined by others. The amount of knowledge and versatility required is perhaps less here than in the other sections of the industry.

Firms differ in the structure of the composing department, but a general pattern can usually be seen. The composing department consists of hand and machine compositors and the proof-reading room (where the readers may or may not have been compositors previously). In addition the department may include a few pressmen who print the proofs which are seen by the customer before the job is printed, and the men who cast the metal ingots for the Monotype machines; these have an entirely different training. Except in small firms each department in the firm has its overseer who is under the authority of the works manager. In the composing department, the overseer divides up the work between the men. When a job is a large one, needing a number of hand compositors, one of the compositors is generally given charge of the job. This man is called a 'clicker' and is given an extra sum of money for this responsibility. Clickers tend to retain their status, particularly in large firms, and even when the job does not recur, further jobs are generally put into their care. The group of men in the charge of the clicker is termed a 'companionship', this 'ship, as it is called, may be added to or reduced in number according to the work available, but it tends to be a fairly permanent group, especially when the job is a recurring one. Not all jobs need several men and where one man is sufficient for the job he is directly responsible to the overseer, thus there may be a number of men who are not attached to any 'ship. If the firm is a large one the different types of composing machine would be formed into separate sections with their own operator-in-charge; they would thus form a sub-group, but under the general sur-veillance of the composing room overseer.

It is difficult to distinguish clear status differentials between these var-ious groups in the composing department. There is a hierarchy of over-seer, clicker, and other journeymen. But whilst the distinction between the overseer and the rest is clear, that between clicker and other jour-neymen may be blurred. Here the relationship is more fluid with status sometimes non-existent or not accorded, depending on such factors as the size and permanence of the 'ship, amount of responsibility and skill entailed in the job being done, or the personality of the clicker. Some status differential may exist, conferred on the clicker not only because of his responsibility but because of his position in the line of communica-tion with management, he is the link with the overseer and he may be directly consulted by the works manager or by editors of journals. There is some general status differential between the machine operators, read-ers and the hand compositors: the operator is regarded as having an extra skill, and the reader as being knowledgeable. But within the firm such esteem is often more specifically based on performance and thus may not be accorded to individuals in these occupations.

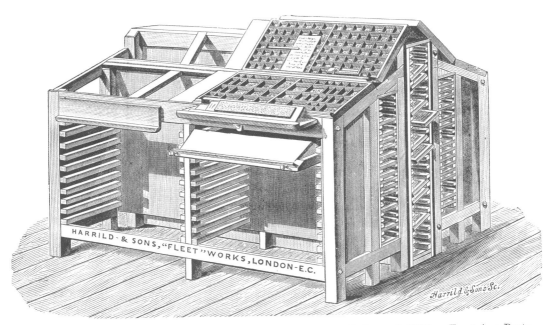

Improved Double Frame, with Double Case Racks, Correcting Galley and Sliding Emptying Rests, Internal Galley Rack, etc., *i.e.* two Double Frames, back to back, with Galley Rack between.

Appendix B

The samples

The survey data are derived from two samples, the main one of journey-men compositors and the other of composing apprentices.

Journeymen

A sample of journeymen compositors was made possible through the help of the London Master Printers' Association (LMPA), and all the compositors were in firms which were members of the LMPA. Drawing the sample from this source had the advantage of including men who were not members of the LTS. A disadvantage is that though member firms of the LMPA cover about ninety per cent of the labour force, many very small firms are not members of the LMPA; but as it is unlikely that compositors in small non LMPA firms are different from compositors in small LMPA firms, little, if any, bias is likely from this factor. Before any interviewing was attempted the LTS was approached to find out whether they had any objection to the proposed interviewing. This facilitated access.

The sample was drawn on the following basis. It had already been decided that it would be desirable to interview about 100 compositors. Though not a sufficient number for detailed analysis it was thought to be fairly adequate for the scope of this study, and it was a number which was possible for one interviewer to deal with (particularly as it was not certain whether compositors would be interviewed at their workplace or whether visits to their homes would be necessary).

It was likely that size of firm would be significant in various ways. Comparison of LMPA statistics on size of firms with those of the LTS showed that the LMPA figures could be taken as fairly representative of the distribution of compositors in the London printing trade. The number of size divisions had to be limited if any analysis by size was to be made, and it was decided to make the following three-fold division for sampling purposes: (i) small firms, those employing fewer than ten compositors (here the work process was likely to be less rationalized, the men in close contact, and the Chapel less highly organized); (ii) medium firms, those employing from ten to 50 compositors (the organization of the work and the Chapel was likely to vary considerably in these firms, but tend towards being more formal); (iii) large firms, those employing more than 50 compositors (here both the work process and the Chapel were likely to be more highly organized). The sample was distributed in the proportion of 25, 36 and 39 for each size group respectively corresponding to the size distribution of the LMPA member firms.

Though the number of compositors to be interviewed in each group had, of course, to be in the same proportion to the 100 as the proportion of compositors in each group was to the total number of compositors, it was necessary to decide what number of firms the sample should cover (bearing in mind the need to limit the number of firms to be approached). At first it seemed desirable to limit the number of men interviewed in each firm to prevent the danger of bias from communication between the respondents, i.e. from feedback; the smaller the firm the lower the number it would be expedient to interview. The number of firms in each group was arrived at by dividing the total number of men required for the size group by the number of men it was preferable to interview for that size group. After the firms were selected, however, it was decided that the same sampling interval should be used for all firms in the size group. This interval was found by dividing the number of compositors required for interviewing into the total number of compositors employed in all the firms in the size group. By the time the firms were selected it was clear that it would be possible to interview the men at the workplace; this meant that the time lag between interviews would be short and there would be little danger of bias through feedback.

The procedure for drawing the sample of firms was as follows. Having given the number of firms required in each size range to the LMPA, the research section of that organization kindly proceeded to draw the sample at random from their alphabetical card index of member firms; these were selected until the required number for each size group was obtained. The procedure had its defects: it cannot be stated with assurance that every firm had equal chance of being selected; this would have been a lengthy task for the cards would have had to be differently arranged. But it seems unlikely that any bias for the purpose of this enquiry is likely to have resulted, and the sample is fairly representative of firms in the London printing trade, other than the newspaper section.

When all the firms were selected, a letter was sent by the LMPA asking whether the firm would grant facilities for interviewing a number of compositors. It was made clear that the interviewer was independent of any organization and was concerned with various features about the social condition of the compositor. The data below shows the number of firms originally selected and the number actually used for drawing the sample of compositors.

Size of chapel	Number of firms			
	In original sample	Used	Refused	Not used
1–10	15	10	4	1
11–50	18	13	1	4
51 +	8	5	0	3

Size of chapel	Total number of compositors in firms used	Number interviewed	Sampling interval
1–10	51	25	2
11–50	283	36	8
51 +	540	39	13
	874		

As can be seen, only five out of the 41 firms selected refused to give access to their compositors, most of these were in very small firms. A further eight firms were not used for various reasons: it was difficult to arrange a convenient time; or they had not replied to the LMPA's letter; or interviewing could not be done at the firm (in addition to the fact that this meant a considerable saving in time, it was preferable to keep the interview situation uniform). Therefore, it was decided not to press firms who had refused or who had not replied, except as a last resort. The fact that there had been a major dispute in the trade during the year might have produced some hesitancy. There did not appear to be anything significant about these firms that would introduce a bias into the sample. This conclusion was reinforced by the fact that two firms in the smallest size group who had not replied to the letter were approached in order to make up the numbers in this group: they had overlooked replying to the letter and were quite happy to grant facilities for the interviews.

The heaviest concentration of firms used in the sample was in the central districts of London. These districts conform to the concentration of the printing industry in general: the East Central and West Central and the South East One area. The firms that were selected but not used in the sample had a geographical distribution not very dissimilar from those used; three-quarters being in these central districts north and south of the Thames.

The procedure at each firm followed a set pattern. A member of the management was first interviewed and information on the following topics was requested: the range of wages paid in the composing department, and additional bonuses; the amount of overtime worked by the compositors; the number of administrative staff who were recruited from the composing and other manual departments; whether recruitment into the composing room was satisfactory in terms of quality of apprentices.

The interview was begun by some general questions about the history of the firm and the kind of work done, and the number of men working in the composing room was checked. All the interviews were pleasant and additional information was often volunteered about special conditions in the firm, relations with the union or the Chapel, and the shortage of labour. Few detailed questions were asked about the nature of the research to be done and in no case was it requested that the questionnaire be seen. After this interview another date was either arranged, or, more frequently, there was an immediate introduction to the FoC of the composing department (in the larger firms the composing room overseer would be introduced first).

It was essential that the compositors were selected with the approval of the Chapel organization. In the first place it was desirable to show the independent nature of the enquiry by getting the acquiescence of both sides of the industry. Secondly, without the Chapel's approval interviewing would not have been allowed. Thirdly, the Chapel list of members would provide a useful basis for the sample, and the FoC could state whether the man's age was suitable and introduce the interviewer. Fourthly, information about the Chapel was to be obtained from the FoC. Generally there was no difficulty. The FoC recalled hearing of the enquiry as a result of the LMPA's letter to the firm; often he had already 'got the feeling' of the Chapel by having asked a few of the members, or had held a Chapel committee meeting, or had decided himself that access to the members could be granted; a letter from the union showed that they were aware of the enquiry.

Refusals were rare. Extra names were collected in case of refusal and then rejected if not used. Altogether only five compositors refused entirely – they had all been asked by the FoC (two of those were predicted, the men being well-known as 'cantankerous'). Each interviewee was told that no record of names was being kept so that anonymity was assured, and that any question could, of course, be refused to be answered. Only in one case was a question refused. Most compositors readily agreed to participate, and many commented afterwards that they enjoyed the interview, were surprised that the questions were not more personal and some even kindly volunteered their names and addresses in case they could be of further help. The time taken in each interview varied from about 20 minutes to three-quarters of an hour. In most cases, all the interviews took place during the one visit, where this was impossible a visit was arranged as soon as possible (usually for the following day) so that any communication among the compositors about the interview could be reduced. The whole of the interviewing took place from December 1959 to February 1960.

The sample of compositors appears to be fairly representative of the London printing trade, excluding the national newspaper section. These were specifically excluded because their generally much higher earnings and peculiar hours were likely to make them somewhat different from other compositors, and they would need to have been considered separately.

Possible sources of bias need to be mentioned. In the first place all the compositors interviewed were on day work. A proportion of London compositors (about ten per cent of the general trade according to the LTS) are engaged on night work; they have higher earnings and peculiar hours. Also, all compositors under 30 were specifically left out of the sample and therefore the age distribution of the sample is not representative of all compositors; where this factor is significant in the way of life it is referred to in the text.

Some estimate of the representativeness of the sample can be made by comparing the age distribution of the sample with London compositors in general (based on information for the same year supplied by the LTS). it should be noted that the percentages in each case are of all those over 30, and not of all compositors (about 75 per cent of all London compositors are over 30 years old).

It will be seen that age distribution is fairly representative; the small bias towards the older age group in the sample may be a result of the absence of night workers – as a man gets older he might be less inclined to work on the night shift. Comparison of the occupations of composi-

Age	Sample	All compositors
	%	%
30–40	28	28
41–50	28	32
51 +	44	40

tors in general with those interviewed can also be made. The size of the sample did not warrant stratification by occupation and occupations are not analysed separately. It is likely that the way of life is different to some extent for the different occupational divisions.

Occupation	Sample	All compositors
	%	%
Working overseers	5	
Store	6	83
Hand compositors	74	
Lino and Intertype	4	11
Mono	11	6
	100	100

The sample's occupational distribution is not precisely representative of London compositors. Though the proportion of machine compositors (Lino, Inter, and Mono) combined, at 15 per cent, is similar to all compositors (machine compositors are about one-sixth of all compositors in the general trade), Mono operators are over represented and there are too few Lino operators. This is because a high proportion of Linotype operators were employed in the newspaper sector, which was deliberately excluded in the sample.

It is difficult to say whether the number of storemen and working overseers is representative, but it would seem that they are not over represented in the sample. The total number of firms in London with composing departments is about 800. Many of these are very small firms without either an overseer or a storeman; large firms however, may have several storemen. It is possible that on average there are between one and two men in these occupations in each firm. This would give a proportion in both these occupations of between eight and 12 per cent – not unlike the sample at 11 per cent.

Thus taking age and occupational distribution it would appear that the sample is not widely different from London compositors as a whole.

Apprentices

The information on apprentices was derived from a questionnaire submitted to all apprentices in their first year and fifth year who were in attendance during the same week in November, at a major specialist printing college in London, the LSP. The majority of composing apprentices in London attend this school and there is no reason why these apprentices are not typical of all composing apprentices of their age. The only major source of bias is the fifth year group. About one-third of those apprentices who should have gone into the fifth year left college at the end of the fourth year. It is possible that the educational attainment and social origins of those who left were lower than those who continued their day-release education; any possible bias from this source is referred to in the text. The questions were asked as part of an enquiry into other aspects about the students, and the questionnaire was filled in by the students during one of their class periods at the school. There were no refusals to fill in the questionnaire and only two had to be rejected for not being answered seriously; this left 142 usable replies. The enquiry was confined to boys apprenticed in London; the number involved represents about ten per cent of the total number of composing apprentices in the area.

Appendix C

The Compositor's Vocabulary

Frequency with which the words were known or used in the 28 firms in the sample

Word	Known	Used regularly	Used rarely
Pie	28	27	1
OT	28	27	0
Bit of fat	28	26	2
Gobbler	27	26	0
Slum	26	23	2
Chopper	26	22	1
GH	25	21	4
Chuff	25	21	3
Trunk out	24	21	1
The 'O'	26	20	2
Trot	25	20	2
Ship	28	19	5
Coach	25	19	3
Cut the line	26	18	3
KD	24	18	3
Wrong cast off	26	17	5
Clicker	28	17	1
Nailing	24	16	7
Space up	21	16	3
Spiking	26	16	2
NF	24	15	7
WF	25	14	4
Cap I	20	14	3
Out	19	14	3
Side/back page	26	13	6
Take	23	13	3
Rounder	24	11	7
Screamer	22	10	3
Dark'un	17	8	5
The organ	23	7	6
No you don't	15	6	6
Slate	18	6	5
Knowing your boxes	18	5	7
Swinger	13	5	2
You can	10	5	2
Wayzgoose	23	3	9
Pica thumper	27	2	11
Miles' Boy	7	2	2
HSE	5	2	0
AHA	5	2	0
Ralph	1	0	0
Bridging	0	0	0

Brief Definitions of Words Submitted

AHA All Hope Abandoned, see HSE

Bit of fat An easy job. It may imply that longer time can be attributed to it than it actually takes.

Bridging Failing to appear at the appointed time and forward no reason for absence.

Cap I Egotism: a person always talking about his achievements may be said to be running out of Cap I's referring to using up the capital letter I in a case of type.

Chopper Being disgruntled and unapproachable.

Chuff Being happy.

Clicker Man in charge of a job (the origin of this word may be that the person 'clicks' for the job, i.e. is fortunate enough to get it, or, more probably, is in charge of a clique).

Coach To ignore another member in the Chapel is expressed as 'having him on the coach'. Also semi-coach, to ignore except for official or work purposes. Sometimes 'got him on' is said or 'he's a conductor' (that is to say, he is on a coach).

Cut the line Stopping work for meal break. Also 'the line is on' is sometimes used for commencing work.

Dark'un or Darkie Working overtime for five or six hours. Sometimes known as a 'ghoster'.

GH Used when an obvious remark is made or for stale news. The letters stand for George Horne (or Hall) who was reputed to know everything that he was told.

Gobbler One who does as much overtime as possible.

HSE Hope Springs Eternal; said when one hopes to be asked to do overtime. Also, AHA (All Hope Abandoned), said when it is obvious that one isn't going to be asked.

KD To keep dark: not to disclose information.

Knowing your boxes Knowing one's job or what one is talking about. (An apprentice has to learn the layout of the boxes in a case of type.)

Miles' Boy Miles was a printer whose apprentice was knowing and artful, who always knew what was going on.

Nailing or 'having the nail box out'. Talking about someone derogatorily behind his back.

NF No fly. One who is quick witted is said to have no flies on him. Similarly one who ignores a pointed remark intended for him is said to be NF. There is a double meaning here: that the person is too quick for a fly to settle on him, or that he doesn't rise to the bait of a fly (as would a fish).

No you don't Said when the information given is not believed.
OT Overtime.
Out To come out – to lose one's temper. 'Getting' or 'drawing him out' – making him lose his temper.
Pica thumper Before composing machines all type was set by hand and those who spent their days speedily putting type into their sticks were known as pica thumpers. Pica is a size of type.
Pie Accidentally mixed up type.
Ralph The Chapel ghost, blamed for misdeeds where the culprit is unknown.
Rounder Working overtime all night.
Screamer Exclamation mark.
Ship (or boat) A companionship of compositors engaged on the same job.
Side page The compositor whose working frame is alongside one's own. Also back page (the man behind); front page (the man in front); front page doubled up (the man after the one in front); diagonal (the compositor working in front of one's side page, also known as shilling stroke).
Slate Having no work. A slate used to be provided for a man to write his name when he had finished a job, so that he could be the next one to receive some work. This system is particularly important when piece work is in operation, when the absence of work means reduced wages.
Slum A secret hoard of materials in short supply.
Space up A metal space between words which has risen and is therefore printing in error. When two men have quarrelled there is said to be a space up between them.
Spiking Copy is spiked at the point where it has been left uncompleted or not used. Also used when type is physically spiked in order to tighten a line – a bad practice.
Swinger The last piece of copy.
Take A large batch of copy may be divided into a number of 'takes' to be distributed to several compositors for setting.
The 'O' The overseer.
The organ A mutual club subscribed to weekly from which loans can be made or which is distributed periodically.
Trot Playing a practical joke on another person or 'leading him up the garden'.
Trunk out Keep your nose out.
Wayzgoose (or beano) Annual outing.
WF A wrong fount, a type of one fount mixed by mistake with another fount; this is often applied to people who are considered odd.

Wrong cast off To make a wrong estimate or judgment; derived from wrongly estimating the area of type which copy will make.

You can Meaning you can do, or have, the thing being talked about. The implication varies with the inflection used; it can be used ironically to mean the opposite.

Other words in the vocabulary*

Barging Taking things that should not be taken; derived from taking sorts of type from one case to another (therefore leaving less in the case used regularly by another compositor).

Daily lie The work docket.

Grassing or smouting Working for more than one employer.

Hammer the job To charge more for a job than it is really worth.

Nose in 'e' box Man who is always busy (this dates from the time when type was all hand set, and a compositor would be constantly picking up 'e' from its compartment in a case of type).

On the square A Freemason.

Overmatter Something extra or that can't be used.

Pudden or Pudding Working during the dinner hour at overtime rates.

Pull a revise To do something again, or to change one's mind about something.

Pull out To work hurriedly.

Stickful To give someone a stickful (referring to a composing stick full of type) is to give him a long harangue.

Whiting it out To put a lot of space into the job; to lengthen a story unnecessarily.

*Further words can be found in *The 'Line' is On* by G.E. Rowles.

Publisher's note

The collectors Stuart and Kath McMinn brought in their wood engraving, shown above, to St Bride Library to establish its date, purpose and provenance. It was signed by Robson J Scott who advertised as a manufacturer of engravers' blocks of all kinds in the *Post Office Directory of Stationers, Printers, Booksellers, Publishers and Paper Makers* of 1872. He had been established twenty-five years, and offered alterations and reparations. He traded in Whitefriars Street (off Fleet Street) and promised personal superintendence of all kinds of work – satisfaction guaranteed. The specific purpose of this image is still not known but it combines the droll tradition of printers' humour with more critical views of the world of publishing. By tradition Chapels called the compositors 'donkeys' and the pressmen 'horses' but the workers fined each other if they used these terms as taunts. An eighteenth century Grub Street Journal showed the compositors and printers with monstrous heads while a writer in the nineteen-twenties refers to non-union labour as 'an idiotic and insulting caravan of hee-haws ... damnable tribe of cloven-hoofed blacklegs.' According to Balzac, in nineteenth century France the compositors were called 'monkeys' and the pressmen 'bears'. This engraving suggests that printers could be seen as unprincipled (like the Vicar of Bray), serving whichever master would pay them.

Bibliography

The bibliography has been compiled for this published edition, and it includes all the works referred to in the preceding notes. However, where these have appeared in later editions than those used for the original research, reference in the notes is made to those later editions – since they will be more easily found in libraries than superseded ones; the edition cited will always be the last version indicated here.

Manuscript and typescript material

Cannon, I.C., 'The Social Situation of the Skilled Worker: a Study of the Compositor in London', Thesis submitted for the Ph.D. Degree of London University, [1961]. London School of Economics Library, theses collection X30,176. St Bride Library, 31180.

Donald Milham Archive. St Bride Library *and* University of Reading.

Hayton, A., 'Women, Work and New Technology: the implications for education and training: the case of desk top publishing', Open University, MA in Education E816, dissertation, 1992. St Bride Library, 55477. Abridged version published as: *Women, Work and New Technology: the case of desktop publishing: implications for education and training*, [London]: Post-16 Education Centre, Institute of Education, 1995, (Working papers, no. 16). St Bride Library, 55478.

Lintas. There are references in chapters 5 and 6 to Lintas Ltd as a source of statistical information. It has not proved possible to establish whether this material still exists.

London School of Economics Library, Webb Trade Union Collection, vols A30–A31.

London Society of Compositors, Emigration Aid Committee, Minute Book of Monthly Meetings, 9 February 1853 to 18 July 1857. Modern Records Centre, MSS.28/CO/1/2/1/1.

Memories and Impressions of Fifty & Sixty Years Ago, by an Old-Timer. [A manuscript written anonymously in the 1940s, by an old compositor who was apprenticed in his eighteenth year.] Given to the author by G.E. Rowles, and now presented to St Bride Library, 55456.

Richards, J.H., 'Social and Economic Aspects of Combination in the Printing
    Trade before 1875', M.A. Thesis, Liverpool University, 1956. Liverpool
    University Library, thesis 1304B.

Journals associated with or promoting the London compositors' trade unions

The Compositors' Chronicle, London, 1840–3.
The Printer, London, 1843–5.
The Typographical Gazette, London, 1846–7.
The Typographical Protection Circular, London, 1849–53.
London Press Journal, London, 1858–9.
Fleet Street Gazette, London, 1874.
The Printer, London, 1883–8.
*The Vigilance Gazette: a monthly journal devoted to the interests of the London
    Society of Compositors*, London, 1888–90.
Printing News, London, 1892–4.
Print: a journal for Printing-house Employés of all grades and departments,
    London, 1896.
Fleet Street, London, 1903.
London Typographical Journal, London: LSC, 1906–63.
Graphical Journal: official organ of the National Graphical Association, Aspley
    Guise, 1964–7.
Print: the official journal of the National Graphical Association, Bedford, 1968–91.

Other printed works

A.R.L., 'Tuition or Trade?', *The English Woman's Journal* (London), May 1860,
    p. 173–83.
Abrams, M., 'Who owns Household Goods?', *Financial Times* (London), 9
    December 1959, p. 10, cols 3–6.
Abrams, M., 'Why Labour has Lost Elections, Part One, Party Images', *Socialist
    Commentary* (London), May 1960, p. 4–9.
Abrams, M., and R. Rose, *Must Labour Lose?*, Harmondsworth: Penguin Books,
    1960.
'An Address to the People', by 'Silverpen', *The People's Newspaper* (London),
    30 May 1847, p. 1, cols 1–2.
Aron, R., *Main Currents in Sociological Thought*, New York: Basic Books, 1965–
    7, 2 vols; new ed., New Brunswick, N.J.: Transaction Publishers, 1998–9,
    2 vols.

Austen-Leigh, R.A., *The Story of a Printing House: being a short account of the Strahans and Spottiswoodes*, London: Spottiswoode & Co., 1911; 3rd ed., Colchester: Spottiswoode Ballantyne, [1989].

Barson, S., and A. Saint, *A Farewell to Fleet Street*, London: Historic Buildings and Monuments Commission for England, 1988.

Bennett, A., *Clayhanger* [A novel], London: Methuen, 1910; new ed., London: Penguin, 2000.

Beveridge, W.H., *Full Employment in a Free Society*, London: Allen & Unwin, 1944.

Birkenshaw, J.W., *Ten Year Technology Forecast of Printing and Publishing 1995–2005*, Leatherhead: Pira International, 1995.

Booth, C., *Life and Labour of the People in London, Second Series, Industry*, London: Macmillan, 1903, 5 vols.

Bowley, A.L., *Wages and Income in the United Kingdom since 1860*, Cambridge: Cambridge University Press, 1937.

Cannon, I.C., 'Ideology and Occupational Community: a Study of Compositors', *Sociology: the journal of the British Sociological Association*, May 1967, p. 165–85.

Cannon, I.C., 'The Roots of Organization among Journeymen Printers', *Journal of the Printing Historical Society*, no. 4 (1968), p. 99–107.

Carr-Saunders, A.M., D.C. Jones and C.A. Moser, *A Survey of Social Conditions in England and Wales as illustrated by statistics*, Oxford: Clarendon Press, 1958.

Cauter, T., and J.S. Downham, *The Communication of Ideas: a study of contemporary influences on urban life*, London: Chatto and Windus, 1954.

Clapham, J.H., *An Economic History of Modern Britain*, Cambridge: Cambridge University Press, 1926–38, 3 vols.

Clapham, M., 'Typographer and comp', *Matrix*, no. 18 (1998), p. 1–10.

Clement Dust Extractor Co., *The Printers' Enemy*: [brochure advertising the Clements Patent Case Dust Extractor], London, [ca. 1913].

Clowes, W.B., *Family business 1803–1953*, London: Clowes, [1953].

Cockburn, C., *Brothers: male dominance and technological change*, London: Pluto Press, 1983; new ed., London: Pluto Press, 1991.

Cockburn, C., 'The Printers and their Skills: a craft destroyed', *Matrix*, no. 3 (1983), p. 94–7.

Cole, G.D.H., *Chartist Portraits*, London: Macmillan, 1941; reissued 1965.

Cole, G.D.H., and R. Postgate, *The Common People 1746–1946*, London: Methuen, 1949; corrected reprint 1956.

'Computer Course', *Graphical Journal*, August and December 1965, p. 266, 397.

'Computer Training', *Graphical Journal*, March 1965, p. 70.

Conference between representatives of the Federation of Master Printers, the London Master Printers' Association ... and representatives of the Printing and Kindred Trades Federation, at De Keyser's Royal Hotel, London, E.C., on Tuesday, January 10, 1911, [London, 1911].

'"Contract out" Percentage Lower: Political Levy', *The Daily Telegraph and Morning Post* (London), 10 November 1959, p. 20, col. 5.

Co-operative and Economical Society, 'The Society's Circular', *The Economist: a periodical paper explanatory of the New System of Society projected by Robert Owen Esq., and of a plan of Association for Improving the Condition of the Working Classes, during their Continuance at their present Employments* (London), 9 March 1822, p. 409–10.

Cornfield, V.M., *The Effect of the Industrial Revolution on the Workers in the Printing Industry in London*, London: London School of Printing, 1928.

'Course on Computer Typesetting', *Members Circular* (BFMP), December 1963, p. 448.

Crosland, A., *Can Labour Win?* London: Fabian Society, 1960, (Fabian Society Tract no. 324).

Dodson, A., 'Shadows in the Composing Room', *Matrix*, no. 21 (2001), p. 167–8.

Duffy, P., *The Skilled Compositor 1850–1914: an aristocrat among working men*, Aldershot: Ashgate, 2000.

Eisenstein, E.L., *Divine Art, Infernal Machine: the reception of printing in the West from first impressions to the sense of an ending*, Philadelphia: University of Pennsylvania Press, 2011.

Estimating for Printers,
9th ed., London: BFMP, 1970.
10th ed., London: BPIF, 1979.
11th ed., London: BPIF, 1980.
13th ed., by H.M. Speirs, London: BPIF, 1989.

Floud, J.E., *Social Class and Educational Opportunity*, London: Heinemann, 1956.

Franklin, B., *Memoirs of the Life and Writings of Benjamin Franklin*, 2nd ed., London: Colburn, 1818, 2 vols.

'Fred's Farewell' [Fred Simmons], *Print: the official journal of the National Graphical Association*, July 1974, p. 2–3.

A General Description of all Trades: digested in alphabetical order: by which Parents, Guardians and Trustees, may, with greater ease and certainty, make choice of Trades agreeable to the Capacity, Education, Inclination, Strength and Fortune of the Youth under their Care, London: T. Waller, 1747.

Gent, T., *The Life of Mr Thomas Gent, Printer, of York, written by himself* [in 1746], London: Thomas Thorpe, 1832.

Gilboy, E.W., *Wages in Eighteenth Century England*, Cambridge, Mass.: Harvard University Press, 1934.

Gillespie, S.C., *A Hundred Years of Progress: the record of the Scottish Typographical Association 1853 to 1952*, Glasgow: STA, 1953.

Glass, D.V., and J.R. Hall, 'Social Mobility in Great Britain: a study of inter-generation changes in status', in: Glass, D.V., *Social Mobility in Britain*, London: Routledge, 1954, p. 177–265.

Goldthorpe, J.H., D. Lockwood, F. Bechhofer, and J. Platt, *The Affluent Worker: industrial attitudes and behaviour*, Cambridge: Cambridge University Press, 1968.

Great Britain, Board of Trade, *Report of an Enquiry by the Board of Trade into the earnings and Hours of Labour of Workpeople of the United Kingdom*, [Part] *VIII, Paper, Printing, &c. Trades ... in 1906*, London: HMSO, 1913, ([Command papers] Cd 6556), (House of Commons papers, sess. 1912/13, v. 108).

Great Britain, Board of Trade, *The Report on the Census of Production for 1954, v. 10, industry J, Newspaper and Periodical Printing and Publishing*, London: HMSO, 1957.

Great Britain, Board of Trade, *The Report on the Census of Production for 1954, v. 10, industry K, Printing and Publishing, Bookbinding, Engraving, etc.*, London: HMSO, 1958.

Great Britain, Department of Employment *Report of the Committee of Inquiry into the Dispute at Odhams (Watford) Limited, involving the International Publishing Corporation, the Society of Lithographic Artists, Designers, Engravers and Process Workers and the National Graphical Association over the handling of photo-composed material*, London: HMSO, 1974.

Great Britain, General Register Office, *Census of England and Wales 1911, vol. 10, Occupations and Industries*, London: HMSO, 1914, ([Command papers] Cd 7018), (House of Commons papers, sess. 1913, v. 78).

Great Britain, General Register Office, *Census of England and Wales 1931, Industry tables*, London: HMSO, 1934.

Great Britain, Medical Research Council, *see* Hill, A.B., *below*.

Great Britain, Medical Research Council and Department of Scientific and Industrial Research, *see* Weston, H.C., *below*.

Great Britain, Ministry of Labour, *Report of an enquiry into Apprenticeship and Training for the skilled occupations in Great Britain and Northern Ireland 1925–1926*, [Part] *I, Printing and Allied Industries*, London: HMSO, 1927.

Great Britain, Ministry of Labour and National Service, *Statistical Information about Men who register under N.S. Acts during the period 19th November to 17th December 1955*, [London: M.L.N.S., 1955], (M. L. Circular Minutes, 117/1955). National Archives, LAB 29/419.

Great Britain, Privy Council, *see* Smith, E., *below*.

Great Britain, Royal Commission on Depression of Trade and Industry 1885–6, *Second Report of the Royal Commission appointed to Inquire into the Depression of Trade and Industry, Appendix, Pt. II*, London, 1886 ([Command papers] C. 4715-I), (House of Commons papers, sess. 1886, v. 22).

Great Britain, Royal Commission on Population 1944–9, *The Trend and Pattern of Fertility in Great Britain: a report on the Family Census of 1946*, by D.V. Glass and E. Grebnik, London: HMSO, 1954, (Papers of the Royal Commission on Population, v. 6).

Greater London Council, *see* Maitland, R., *below*.

Greg, W.W., and E. Boswell, *Records of the Court of the Stationers' Company 1576 to 1602, from Register B*, London: Bibliographical Society, 1930.

Gregory, W., 'Are we still Christians?, Second Article', *News Chronicle and Daily Dispatch* (London), 16 April 1957, p. 4, cols 3–7.

Halévy, E., *A History of the English People*, London: T. Fisher Unwin, 1924–34, 5 vols; 2nd ed. as: *A History of the English People in the Nineteenth Century*, London: Benn, 1949–52, 6 vols in 7.

Hall, J.R., and D.V. Glass, 'Education and Social Mobility', in: Glass, D.V., *Social Mobility in Britain*, London: Routledge, 1954, p. 291–307.

Hamilton, H., *History of the Homeland: the story of the British background*, London: Allen & Unwin, 1947.

Hansard, T.C., *Typographia: an historical sketch of the origin and progress of the art of printing, with practical directions for conducting every department in an office, with a description of stereotype and lithography*, London: Baldwin, Cradock and Joy, 1825; facsimile reprint, London: Gregg, 1966.

Hill, A.B., *An Investigation into the Sickness Experience of Printers (with special reference to the incidence of tuberculosis)*, London: HMSO, 1929, (Industrial Fatigue Research Board, report no. 54).

Hobsbawm, E.J., 'The Labour Aristocracy in Nineteenth-century Britain', in: *Democracy and the Labour Movement: essays in honour of Dona Torr*, edited by J. Saville, London: Lawrence & Wishart, 1954, p. 201–39; reprinted in: E.J. Hobsbawm, *Labouring Men: studies in the History of Labour*, London: Weidenfeld & Nicolson, 1986, p. 272–315.

Holyoake, G.J., *The Life and Character of Henry Hetherington*, London: J. Watson, 1849. LSE Library, CT/338.

Hovell, M., *The Chartist Movement*, edited and completed with a memoir, by T.F. Tout, Manchester: University Press, 1918; 3rd ed., Manchester: Manchester University Press, 1966; facsimile reprint, Aldershot: Gregg, 1994.

Howe, E., *The British Federation of Master Printers 1900–1950*, London: BFMP, 1950.

Howe, E., *From Craft to Industry: aspects of the London printing trade 1700–1900*, London: North-Western Polytechnic Department of Printing, 1946.

Howe, E., *The London Compositor: documents relating to wages, working conditions and customs of the London printing trade 1785–1900*, London: Bibliographical Society, 1947.

Howe, E., and J. Child, *The Society of London Bookbinders 1780–1951*, London: Sylvan Press, 1952.

Howe, E., and H.E. Waite, *The London Society of Compositors: a centenary history*, London: Cassell, 1948.

Jackson, W.A., *Records of the Court of the Stationers' Company 1602 to 1640*, London: Bibliographical Society, 1957.

Johnson, S., 'An Account of the Life of the Late Mr Edward Cave' [anonymously], *Gentleman's Magazine* (London), February 1754, p. 55–8; reprinted (revised) in *The Works of Samuel Johnson, LL.D.*, new ed., with an essay on his life and genius by Arthur Murphy, London: T. Longman, 1796, 12 vols, v. 12, p. 210–19.

'Joint Apprenticeship Study', *Members Circular* (BFMP), November 1973, p. 254–5.

'Journeymen Printers', [believed to be by Francis Place], *The Gorgon: a weekly political publication* (London), 28 November 1818, p. 217–23.

Jury, D., *Letterpress: the allure of the handmade*, Mies: RotoVision, 2004; reissued as *Letterpress: new applications for traditional skills*, Mies: RotoVision, 2006.

Knight, C., *The Old Printer and the Modern Press*, London: John Murray, 1854.

Knowles, K.G.J.C., and D.J. Robertson, 'Differences between the Wages of Skilled and Unskilled Workers 1880–1950', *Bulletin of the Oxford University Institute of Statistics*, April 1951, p. 109–27.

Laski, M., *The Village* [A novel], London: Cresset Press, 1952.

Lee, A.J., *The Origins of the Popular Press in England 1855–1914*, London: Croom Helm, 1976.

Linklater, E., *Private Angelo* [A novel], [London]: privately printed, 1957; with accompanying greetings card. St Bride Library, 30179.

Linton, W.J., *James Watson: a memoir of the days of the fight for a free press in England and of the agitation for the People's Charter*, Manchester: Heywood & Son, [1880]; facsimile reprint, New York: Augustus M. Kelley, 1971.

Linton, W.J., *Memories*, London: Lawrence & Bullen, 1895.

Lipset, S.M., M.A. Trow, and J.S. Coleman, *Union Democracy: the internal politics of the International Typographical Union*, New York: Free Press, 1956.

Littleton, S.M., *The Wapping Dispute*, Aldershot: Avebury, 1992.

London Society of Compositors, *Annual Report* (London), 38th, 1885.

London Society of Compositors, *An Invitation to join the London Society of Compositors*, London: LSC, [1915].

London Society of Compositors, 'To the Non-Society Compositors of London
   and its Vicinity', London: LSC, 1884. A copy is bound in the St Bride
   Library volume of *The Printer*, 1883–5, after p. 26.

'The London Society of Compositors', by 'Scourge', *The Bee-hive Newspaper:
   a journal of general intelligence advocating industrial interests* (London),
   10 October 1863, p. 1, cols 1–2, (Sketches of the London trades, no. 2).

London Society of Compositors Parliamentary Labour Association, *A retrospect,
   15 March 1909 to 30 June 1916*, London: LSC, 1916.

The London Strike, contributed to the British and Colonial Printer and Stationer,
   by a Master Printer, London: Federation of Master Printers, [1911].

London Trade Society of Compositors, *Annual Report* (London), 11th, 1828.

London Union of Compositors, *Annual Report* (London), 1840.

London Union of Compositors, *Report of the General Trade Committee to the
   Compositors of London*, London, 1834.

M.M.H., 'A Ramble with Mrs Grundy: a visit to the Victoria Printing Press', *The
   English Woman's Journal* (London), June 1860, p. 269–72.

McAra, T.W., 'Reminiscences of Print and Fleet Street', *The Annual Craft
   Lectures for 1927–1928 arranged by the Stationers' Company and Printing
   Industry Technical Board* [*Stationers' Craft Lectures*] (London), p. 13–32.

McKenzie, R., and A. Silver, *Angels in Marble: working-class Conservatives in
   urban England*, London: Heinemann, 1968.

Maitland, R., *London's Printing and Publishing Industry*, London: Greater
   London Council, 1980, (Reviews and Studies series, v. 5).

Marsh, D.C., *The Changing Social Structure of England and Wales 1871–1951*,
   London: Routledge, 1958.

Martin, F.M., 'An Inquiry into Parents' Preferences in Secondary Education', in:
   Glass, D.V., *Social Mobility in Britain*, London: Routledge, 1954, p. 160–74.

Martin, F.M., 'Some Subjective Aspects of Social Stratification', in: Glass, D.V.,
   Social Mobility in Britain, London: Routledge, 1954, p. 51–75.

Marx, K., *Selected Writings in Sociology and Social Philosophy*, edited by T.B.
   Bottomore and M. Rubel, London: Watts & Co., 1956.

Marx, K., and F. Engels, 'Manifesto of the German Communist Party' [First
   English translation], *Red Republican* (London), 9 November 1850; new ed.
   as *The Communist Manifesto*, edited with an introduction and notes by D.
   McLellan, Oxford: Oxford University Press, 1992, (World's Classics).

Melvern, L., *The End of the Street*, London: Methuen, 1986.

Mosley, J., 'The Technologies of Print', *The Oxford Companion to the Book*,
   Oxford: Oxford University Press, 2010, p. 89–104.

Moxon, J., *Mechanick Exercises: or, the Doctrine of Handy-Works, Applied to the Art of Printing: the second volumne*, London: printed for Joseph Moxon, 1683[–4]; standard modern edition as *Mechanick Exercises on the whole Art of Printing (1683–4)*, edited by H. Davies & H. Carter, 2nd ed., London: Oxford University Press, 1962; facsimile reprint, New York: Dover, 1978.

Musson, A.E., *The Congress of 1868: the origins and establishment of the Trades Union Congress*, London: TUC, 1955.

Musson, A.E., *The Typographical Association: origins and history up to 1949*, London: Oxford University Press, 1954. NB. There are two versions of this work, issued under identical titles, by the same publisher, in the same year, but with different pagination, one 255mm tall, the other 223mm; it is the taller version that is cited here.

National Graphical Association, *Report of the Delegate Meeting held in the Spa Ocean Room, Scarborough, on June 26th 1972 and the four following days*, [Bedford, 1972].

The New Survey of London Life & Labour, London: P.S. King, 1930–5, 9 vols.

Nichols, J., *Literary Anecdotes of the Eighteenth Century*, London: printed for the Author, 1812–16, 9 vols; facsimile reprint, New York: AMS Press, 1966, 9 vols.

'Photo-composing', *Members Circular* (BFMP), February 1958, p. 38.

Plant, M., *The English Book Trade: an economic history of the making and sale of books*, London: Allen & Unwin, 1939; 3rd ed., London: Allen & Unwin, 1974.

Pottinger, D.T., *The French Book Trade in the Ancien Regime*, Cambridge, Mass.: Harvard University Press, 1958.

The Printer's Guide to Health and Safety [prepared by the Printing Industry Advisory Committee], Sudbury: HSE Books, 1998; 2nd ed., Sudbury: HSE Books, 2002.

Randle, J., 'Hot-metal Typesetting in 2000', *Matrix*, no. 3 (1983), p. 142.

'Rattening in the Printing Trade' [Letter to *The Times*, signed] O. and Co., *The Times* (London), 12 August 1868, p. 10, col. 5.

Report of the Committee appointed at a Meeting of Journeymen, chiefly Printers, to take into consideration certain propositions submitted to them by Mr George Mudie, having for their object a System of Social Arrangement, calculated to effect Essential Improvements in the Condition of the Working Classes, and of Society at Large, London: at the Medallic Cabinet, [1821].

Sale, W.M., *Samuel Richardson, Master Printer*, Ithaca, N.Y.: Cornell University Press, 1950.

Schoyen, A.R., *The Chartist Challenge: a portrait of George Julian Harney*, London: Heinemann, 1958.

Sessions, M., *The Federation of Master Printers: how it began*, London: Sessions, 1950.

Seybold, J.W., *Fundamentals of Modern Photo-composition*, Media, Pa.: Seybold Publications, 1979.

Seybold Report (United States), [title varies slightly], 30 August 1971– .

Smith, C.M., *The Working Man's Way in the World: being the autobiography of a journeyman printer*, London: Cash, [1853]; reissued with cancel title-pages in 1854 and 1857; facsimile reprint of 1857 issue, London: Printing Historical Society, 1967.

Smith, E., 'Report by Dr Edward Smith on the Sanitary Circumstances of Printers in London', Appendix no. 11 to the *Sixth annual report of the Medical Officer of the Privy Council, 1863*, London, 1864, ([Command papers, 3416]), p. 383–415, (House of Commons papers, sess. 1864, v. 28).

'Society for Promoting the Employment of Women, in connection with the National Association for the Promotion of Social Science', *The English Woman's Journal* (London), August 1860, p. 388–96.

Speirs, H.M., *Print Estimators: the handbook*, London: BPIF, 1996.

'Staffing of Typewriters and Tape-producing Keyboards', *Members Circular* (BFMP), September 1968, p. 226–7.

Strachey, J., *Contemporary Capitalism*, London: Gollancz, 1956.

'Structure of Printing Education in State of Flux', *Members Circular* (BFMP), December 1973, p. 276–7.

Sutcliffe, J.H., 'The Care of the Printer's Eyesight', *Saint Bride Trade Lectures: a series of lectures delivered at Saint Bride Foundation Institute during the session 1919–20*, London: printed by students of the Saint Bride Foundation Printing School, 1920, p. 17–19.

Sykes, A.J.M., 'Trade-union Workshop Organization in the Printing Industry: the Chapel', *Human Relations: a quarterly journal of studies towards the integration of the social sciences* (London), February 1960, p. 49–65.

Thomas, H., *The Beginnings of Printing in London: souvenir of the Lord Mayor's Show 1928*, London: Lanston Monotype Corporation, 1928.

Timperley, C.H., *A Dictionary of Printers and Printing*, London, 1839; reissued with a supplement as *Encyclopaedia of Literary and Typographical Anecdote*, London: Bohn, 1842; facsimile reprint of 1842 issue, New York: Garland, 1977.

'To Merge or Not to Merge', *Members Circular* (BFMP), September 1963, p. 329.

Wallis, L.W., *A Concise Chronology of Typesetting Developments 1886–1986*, London: Wynkyn de Worde Society, 1988.

Wallis, L.W., *Electronic Typesetting: a quarter century of technological upheaval*, [Gateshead]: Paradigm Press, 1984.

Webb, R.K., *The British Working Class Reader 1790–1848: literacy and social tension*, London: Allen & Unwin, 1955.

Webb, S., and A. Freeman, *Seasonal Trades*, London: Constable, 1912.

Webb, S., and B. Webb, *The History of Trade Unionism*, London: Longmans, Green, 1894; rev. ed., extended to 1920, London: Longmans, Green, 1920; facsimile reprint, New York: AMS Press, 1975.

Webb, S., and B. Webb, *Industrial Democracy*, London: Longmans, Green, 1897, 2 vols; new ed., London: Longmans, Green, 1920; facsimile reprint, Basingstoke: Palgrave Macmillan, 2003.

Weber, M., *From Max Weber: essays in sociology*, translated, edited and with an introduction by H.H. Gerth and C.W. Mills, London: Kegan Paul, 1947 [1948].

Weston, H.C., and A.K. Taylor, *The Relation between Illumination and Efficiency in Fine Work (typesetting by hand): joint report of the Industrial Fatigue Research Board* [of the Medical Research Council] *and the Illumination Research Committee* [of the Department of Scientific and Industrial Research], London: HMSO, 1926.

Whittock, N., *The Complete Book of Trades: or the parents' guide and youths' instructor*, by N. Whittock [et al.], London: Thomas Tegg, 1842.

Williams, G., *Recruitment to Skilled Trades*, London: Routledge, 1957.

Williams, R., *Culture and Society 1780–1950*, London: Chatto & Windus, 1958.

'Women and Work', *Victoria Magazine*, November 1879, p. 79–93.

Zweig, F., *The British Worker*, Harmondsworth: Penguin Books, 1952.

Online resources

Edwards, S., J. Lockheart, and M. Raein, *The Codex Project*, [a paper given at] Twentieth Century Graphic Communication: technology, society and culture: first annual Friends of St Bride Library conference, 24 & 25 September 2002. Available online at: http://stbride.org/friends/conference/twentiethcenturygraphiccommunication/Codex.html, accessed 7 November 2010.

Murdoch, R., *The Publishing Revolution: a view from the inside*, Wriston Lecture of the Manhattan Institute for Policy Research, 9 November 1989, http://www.manhattan-institute.org/html/wl1989.htm, accessed 7 November 2010; an edited version of this lecture was printed in City Journal (New York), Autumn 1990, now available at http://www.city-journal.org/html/issue1_1.html.

Index

advertising 39, 40, 103, 133, 156
age 204–6, 258–9
Aldersgate area 33, 42
Apple Macintosh 227–8, 237
apprentices: breakdown of system 49–50, 232–3, 235, 239; Chapel customs and 181–3, 203; completion of time 182–3; decline in numbers 128; education 108, 142–3; foreign 19; hours 32; increasing specialization 41; indentured to journeymen 23; indoor (living-in) 22, 49, 55; outdoor 49, 55; payment of premiums for 27–8, 29–30, 54–5, 89, 111–12, 207–8; ratio to journeymen 80, 81, 130; regulation of numbers 21, 24, 25, 50, 72, 79, 81, 109, 128; sample surveyed 260; selection scheme 251; social origin 28–30, 141; Stationers' Company's weakening control over 41–2, 87; term 27, 130, 232, 251; training 81, 251; turn-overs 21; union control of 104; welfare 108; *see also* boy labour; recruitment, source of
artisans 28, 29, 30, 53, 54, 56, 87, 208
artistic ability 136–7
aspirations 150–8

bang outs 58, 180–1, 182–3, 197, 198, 199, 200, 203
benefits 41, 50, 58, 67, 82, 90, 109, 117, 129, 178–9, 216, 217
Bennett, Arnold 86
big business, attitudes to 162
births 31, 32
Board of Trade 75–6, 89
Boer War 98
bonuses 130, 133, 134
bookbinders 99, 106

books: cheap 39–40, 50, 71; increasing demand for 39; and new technology 229
booksellers 33, 49
bookwork, wages for 42, 73
Bowerman, C. W. 95, 96
Bowyer, William 52
boy labour 48–50, 52, 55, 65, 80, 81, 87–8, 104, 108, 208, 209, 210, 219
British Federation of Master Printers (BFMP) 106, 128, 130, 131, 230–1
British Printing Industries Federation (BPIF) 226–7, 231, 233
British Printing Society 243
building industry 106–7

call books 82
Cambridge, University of 19, 25
capitalism 92, 98, 214
car ownership 149, 168
carpenters 23, 92, 138
'Case and Proposals of the Free Journeymen Printers in and about London' 21, 24
casual work 25, 26, 80
Cave, E. 27, 34
censorship, state 20
censuses 41, 71–2, 86, 104, 127, 226
Chapels 31–3, 58–9, 176–87, 208; aid and benefits 50–1, 177–9; customs and rituals 31, 32, 58–9, 179–84, 198–9, 203; dinners 180; emphasis on equality 177; entrance money 32, 58–9; fines 32, 58; and General Strike 117; and growth of LSC 90; and holiday pay 84; influence of wider community 202; language 184–7, 199–200; and new technology 238; officers 176, 193, 195, 196; organization 176; outings 180, 200; pass